DISCOVERING YOURSELF

DISCOVERING YOURSELF

Living the Work You Were Meant to Do

ORISON SWETT MARDEN

Published 2020 by Gildan Media LLC
aka G&D Media
www.GandDmedia.com

DISCOVERING YOURSELF. Copyright © JMW Group Inc. All rights exclusively licensed by JMW Group Inc., jmwgroup@jmwgroup.net.

No part of this book may be used, reproduced or transmitted in any manner whatsoever, by any means (electronic, photocopying, recording, or otherwise), without the prior written permission of the author, except in the case of brief quotations embodied in critical articles and reviews. No liability is assumed with respect to the use of the information contained within. Although every precaution has been taken, the author and publisher assume no liability for errors or omissions. Neither is any liability assumed for damages resulting from the use of the information contained herein.

Front cover design by David Rheinhardt of Pyrographx

Interior design by Meghan Day Healey of Story Horse, LLC

Library of Congress Cataloging-in-Publication Data is available upon request

ISBN: 978-1-7225-0333-8

10 9 8 7 6 5 4 3 2 1

CONTENTS

HOW TO USE THIS BOOK 7
PREFACE 13

PART I
PREPARATION

CHAPTER I   The Victorious Attitude   19
CHAPTER II   "According to Thy Faith"   27
CHAPTER III   Doubt the Traitor   37
CHAPTER IV   Making Dreams Come True   47
CHAPTER V   A New Rosary   60
CHAPTER VI   Making Yourself a Prosperity Magnet   74
CHAPTER VII   The Suggestion of Inferiority   85
CHAPTER VIII   Where Your Supply Is   93
CHAPTER IX   You Are Headed Toward Your Ideal   104
CHAPTER X   Education Under Difficulties   110
CHAPTER XI   Misfit Occupations   135
CHAPTER XII   "This One Thing I Do"   148

CONTENTS

PURSUIT

CHAPTER XIII   Enthusiasm   159

CHAPTER XIV   Doing Everything to a Finish   170

CHAPTER XV   The Help Yourself Society   183

CHAPTER XVI   "I Will!"   194

CHAPTER XVII   Something Touched Him   203

CHAPTER XVIII   How to Find Oneself   209

PART III
LIFE STORIES OF SUCCESSFUL MEN AND WOMEN TOLD BY THEMSELVES

INTRODUCTORY NOTE   221

CHAPTER XIX   Marshall Field   223

CHAPTER XX   Bell Telephone Talk   230

CHAPTER XXI   What Miss Mary E. Proctor Did to Popularize Astronomy   239

CHAPTER XXII   The Story of John Wannamaker   245

CHAPTER XXIII   Giving Up Five Thousand Dollars a Year to Become a Sculptor   260

CHAPTER XXIV   John D. Rockefeller   266

CHAPTER XXV   A Talk With Edison   281

CHAPTER XXVI   Carnegie as a Metal Worker   294

CHAPTER XXVII   Herreshoff, The Yacht Builder   309

CHAPTER XXVIII   A Successful Novelist: Fame After Fifty   327

CHAPTER XXIX   John Burroughs at Home: The Hut on the Hill Top   333

CHAPTER XXX   How James Whitcomb Riley Came to be Master of the Hoosier Dialect   342

SELF-ASSESSMENT   348

HOW TO USE THIS BOOK

"The mass of men lead lives of quiet desperation." Henry David Thoreau, *Walden*.

It is of such great importance to thoughtfully choose our careers—to respond to that which is literally our vocation, our "calling." But for a variety of reasons, many of us have not chosen the work that we are in, it is not our true calling. Many of us took jobs based on "the first decent offer that came along" (based on whatever standards we had at the time for "decent"). In time, we then "moved up." But more often than not, "moving up" means moving up in salary, not moving up in personal satisfaction. And so from time to time we feel a tug, a pulling, and looking around we see the horizon behind us receding—our once cherished dreams of the person we *wished* to be is slipping further away. Behind us, and becoming dimmer in the waning light of that distant horizon, is the ballet dancer we wanted to be . . . the writer . . . the forest ranger . . . the butcher, the baker, or the candlestick maker.

But what can we do? We have a family to support. Children to put through college. A mortgage to pay. Bills to pay. And if we can stay at the work we're doing, we'll be eligible for the company's profit-sharing plan in another year. Moreover, isn't it too late in our lives to be a ballet dancer? To take the writing classes or attend the writing conferences necessary for us to learn the craft of the novel and become novelists?

Perhaps.

Perhaps it's true that we can no longer be the ballet dancer we once wanted to be. But the novelist? That's not so self-evidently gone forever.

And nor is something else, something that may not be that ballet dancer but which is nonetheless still tugging at us, still pulling at us something that is still telling us that there's another direction for our lives, and if we will only take it, we will be more than just successful in the worldly sense, we will be whole.

Orison Swett Marden says that we must not only heed that call, but that we have a certain obligation to do so—that not only our personal happiness and success, but the very "welfare of the whole fabric of society" depends on our doing so. Because if each of us is whole, then the world will be whole. Or, to put that differently: Until each of us is whole—experiencing our fulfillment—the very world we live in cannot be whole—an experience of fulfillment, for us as well as for others.

And for that, it is never too late.

We have, then, a responsibility to ourselves and others to live our lives as works of art. For if I live my life as a work of art, then I not only bring art into my world, but into yours as well. And if my neighbor lives his or her life as a work of art, then he or she will not only bring art into his or her life, but mine as well. And so on and so forth, until one day the whole world became a work of art.

Nothing short of that, Marden makes clear, will ever provide us with a world in which there is peace. For if we don't feel a sense of peace, a sense of fulfillment within ourselves, then we will not be able to achieve it anywhere else.

It was Marden's intent in acquiring these interviews that they should instruct and inspire . . . instruct and inspire by example, and by example demonstrate to us the worthwhileness of each of us finding our own road, as well as the understanding that the road is not straight for anyone . . . except in the important sense that once we enter upon it, it keeps moving us straight into the innermost yearnings and inclinations of our lives.

Read the interviews first just for the pleasure and unique opportunity to hear the voices of some of America's leading figures from a variety of careers. (The interviews were originally printed in *Success* magazine; Marden later edited and collected them in book form, and they are presented here in that latter format and style.) Then read them again, and this time pay close attention to the implicit and explicit insights that the various people give as to the process they had to pursue, the decisions they had to make, the habits they had to develop in order to attain the lives they desired. Then find the way that you can integrate these habits, traits, beliefs into your own life, in order that you may attain the life you desire.

And don't be lulled into the mistaken notion that these people had it easier "back then," that it was easier to shape one's destiny "in those days." Yes, there might have been less competition in certain pursuits, and yes the United States was younger then, and so there were particularly unique opportunities then that there may not be now. But go back to that quote of Henry David Thoreau's that begins this section, and remember that it was written *before* any of the people in Part III began and succeeded in their careers. Regardless of what opportunities there were or weren't "back then," in other words, the majority of people were not pursuing them, and the people you'll read about in Part III still had to take pains to stand out from their friends, family, and neighbors who were not finding lives of fulfillment.

In Part I of this book—"Preparation"—Marden discusses the things we must do to prepare ourselves for the lives we wish to live—the mental, emotional, psychological habits we must acquire or break in order to make ourselves available for our lives.

It's of interest to notice that the matters that Marden writes about in Part I are not aptitudes we must learn, but personality traits. Here we see why Orison Swett Marden held such a commanding role as the leading motivational/self-help writer. In writing about personality traits rather than aptitudes as the concerns we needed to look at for life and career satisfaction, Marden was foreshadowing what today has become a well-researched fact: that contentment in work has less to do with aptitudes than with self-expression. Put differently, that we should not think of work as being the opposite of self-expression—or if we do, we do so at our own discontent.

In Part II—"Pursuit"—Marden discusses the activities, the ways of thinking, that will help guide us into that choice of life we've decided upon.

Part III—"Life Stories of Successful Men and Women Told By Themselves"—is arguably the crux of the book. Indeed, Parts I and II could be seen as a distillation of the traits, habits, etc., of the true-life success stories recounted in Part III. If a picture is truly worth a thousand words, here are the pictures—the stories of men and women, told in their own words, many of whom you will recognize by name, who lived the lives they chose for themselves. These are not, though, stories of lives made easy, although history has tended to make the lives of these people seem more effortless, more well-fitted, than perhaps most of ours are. But you'll see that the people in Part III overcame hardships, rejection, handicaps—sometimes handicaps of circumstance and sometimes physical—and had to make sacrifices and take risks. Some entered the bumpy roads toward their goals early; some didn't locate the road until late.

And then remember, too, that there are more millionaires in America today than ever in its history—not that money is or should be a standard of fulfillment, but that indicates that there are still plenty of opportunities . . . for entrepreneurs, the self-employed, whomever.

There are no "action steps" or "tests to determine your calling" in Parts I–III of this book. There aren't, because as Marden points out, ultimately the way to identify the path of one's life is to look within—to "know thyself"—and that's an individual process.

Moreover, virtually all of us know the answer to the question "What's my right place in life?" We know it because virtually all of us know, in expressing our feeling of a lack of wholeness, what it would be in our lives that would make us feel whole. The answer to that is not to be found in easy answers like "More money," or "To be younger," because all of us know that just having more money would not truly fulfill our soul's yearnings. Remember: When we wanted to be that ballet dancer, that musician, that artist, that history teacher—even that lawyer or doctor—it wasn't because that lifestyle was going to make the most money for us.

Nor is the answer to that question about what would make us feel whole the easy answer, "If only I were younger." After all, if and when we do say we'd like to be younger, we invariably add, "knowing the things I now know." So it's not truly the years we want back, but the opportunity to fill them rightly.

That's the goal, the purpose, of this book—to give you the opportunity to not only believe that you *can*, but to encourage you take steps to fill the years of your life rightly.

As Marden says, "Everything in nature is naturally beautiful, and each thing is necessary in its place. Find *your* place, and fill it."

Wishing you the best. . . .

—The Editor

PREFACE

The demand during its first two years for nearly an edition a month of *Peace, Power, and Plenty*, the author's last book and its republication in England, Germany, and France, together with the hundreds of letters received from readers, many of whom say that it has opened up a new world of possibilities to them by enabling them to discover and make use of forces within themselves which they never before knew they possessed, all seem to be indications of a great hunger of humanity for knowledge of what we may call the new gospel of optimism and love, the philosophy of sweetness and light, which aims to show how one can put oneself beyond the possibility of self-wreckage from ignorance, deficiencies, weaknesses, and even vicious tendencies, and which promises long-looked for relief from the slavery of poverty, limitation, ill-health, and all kinds of success and happiness enemies.

The author's hope in this volume is of arousing the readers to discover the wonderful forces in the Great Within of themselves, which, if they could unlock and utilize, would lift them out of the region of anxiety and worry, eliminate most, if not all, of the discords and frictions of life, and enable them to make of themselves everything they ever imagined they could and longed to become.

The book teaches the divinity of right desire; it tries to show that the Creator never mocked us with yearnings for that which we have no ability or possibility of attaining; that our heart longings and aspirations are prophecies, forerunners, indications of the existence of the obtainable reality, that there is an actual powerful creative force in our legitimate desires, in believing with all our hearts that no matter what the seeming obstacles, we shall be what we were intended to be and do what we were made to do; in visualizing, affirming things as we would *like* to have them, as they *ought* to be; in holding the ideal of that which we wish to come true, and only that, the ideal of the man or woman we would like to become, in thinking of ourselves as absolutely perfect beings possessing superb health, a magnificent body, a vigorous constitution, and a sublime mind. It teaches that we should strangle every idea of deficiency, imperfection, or inferiority, and however much our apparent conditions of discord, weaknesses, poverty, and ill-health may seem to contradict, cling tenaciously to our vision of perfection, to the divine image of ourselves, the ideal which the Creator intended for His children; should affirm vigorously that there can be no inferiority or depravity about the man God made, for in the truth of our being we are perfect and immortal; because our mental attitude, what we habitually think, furnishes a pattern which the life processes are constantly weaving, outpicturing in the life.

The book teaches that fear is the great human curse, that it blights more lives, makes more people unhappy and unsuccessful than any other one thing; that worry-thoughts, fear-thoughts, are so many malignant forces within us poisoning the very sources of life, destroying harmony, ruining efficiency, while the opposite thoughts heal, soothe instead of irritate, and increase efficiency and multiply mental power; that every cell in the body suffers or is a gainer, gets a life impulse or a death impulse, from every thought that enters the mind, for we tend to grow into the image, of that which we think about most, love the best; that the body is really our thoughts, moods, convictions objectified, outpictured, made visible to the eye. "The Gods we worship write their names on our faces." The face is carved from within by invisible tools; our thoughts, our moods, our emotions are the chisels. It is the table of contents of our life history; a bulletin board upon which is advertised what has been going on inside of us.

The author believes that there is no habit which will bring so much of value to the life as that of always carrying an optimistic, hopeful attitude of really *expecting* that things are going to turn out well with us and not ill, that we are going to succeed and not fail, are going to be happy and not miserable.

He points out that most people neutralize a large part of their efforts because their mental attitude does not correspond with their endeavor, so that although working for one thing, they are *really expecting* something else, and what we expect, we tend to get; that, there is no philosophy or science by which we can arrive at the success goal when we are facing the other way, when every step we take is on the road to failure, when we talk like a failure, act like a failure, for prosperity begins in the mind and is impossible while the mental attitude is hostile to it.

No one can become prosperous while he or she really expects or half expects to be always poor, for holding the poverty-thought keeps us in touch with poverty-producing conditions.

This book teaches that everybody ought to be happier than the happiest of us are now; that our lives were intended to be infinitely richer and more abundant than at present; that we should have plenty of everything which is good for us; that the lack of anything which is really necessary and, desirable does not fit the constitution of any right-living human being, and that we shorten our lives very materially through our own false thinking, our, bad living, and our old-age convictions, and that to be happy and attain the highest efficiency, each of us must harmonize with the best, the highest thing in ourselves.

—December, 1910
O. S. M.

PART I

PREPARATION

CHAPTER I
The Victorious Attitude

To be a conqueror in appearance, in one's bearing, is the first step toward success. It inspires confidence in others as well as in oneself. Walk, talk and act as though you were a somebody, and you are more likely to become such. Move about among others as though you believe you are a person of importance. Let victory speak from your face and express itself in your manner. Carry yourself like one who is conscious of having a splendid mission, a grand aim in life. Radiate a hopeful, expectant, cheerful atmosphere. In other words, be a good advertisement of the winner you are trying to be.

Doubts, fears, despondency, lack of confidence, will not only give you away in the estimation of others and brand you as a weakling, a probable failure, but they will react upon your mentality and destroy your self-confidence, your initiative, your efficiency. They are telltales, proclaiming to every one you meet that you are losing out in the game of life. A triumphant expression inspires trust, makes a favorable impression. A despondent, discouraged expression creates distrust, makes an unfavorable impression.

If you don't look cheerful and appear and act like a winner nobody will want you. Every one will turn a deaf ear to your plea for work. No matter if you are jobless and have been out of work for a long time you must keep up a winning appearance, a victorious attitude, or you will lose the very thing you are after. The world has little use for whiners or long-faced failures.

It is difficult to get very far away from people's estimate of us. A bad first impression often creates a prejudice that it is impossible afterwards wholly to remove. Hence the importance of always radiating a cheerful, uplifting atmosphere, an atmosphere that will be a commendation instead of a condemnation. Not that we should deceive by trying to appear what we are not, but we should always keep our best side out, not our second best or our worst. Our personal appearance is our show window where we insert what we have for sale, and we are judged by what we put there.

The victorious idea of life, not its failure side—its disappointed side—the triumphant, not the thwarted-ambition side, is the thing to keep ever uppermost in the mind, for it is this that will lead you to the light. You must give the impression that you are a success, or that you have qualities that will make you successful, that you are making good, or no recommendation or testimonial however strong will counteract the unfavorable impression you make.

So much of our progress in life depends upon our reputation, upon making a favorable impression upon others, that it is of the utmost importance to cultivate mental forcefulness. It is the mind that colors the personality, gives it its tone and character. If we cultivate willpower, decision, positive instead of negative thinking, we cannot help making an impression of masterfulness, and everybody know that this is the qualification that does things. It is masterfulness, force, that achieves results, and if we do not express it in our appearance people will not have confidence in our achieving ability. They may think that we can sell goods behind a counter, work under orders, carry out some mechanical routine with faithfulness and precision, but they will not think we are fitted for leadership, that we can command resources to meet possible crises or big emergencies.

Never say or do anything which will show the earmarks of a weakling, of a nobody, of a failure. Never permit yourself to assume a poverty-stricken attitude. Never show the world a gloomy, pessimistic face, which is an admission that life has been a disappointment to you instead of a glorious triumph. Never admit by your speech, your appearance, your gait, your manner, that there is anything wrong with you. Hold up your head. Walk erect. Look everybody in the face. No matter how poor you may be, or how shabby your clothes, whether you are jobless, homeless, friendless even, show the world that you respect yourself, that you believe in yourself, and that, no matter how hard the way, you are marching on to victory. Show by your expression that you can think and plan for yourself, that you have a forceful mentality.

The victorious, triumphant attitude will put you in command of resources which a timid, self-depreciating, failure attitude will drive from you.

This was well illustrated by a visitor to the Athenæum Library in Boston. Ignorant of the fact that members only were entitled to its special privileges, this visitor entered the place with a confident bearing, seated herself in a comfortable window seat, and spent a delightful morning reading and writing letters. In the evening she called on a friend and in the course of conversation, referred to her morning at the Athenæum.

"Why, I didn't know you were a member!" exclaimed the friend.

"A member! No," said the lady. "I am not a member. But what difference does that, make?"

The friend, who held an Athenæum card of membership, smiled and replied:

"Only this, that none but members are supposed to enjoy the privileges of which you availed yourself this morning!"

Had the lady in Boston had any doubt of her right to enter the Athenæum and to freely use all its conveniences, her manner would have betrayed it. The library attendants would have noticed it at once, and have asked her to show her card of membership. But her assured air gave the impression that she was a member. Her victorious attitude dominated the situation, and put her in command of resources which otherwise she could not have controlled.

The spirit in which you face your work, in which you grapple with a difficulty, the spirit in which you meet your problem, whether you approach it like a conqueror, with courage, a vigorous resolution, with firmness, or with timidity, doubt, fear, will determine whether your career will be one grand victory or a complete failure.

It is a great thing so to carry yourself wherever you go that when people see you coming they will say to themselves, "Here comes a winner! Here is someone who dominates everything he or she touches."

Thinking of yourself as habitually lucky will tend to make you so, just as thinking of yourself as habitually unlucky, and always talking about your failures and your cruel fate will tend to make you unlucky. The attitude of mind which your thoughts and convictions produce is a real force which builds or tears down. The habit of always seeing yourself as a fortunate individual, the feeling grateful just for being alive, for being allowed to live on this beautiful earth and to have a chance to make good will put your mind in a creative, producing attitude.

We should all go through life as though we were sent here with a sublime mission to lift, to help, to boost, and not to depress and discourage, and so discredit the plan of the Creator. Our conduct should show that we are on this earth to play a magnificent part in life's drama, to make a splendid contribution to humanity.

The majority of people seem to take it for granted that life is a great gambling game in which the odds are heavily against them. They look on the probability of their winning out in the life game in any distinctive way as highly improbable. When they look around and see how comparatively few of the multitudes of men and women in the world are winning they say to themselves, "Why should I think that I have a greater percentage of chance in my favor than others about me? These people have as much ability as I have, perhaps more, and if they can do no more than grub along from hand to mouth, of what use is it for me to struggle against fate?" This conviction colors their whole attitude, and is responsible for innumerable failures.

What would you think of an actor who was trying to play the part of a great hero, but who insisted on assuming the attitude of a coward and thinking like one; who wore the expression of a man who did not believe he could do the thing he had undertaken, who felt that he was out of place, that he never was made to play the part he was attempting? Naturally you would say the man never could succeed on the stage, and that if he ever hoped to win success, the first thing he should do would be to try to think himself the character, as well as to look the part, he was trying to portray. That is just what the great actor does. He flings himself with all his might into the role he is playing. He sees himself as, and feels that he is actually, the character he is impersonating. He lives the part he is playing on the stage, whether it be that of a beggar or a hero. If he is playing the part of a hero he acts like a hero, thinks and talks like a hero. His very manner radiates heroism. And vice versa, if the part he takes is that of a beggar, he dresses like one, thinks like one, bows, cringes and whines like a beggar.

Similarly, you will be judged by the role you are performing in life and how you are performing it. If you are trying to be successful you must act like a successful person, carry yourself like one, talk, act and think like a winner: You must radiate victory wherever you go.

You must maintain your attitude by believing in the thing you are trying to do. If you persist in looking and acting like a failure or a very mediocre or doubtful success, if you keep telling everybody how unlucky you are, and that you do not believe you will: win out because success is only for a few, that the great majority of people must be hewers of wood and drawers of water, you will be about as much of a success as the actor who attempts to personate a certain type of character while looking, thinking and acting exactly like its opposite.

It always pains me to hear everyone who ought to be full of hope and high promise express a doubt as to the future career. To hear such a person about possible failure sounds like treason to his or her creator. Talking about failure is like beauty talking about ugliness; like superb health dwelling upon weakness and disease; like perfection dwelling upon imperfection. It is in our nature act as it is in all of Nature: to climb, to look up. The very atmosphere of our souls should breathe hope, superb promise of the future.

Just think what would happen if all of the down-and-outs-today, all of the people who look upon themselves as failures or as dwarfs of what they ought to be, could only get this victorious, this triumphant, idea of life, if they could only once glimpse their own possibilities and assume the triumphant attitude! They would never again be satisfied to grovel. If they once got a glimpse of their divinity, once saw themselves in the sublime robes of their power, they never again would be satisfied with the rags of their poverty.

But instead of such a true and noble purpose, of trying to improve their condition, to get away from their failure, poverty-stricken atmosphere, so many cling the more closely to their false sense of hopelessness and sink deeper and deeper in the quagmire of their own making.

Everywhere we find people grumbling at everything, complaining that "life is not worth living," that "the game is not worth the candle," that "life is a cheat, a losing game."

Life is not a losing game. It is always victorious when properly played. It is the players who are at fault. The great trouble with all failures is that they were not started right It was not drilled into the very texture of their being in youth that what they would get out of life must be created mentally first, and that inside the man, inside the woman, is where the great creative processes of life are carried on.

By a psychological law we attract that which corresponds with our mental attitude, with our faith, our hopes, our expectations, or with our doubts and fears. It is what we do with our brains that counts. Our manner and our appearance are determined by our mental outlook. If we see only failure ahead we will act and look like failures. We have already failed. If we expect success, see it waiting for us a little bit up the road, we will act and look like successes. We have already succeeded. The failure attitude loses; the victorious attitude wins.

There are times when we cannot see the way ahead, when we seem to be completely enveloped in the fogs of discouragement, disappointment and failure of our plans, but we can always do the thing that means salvation for us—and that is to persistently, determinedly, everlastingly to face towards our goal whether we can see it or not. This is our only chance of over coming our difficulties. If we turn about face, turn our back, on our goal, we are headed toward disaster.

No matter how many obstacles may block your path, or how dark the way, if you look up, think up, and struggle up, you can't help succeeding. Whatever you do for a living, whatever fortune or misfortune may come to you, hold the victorious attitude and push ahead.

A captain might as well turn about his ship when he strikes a fog bank, because he cannot see the way ahead of him, and still expect to make his distant harbor, as for you to drop your victorious attitude and face the other way just because you have run into a fog bank of disappointment or failure. The only hope of the captain's reaching his destination is in being true to the compass that guides him in the fog and darkness as well as in the light. He may not see the way, but he can follow his compass. That we also can do by holding the victorious attitude towards life, the only attitude that can insure safety and bring us into port.

CHAPTER II
"According to Thy Faith"

"I shall study law," said an ambitious youngster, "and those who are already in the profession must take their chances!"

The divine self-confidence of youth, the unshaken faith that believes all things possible, often makes cynics and world-weary people smile. Yet it is the grandest, most helpful attribute of man, the finest gift of the Creator to the race. If we could retain through life the faith of ambitious, self-confident, untied youth, its unquestioning belief in its ability to carve out its ideal in the actual, what wonders we should all accomplish! Such faith would enable us literally to remove mountains.

All through the Scriptures, faith is emphasized as a tremendous power. It was by faith that Moses led the children of Israel out of Egypt, through the waters of the Red Sea, and through the wilderness. It was by faith that Elijah, Isaiah, Daniel, and all of the great prophets performed their miracles.

Faith was the great characteristic of Christ Himself: The word was constantly on His lips, "According to thy faith be it unto thee." He often referred to it as the measure of what we receive in life, also as the great healer, the great restorer. Whenever He healed He laid the entire emphasis upon the faith of the healer and the one healed. "Thy faith hath made thee whole," "Believe only and she shall be made whole," "Thy faith hath saved thee." Or He reproved His, disciples for the lack of faith which prevented them from healing, as when He addresses them, "O faithless and perverse generation, how long shall I be with you and suffer you."

Faith believes; doubt fears. Faith creates; doubt destroys. Faith opens he door to all things desirable in life; doubt closes them. Faith is an arouses, an awakener of our creative forces. It opens the door of ability, and arouses creative energies. Faith is the link in the Great Within which connects each of us with the Great Force. Our faith puts us in touch with Infinite Power, opens the way to unbounded possibilities, limitless resources. No one can rise higher than his or her faith. None can do a greater thing than they believe they can. The fact that a person believes implicitly that he or she can do what may seem impossible to others, shows there is something within that person that has gotten a glimpse of power sufficient to accomplish his or her purpose.

Those who have achieved great things cannot account for their faith; they cannot tell why they had an unflinching belief that they could do what they undertook. But the mere fact of such belief was evidence that they had had a glimpse of interior resourcefulness, reserve power and possibilities which would warrant that faith; and they have gone ahead with implicit confidence that they would come out all right, because this faith told them so. It told them so because it had been in communication with something that was divine, that which had passed the bounds of the limited and had veered into the limitless.

Men and women who have left their mark on the world have been implicit followers of their faith when they could see no light.

Their unseen guide has led them through the wilderness of doubt and hardship into the promised land.

When we begin to exercise self-faith, self-confidence, we are stimulating and increasing the strength of the faculties which enable us to do the thing we have set our heart on doing. Our faith—causes us to concentrate on our object, and thus develops power to accomplish it. Faith tells us that we may proceed safely, even when our mental faculties see no light or encouragement ahead. Our faith is a divine leader which never misdirects us. But we must always be sure that it is faith, and not merely egotism or selfish desire that is urging us. There is a great difference between the two, and no one who is true to himself or herself can possibly be deceived.

When we are doing right, when we are on the right track, our faith in the divine order of things never wavers. It sustains in situations which drive the self-centered egoist to despair.

Those who do not see the design of promise and hope and achievement everywhere, who do not see the mighty Intelligence back of every created thing, cannot have that sublime faith which buoys up the great achievers.

Our supreme aim should be to get the best from life, the best in the highest sense that life has to give, and this we cannot do without superb faith. What we accomplish will be large or small according to the measure of this faith. The skeptic, the pessimist, has no bulwark of faith, none of the divine enthusiasm that faith gives, none of the zeal that carries the person of faith unscathed through the most terrible trials.

Without confidence in the beneficence of the great universal plan we can not have much confidence in ourselves. To get the best out of ourselves we must believe that there is a current within us running heavenward, however much our surroundings may seem to contradict this. We must believe that everything will work together for good, however much wars and crime, poverty, suffering and wretchedness all about us may seem to deny this.

The abiding faith that things will turn out right in the end has always been strong in men and women who have done great things in the world, especially in those who have achieved grand results in spite of the most severe trials and tribulations.

It takes sublime faith to enable us to fight our way through "insuperable" difficulties, to bear up under discouragements, afflictions and seeming failure without losing heart; and it is just such faith that has characterized every great soul who has ever made good. Whatever other qualities they may have lacked, great characters have always had sublime faith.

Some of the most important reforms in history have been brought about by very fragile, delicate men and women, not only without outside encouragement, but in the teeth of the most determined opposition. They have agitated and agitated, hoped and hoped, and struggled and struggled, until victory came. No one could even attempt the herculean tasks they accomplished without that instinctive, abiding faith in and perception of a life which would work in harmony with honesty, with earnestness, with integrity of purpose, in a persistent struggle for the right, but which would never sanction wrong.

Think of what the faith of inventor, scientists, and artists has done! It kept them at their tasks, kept them nerved and encouraged in the face of starvation, kept them at their work when their families had gone back on him, when their neighbors had denounced him and called them insane. Think of what the faith of Columbus, of Beethoven, of Edison has accomplished for mankind!

Faith has built our railroads, has revealed the secrets of nature to science, has led the way to all our inventions and discoveries, and has brought success out of the most inhospitable conditions and iron environments. We owe everything that has been accomplished to faith, and yet when we come to its practical application in our everyday affairs how few of us avail ourselves of this tremendous force! The vast majority are looking for some outside power to help, when we ourselves hold the key which has ever unlocked, and ever will unlock, all barred doors to aspiring souls.

It is not alone in our life work, or in great or special undertakings that faith is necessary. We need it every moment of our lives, in everything, great and small, that concerns us It is just as necessary to your health as it is to your success. To build up the faith habit, the habit of believing in yourself, in your ability, of believing that you are victory organized and that you are going to attain your ambition, is to blaze a path to success.

We begin to deteriorate, to go toward failure, not when we lose all of our material possessions, not when we fail in our undertakings, but when we lose faith in ourselves, in our ability to make our dreams come true.

The reason why faith works such marvels is that it is the leader of all the other mental faculties. They will not proceed until faith goes ahead. It is the basis of courage, of initiative, of enthusiasm. Much of Napoleon's power and early success came from his tremendous faith in his mission, the conviction that he was a man of destiny, that he was born under a lucky star, born to conquer. Shorn of his mighty belief in his star, stripped of the faith that he was born to rule, he would have been no more of a power in human affairs than the dullest private in the ranks of his army. When warned by his generals not to expose himself to the enemy, he would reply that the bullet or the cannon had not been cast which could kill Napoleon. This invincible belief in his destiny added wonderfully to his natural powers.

It was her conviction that she was chosen of God to free France from its enemies that made Joan of Arc, the simple, ignorant peasant girl of Domrèmy, the savior of her country. Her mighty faith in her divine mission gave her a dignity and a miraculous force of character, a positive genius, that made all the commanders of the French army obey her as private soldiers obey their superior officers. Faith in herself and in her mission transformed the peasant maiden into the greatest military leader of her time.

There is no doubt that every human being comes to this earth with a mission. We are not accidental puppets thrown off to be buffeted by luck or chance or cruel fate. We are a part of the great universal plan. We were made to fit into this plan, to play a definite part in it. We come here with a message for humanity which no one else but ourselves can deliver, and faith in our mission, the belief that we are important factors in the great creative plan, that we are, in fact, co-creators of life is what enables us to perform the "impossible."

We see this sort of instinctive faith illustrated by the lower animals. Take the hen, for example. See how patiently she sits on the eggs week after week until the chickens are hatched. She cannot see the chickens when she begins to sit, but her instinct that they will come if she does her part induces her to give up her liberty for weeks, and to go sometimes for days without food, that she may keep the eggs at the right temperature in order to produce the chickens.

The trouble with most of us is that we do not have sufficient faith in the creative power of the vigorous determination to do a thing, in the persistent endeavor backed by self-faith to accomplish what we desire. We give up too easily under discouragement. We haven't sufficient stamina and grit to push on under disheartening conditions. We want to see clear through from the beginning to the end of whatever we undertake. We refuse to have faith. Yet much of the time throughout life we may have to work without any goal in sight, or at least without any clear light to see it. But if the mental attitude is right we know that, somehow, we shall attain our heart's desire.

When we see our ambition, our aspiration, our goal, it is as if we have been shown a program which we are capable of carrying out, a table of contents of our capabilities, the signs of the corresponding realities—for faith is not an idle dream, an illusive picture of the imagination. Our ideals and aspirations, soul yearnings and heart-longings are not mockeries for the things which have no possible realities. Faith is not a cheat. There is ability to match the faith.

There is something about devotion to one's inward vision, the intense desire and concentrated effort to fulfill what we believe, to be our mission here, that has a solidifying influence upon the character, gives poise and peace of mind and also helps us to realize our vision.

The probabilities are that the iceberg which sent the *Titanic*, with sixteen hundred souls to the bottom of the ocean did not even undergo a tremor at the shock. More than seven-eighths of its huge bulk was below the water, deep down in the eternal calm of the sea, beyond the reach of storm or tempest. Like the giant iceberg, faith reaches down into the serene within of us, into the eternal calm of the soul. It is not disturbed by the surface commotions. A life poised on faith rides steadily, triumphantly, through the tempests and the hurricanes of existence:

You will constantly be confronted with things which tend to destroy your faith in yourself. There are many times in life when about all we can do is to hold on to the hand of the faith until we have run through the storm zone. We have to learn to turn away from the heart-breaks of life and to face toward the light. We have to disregard the criticisms and the discouragement of others, as well as the assaults of fear and doubt, and press on to our goal.

If you go in business for yourself, if you are struggling to get an education, if you are making desperate efforts to realize your ambition, whatever it is, you will find plenty of pessimists who will predict your failure. They will tell you that you never can build up a business without a lot of capital and outside help in these times of terrific competition, that you cannot work your way through college, that you can never be whatever you are dreaming of and longing to be. You will meet plenty of obstacles and much opposition, and it will take a very stiff backbone, a lot, of sand and grit to keep pushing on towards your goal against great odds, but faith is more than a match for all these. Nothing else will enable you to win out.

Remember it is not other people's faith in you but your faith in yourself that counts most. It is a good thing to have other people's good opinion, to have their confidence in us, their faith in the success of our efforts, but it is not imperative. Our own is. No one ever gets anywhere or does anything great in this world without faith in himself or herself, without a superb belief that he or she is on the right track, that he or she is doing the thing he or she was made, to do, that he or she is going to stick to it through thick and thin to the end. It takes faith to look beyond obstacles—to see the way over difficulties, to brave opposition and to allow nothing to swerve us from our course.

You cannot keep any one from succeeding who has an unshakable faith in his or her mission. You cannot crush the faith that wrestles with difficulties, that never weakens under trials or afflictions, that pushes on when everybody else turns back, that gets up with greater determination every time it is knocked down.

In the sacred Confucian scriptures we are told that a very devoted disciple of Confucius, on a pilgrimage to his master, was stopped on his journey by a broad river. As he could not swim and could not procure a boat, the zealous disciple resolved that he would walk on the water.

Believing that the necessity of seeing his master was most urgent, and, being filled with zeal in the performance of his mission, he boldly made the attempt—and succeeded. The record of this miracle is supposed by followers of Confucius to be just as authentic as the Bible account of the walking of Christ on the water.

If, like this zealot, you have faith in your power to overcome difficulties, nothing can keep you from your goal.

To feel that you have a divine mission that no one else can perform, that you came here with a sacred message for mankind, and that it is up to you to deliver it, will add a wonderful motive for effectiveness in your life work. The consciousness that you are keeping faith with yourself, that you are keeping faith with a splendid life purpose, with your holiest vision, gives a satisfaction which nothing else can afford.

Cling to your faith no matter what happens It is your best friend. Like the magnetic needle on the ship's deck, which will find the north star, no matter, how dense the fog, how dark the night, or how threatening the tempest, your faith, even though you cannot see, will find the way. It sees the open road, beyond the mountain of difficulties which shuts out the vision of the other faculties.

We are just beginning to see that faith is as much a real force as is electricity. It is faith that removes mountains—mountains of difficulty, of opposition, of doubt, of distrust. It clears the track of all obstructions. It makes stepping stones of stumbling blocks. Faith is the most powerful, the most sublime of human attributes. Without it the bottom would drop out of civilization. It is the fundamental principle of life. Faith is the basis of health, of success, of happiness, of love itself. It believes in, hopes, trusts, clings to the loved one in spite of all faults and sins. It is faith that heals, that achieves, that hopes.

Let no one shake your faith in yourself. Faith is your bracer, the trusty leader that will never fail to guide you to the home of your heart's desire.

If you are filled with a great faith you will not fear, though you walk through the valley of the shadow. Though the way, may be dark faith will lead you into the light. The Power that has sustained you every moment of your existence, and without which you could not exist a fraction of a second, will certainly not leave you in your greatest need.

If you bade your child jump into your arms, your child would not hesitate even though it was so dark that he or she could not see you. Your would jump because of his or her faith in you. Your child would know that he or she would be perfectly safe in doing whatever you told him or her.

Why should you not have the same faith to jump with equal confidence into the outstretched arms of the aspiration that calls you?

CHAPTER III
Doubt the Traitor

I used to go trout fishing with two men, one of whom was always saying that he never had any luck fishing, that he somehow didn't have the knack, and never expected to catch many fish. This doubt totally unfitted him for successful trout fishing. He didn't take enough interest in the sport to study the habits and the haunts of the trout. He did not know the likely places in streams and rivers to drop his hook. He did not know the best kinds of bait to use. His doubt of his ability led to indifference, and this made him a failure as a trout fisher. The other man never had a doubt of success. If there were any trout to be caught he felt sure he would catch them. For years he had made a study of trout habits. He could tell which side of the big rocks to cast his hook, and he knew how to cast it in a way that would tempt he trout. Fishing in the same stream alongside the doubtful, indifferent fisherman he would catch ten times as many fish.

If there is a great big doubt in your self-faith, if you have left a bridge standing for your retreat in case of defeat, if you lack clean-cut, firm decision, if there is any interrogation point in your confidence in yourself, there will be a limp in your success gait, and you will not be able to rise out of mediocrity.

Our worst enemies are not outside but inside of us. We each harbor a traitor who is always on the watch to thwart us in our ambitions, to turn us aside from our aims. That traitor is doubt. You must make up your mind at the very outset of your career that you will always be followed about by certain mental enemies, mental traitors, which will try to dissuade you from doing the highest or biggest thing possible to you. Doubt is one of the most insistent of these, and will dog your steps to your grave. The man or woman who is not strong enough to resist its insidious attacks will never do what he or she is capable of doing—was sent into the world to do.

No one who is not bigger than his or her doubts can ever accomplish anything great or worth while, because this subtle enemy kills initiative and self-confidence, and without these dominant qualities no human being can measure up to his or her possibilities.

But for doubt, which strangles the very beginning of things, initiative instead of being so rare would be a common virtue among all classes. Nine out of ten average individuals are held back from testing their powers by the suggestions of doubt. If it were possible to drive from the human mind this specter which stands at the door of our hopes, which throws its baleful shadow across our vision, we would forge ahead by leaps and bounds. This miserable traitor under the guise of a friend, is holding downs millions of men and women below the level of their powers, keeping them from beginning things which they are capable of doing, but which doubt warns them at their peril not to attempt.

Doubt makes more people afraid to start out on a course they know they ought to pursue than any other thing. Standing right at the gateway of our choice, at the parting of the ways, when we have fully resolved to take the path that is best for us, a hard and forbidding one compared with the easy way along the line of least resistance, doubt calls a halt. It bids us pause and think once more, asks us to look again at the rugged path we have chosen and consider whether we really want to pay the price of our choice, to take that turning when the other looks so much brighter and pleasanter and is so very much easier.

This is the point of cleavage which marks the beginning of failure for the timid soul who is not bigger than his or her doubt. The suggestions pushed into our minds by this enemy make us hesitate. We are moved to "stop, look, and listen." We begin to reconsider, to look again at the obstacles ahead, and the longer we look, the bigger they grow. We become frightened, fear we cannot do the thing that at first seemed possible, and finally turn aside to the easier path of mediocrity and commonness.

Talk about drug victims and slaves of drink! Doubt has more victims than even these terrible enemies of the race. We see those victims everywhere—in menial and lowly positions, perpetual clerks, discontented hewers of wood and drawers of water—paralyzed at the very gateway of their career by that fatal trait which they have never learned how to strangle, to neutralize with its opposites: faith, hope, confidence, assurance.

How many thousands of employees plodding along in mediocrity today could have been in business for themselves but for this great enemy inside of them! How many today who are clerks, bookkeepers, or other subordinates, might have been managers, superintendents or proprietors themselves but for the work of this damnable traitor!

When opportunity presented itself these doubters were afraid. They waited for certainty.

They dared not take chances. They did not realize that opportunity is a maiden or beau who admires the bold, courageous, self-confident suitor. They did not wake up in time to the fact that opportunity will not trust itself to the timid, the hesitant, the over-cautious suitor. When too late they realized that while the doubter is wavering and hesitating, wondering if he or she dare try to win, the daring, intrepid wooer steps in and wins.

Doubt tells the poor boy and girl who long for an education that it is foolish for them to think of going through school and college without money or without somebody to help them. It tells them that there are many more poor boys and girls in every school and college who are trying to pay their way than will ever find opportunities to make their education available. It is always whispering to them that there is a big waiting list of men and women who were graduated years ago everywhere looking and waiting, trying in vain to get something to do to earn back the amount they spent on their education.

No matter what you attempt to do what new enterprise you may undertake, what progressive plans you may make, the traitor doubt will bob up and call a halt, will try to dissuade you from your purpose. It will suggest to you how many others have undertaken similar things and have gone to the wall, failing to accomplish what they expected. It will tell you that you had better go slow, that it is foolish to go into business in times like these, that you should wait until you are better prepared, until you have more capital—in short, that there are stumbling blocks in the way, and that you must consider the step very carefully before you venture to decide.

It does not matter what we plan to do, doubt is always there ready to knock down our resolutions, and, if possible, to discourage us even from attempting to put our plans in execution. Who could ever estimate how many superb inventions and discoveries, which would have helped emancipate the race from drudgery and hard conditions, have been sidetracked by this traitor!

Doubt kills activity, discourages ambition and destroys or neutralizes the biggest brain power. It would make a pigmy of an Edison. By filling his mind full of doubt of his own creative power, a, hypnotist could make a Shakespeare believe he was a fool—could inject a doubt into the mind of a Napoleon that would cut his genius down to the mediocrity of a common soldier.

This arch traitor of mankind is so closely related to fear that it is almost impossible to draw a dividing line between the two. They are twins. Wherever doubt can get a foothold it introduces its brother fear, and fear brings with it all of its relatives: worry, anxiety, discouragement—the whole failure family. A single day of doubts, of fears, of unbeliefs, of the crime of self-deprecation, will drive away from us all that we have attracted to ourselves in many months.

Those who would do anything worthwhile in this world must have a vision and the courage to match it. Courage is the great leader in the mental realm. Whatever paralyzes it strangles the initiative, kills the ability to do things. Doubt is its greatest enemy. It suggests caution at the very moment when everything depends on boldness.

Caution is an admirable trait, but when carried to excess it ceases to be a virtue and comes perilously near being a vice. It may render ineffective many noble qualities. There are a great many people who seem to be courageous enough, but an excessive development of caution holds everything in abeyance to wait for certainty. I know those who wait and wait, never daring to undertake anything where there is risk, even though their judgment tells them they ought to go ahead.

We are creatures of habit, and the constant raising of doubts in our minds as to our ability to do what we want to do in time becomes a habit of thinking we can't. And when we think we can't, we can't.

Why delay beginning the thing that you know perfectly well you ought to do? What are you afraid of? Failure in an honorable attempt is preferable to forever postponing the thing that you ought to do. Do you have a horror of possible failure? Do you shrink from the possible humiliation of losing out in your venture? What is it that enlarges your doubt and holds you back? Are you carrying a great excess of baggage, clinging to unnecessary things which handicap you?

I have heard of a sailor who lost his life in that way. He was one of the crew of a ship that was carrying a large quantity of gold nuggets to a distant port. The ship ran upon a rock, and when all hope of saving her or her precious cargo was gone, the captain ordered everybody to leave the sinking ship. The last boat was ready to push off, but this sailor refused to get into it until he had loaded himself with gold nuggets. He said he had been a poor man all his life, and now he was going to be rich at last. He would take away with him just as much of the sinking wealth as he could carry. Heedless of the warning of the captain and his companions that they would not wait for him, he loaded himself with gold. Then, the boats having pushed away, he jumped overboard and tried to save himself by clinging to pieces of the wreck. But, owing to the weight he carried, he could neither float nor swim, and so the wealth he felt he could not leave behind—*that he doubted could be his in any other way*—carried him down to death.

Your doubt of your success is probably your biggest handicap. But it would be a thousand times better to make mistakes by forging ahead too rapidly, by undertaking more than we can carry out, than to be forever hovering upon the edge of doubt, delaying, postponing, waiting for certainty, until we become slaves of a habit which we cannot break. That habit of putting off, of waiting to see how things are going to turn out, to see if something more certain, something with less risk will not turn up, is fatal to initiative, fatal to leadership, fatal to efficiency.

All history shows that while experience increases wisdom, it does not always increase faith. The inexperienced youth will often undertake things which stagger the older and more experienced. Confidence is characteristic of youth; but after a few setbacks and disappointments, many begin to wonder whether, after all, their first confidence was based upon good judgment, whether their enthusiasm and faith were not the result of lack of experience, and then they begin to doubt and to fear that this voice of ambition which is ever beckoning them on and upward is not reliable. They say to themselves: "What if this should be merely a mirage to lure me on the rocks," and before they realize it they are weaving doubts and fears and over-caution into a habit that has ruined multitudes of careers, a habit that is responsible for a larger percentage of unused ability, of locked-up powers than any other one thing.

Have *you* done the biggest thing you are capable of doing? Is it not possible that there is something within you, some unworked mental territory which, if cultivated; would lead you out into that wider field you dreamed of when a youth? How long have you been just an ordinary employee? Do you realize that habit is getting a tremendous grip upon you, and that before you realize it you may be a "perpetual clerk"? Why do you go on year after year in the same old rut, doing the same old thing in the same old way because doubt whispers it would be rash to try new ways, new ideas?

The longer you remain in one position, doing the same thing without promotion, the stronger the inertia habit will grip you, the bigger will grow your doubt as to the wisdom of making a change. It is a dangerous thing to get into a rut. Bestir yourself and begin to put into operation that plan which has so long haunted you, but which doubt has been telling you is not feasible, is not practicable.

Are you not tired of the traitor doubt? Why not turn it out of your mental house?

Neutralize it with a great splendid faith in yourself, in your mission.

If I believed in a real devil, I think it would be that unseen monitor, that mysterious something within us which whispers doubt, which tells us to hold on, to be careful, to go slow—which pulls us back when we are attempting to reach out, trying to do the thing we long to do. You know that the devil which has followed you through life, which has blocked your progress, put out the lights in your path, tortured you and undermined your confidence in yourself, has been the devil of doubt. It has been the whispering fiend which told you that you could not do this and you could not do that, which stepped in and killed your initiative when you were about to begin to do that which your ambition had hoped to accomplish.

Don't let this enemy thwart and baffle you any longer. Have a good heart to heart talk with yourself and break the habit chain of unbelief in self with which it has bound you. Say to yourself, "I will not listen any longer to the voice of this fiend. I will not allow it to spoil my plan for myself. There is some thing inside of me which insists that I was planned for victory, not for defeat, for happiness, not for misery, for peace of mind not for a life of worry, anxiety, and fear. I do not believe that I was placed here to be a mere puppet of circumstances. Faith, hope and confidence are my helpers. Doubt is a child of fear, and fear has the great majority of human beings hypnotized, so that they do not dare to forge ahead, do not dare to undertake take the things they are perfectly capable of accomplishing. From henceforth it has no power over me. I will not listen to its treacherous voice."

Undoubtedly, if you would succeed, you must avoid rashness as well as over-caution. But when you have fully considered in all its bearings whatever project you are about to undertake, and have decided on your course, don't let any fears or doubts enter your mind. Commit yourself to your undertaking, and don't look back to see if you could have done something else, or started in some other way. Push on and don't be afraid.

After you have launched out in an enterprise, have committed yourself, pride will step into the situation and push you on through hardships which would have discouraged and turned us aside before you had fully committed yourself. When you have taken the plunge, made the venture, you have said to the world, "Now, watch me make good. I have made up my mind to put this thing through, and I am not going to turn back." Our confidence grows as we advance and then it is comparatively easy, even under difficulties, to keep forging ahead.

Make up your mind that you are going to be a conqueror in life, that you are going to be the king or queen of your mental realm, and not a slave to any treacherous enemy, that you will follow the course of your calling no matter how forbidding or formidable the difficulties in the way, that you will take the turning which points toward the goal of your ambition, no matter who or what may bar your onward path. Don't let doubt balk your efforts. Don't let it paralyze your beginning and make you a pigmy so that you will not half try to make good when you have a waiting giant in you.

There will be many occasions for doubt as you pursue your chosen career—family and friends may caution you against your pursuit; impediments, setbacks may occur. The former is unfortunate, the latter is natural.

"Every condition, be it what it may," writes William Channing, the great Unitarian minister whose writings influenced writers such as Emerson, "has hardships, hazards, pains. We try to escape them; we pine for a sheltered lot, for a smooth path, for cheering friends, and unbroken success. But Providence ordains storms, disasters, hostilities, sufferings; and the great question whether we shall live to any purpose or not, whether we shall grow strong in mind and heart, or be weak and pitiable, depends on nothing so much as on our use of the adverse circumstances. Outward evils are designed to school our passions, and to rouse our faculties and virtues into intenser action. Sometimes the seem to create new powers. Difficulty is the element, and resistance the true work of the individual. Self-culture never goes on so fast as when embarrassed circumstances, the opposition of others or the elements, unexpected changes of the times, or other forms of suffering, instead of disheartening, throw us on our inward resources, clear up to us the great purpose of life, and inspire calm resolution. No greatness or goodness is worth much, unless tried in these fires." Confidence, self-assurance, self-faith, then—these are the great friends which will kill the traitor doubt.

CHAPTER IV
Making Dreams Come True

Washington, in a letter written when he was but twelve years old, said: "I shall marry a beautiful woman; I shall be one of the wealthiest men in the land; I shall lead the army of my colony; I shall rule the nation which I help to create."

General Grant, in his *Memoirs*, says that as a boy at West Point, he saw General Scott seated on his horse, reviewing the cadets, and something within him said, "Ulysses, some day you will ride in his place and be general of the army."

Every one knows how those boyish visions were realized by the mature men.

The late J. Pierpont Morgan's fortune was built largely by the dynamic forcefulness of his thought, of his mental visualizing, the nursing of his youthful visions. He was a man of varied and aesthetic tastes, but he concentrated upon finance and he became the world's master in its science.

Ancient Greece concentrated on beauty and art, and she became the great beauty model and art teacher of the world. The Roman Empire concentrated upon power—and became mistress of the world. England concentrated on the control of the seas and commerce, and she became the ruler of the seas and the greatest commercial nation in the world.

Whatever you concentrate upon you tend to get, because concentration is just as much of a force as is electricity. The person who concentrates upon law, thinks law, dreams law, reads everything he or she can get hold of relating to law, steals into courts listens to trials at every chance he gets, is sure to become a lawyer.

It is the same with any other vocation or art—medicine, engineering, literature, music; any of the arts or sciences. Those who concentrate upon an idea, who continue to visualize their dreams, to nurse them, who never lose sight of their goal, no matter how dark or forbidding the way, get what they concentrate on. They make their minds powerful magnets to attract the thing on which they have concentrated. Sooner or later they realize their dreams.

If you can concentrate your thought and hold it persistently, work with it along the line of your greatest ambition, nothing can keep you from its realization. But spasmodic concentration, spasmodic enthusiasm, however intense, will peter out. Dreaming without effort will only waste your power. It is holding your vision, together with persistent, concentrated endeavor on the material plane, that wins.

There are thousands of devices in the patent office in Washington which have never been of any use to the world, simply because the inventors did not cling to their vision long enough to materialize it in perfection. They became discouraged. They ceased their efforts. They let their visions fade, and so became demagnetized and lost the power to realize them. Other inventors have taken up many such "near" successes, added the missing links in their completion and have made them real successes,

Everywhere there are disappointed men and women who have soured on life because they could not get what they longed for—a musical or art education, the necessary training for authorship, for law or medicine, for engineering, or for some other vocation to which they felt they had been called. They are struggling along in an uncongenial environment, railing at the fate which has robbed them of their own. They feel that life has cheated them, when the truth is they have cheated themselves. They never got the spindle and distaff ready that would have drawn to them the flax for the spinning of a happy and complete life web. They did not insistently and persistently send out their desires and longings; they did not nurse them and positively refuse to give them up; above all, they did not put forth their best efforts for their realization.

Three things we must do to make our dreams come true: Visualize our desire; Concentrate on our vision; Work to bring it into the actual. The implements necessary for this are inside of us, not outside. No matter what the accidents of birth or fortune, there is only one force by which we can fashion our life material—mind.

Of two boys or two girls in the same wretched environment, one picks up an education, trains himself or herself for place and power, while the other grows up a nobody. It is all in the boy or the girl. Each has similar material to work in. One transmutes it into gold; the other into lead.

Two sailors force the same breeze to send their boats in opposite directions. It is not the wind, but the set of the sail that determines the port.

The power that makes our desire, our vision, a reality is not in our environment or in any condition outside of us, it is within us.

There is some unseen, unknown, magnetic force developed by a long-continued concentration of the mind upon a cherished desire that draws to itself the reality which matches the desire. We cannot tell just what this force is that brings the thing we long for out of the cosmic ether and objectifies it, shapes it to correspond with our longing. We only know that it exists. The cosmic ether everywhere surrounding us is full of undreamed of potencies and the strong, concentrated mind reaches out into this ether, this sea of intelligence, attracts to it its own, and objectifies the desire.

All human achievements have been pulled out of the unseen by the brain, through the mind reaching out and fashioning the wealth of material at its disposal into the shapes which matched the wishes, the desires, of the achievers.

All the great discoveries, great inventions, great deeds that have lifted us up from our animal existence have been wrought out of the actual by the perpetual thinking of and visualizing of these things by their authors. These grand characters clung to their vision, nursed it until they became mighty magnets that attracted out of the universal intelligence the realization of their dreams.

Most revolutionary inventions have evolved from a flash of thought. The sewing machine, for example, started with a simple idea, which the inventor held persistently in his mind until through his efforts the idea materialized into the concrete reality. Elias Howe used to watch his wife making garments, sewing, sewing far into the night, and it set him thinking, questioning whether such: drudgery was really necessary. As he watched her busy needle fly back and forth, he began to wonder if this same work which it took his wife so long to do could not be done with less labor and in half the time by some sort of mechanical contrivance. He kept nursing his idea, thinking what a splendid thing it would be if some one could relieve millions of women from this toil, which frequently had to be done at night after a day of hard work. He began to experiment with crude devices, clinging to his vision through poverty and the denunciation of friends, who thought the man must be crazy to spend his time on "such a fool idea." But at last his vision materialized into a marvelous reality, a perfected machine which emancipated the world from infinite drudgery.

The idea of the telephone was flashed into the mind of Professor Alexander Bell by the drawing of a string through a hole in the bottom of a tin can, by means of which he found that the voice could be transmitted. The idea took such complete possession of the inventor that it robbed him of sleep and, for a time made him poor. But nothing could rob him of his vision or prevent him from struggling to work it out of the visionary stage into the actual.

I lived near Professor Bell, in the next room, indeed, while he worked on his invention. I saw much of his struggle with poverty, heard the criticisms and denunciations of his friends, as he persisted in his visionary work until the telephone became a reality—a reality without which modern life could not be conducted.

All of Edison's inventions, those of every inventor, have been wrought out on the same principle that gave us the sewing machine and the telephone. They all started in simple ideas, in dream visions which were nursed and worked into actualities.

The brain cells grow in response to desire. Where there is no desire there is no growth. The brain develops most in the direction of the leading ambition, where the mental activities are the most pronounced. The desire for a musical career, for instance, develops he musical brain cells. Business ambition develops that part of the brain which has to do with business, the cells which are brought into action in executive management, in administering affairs, in money making. Wherever we make our demand upon the brain by desire that part responds in growth.

For years a poor country boy builds air castles of his future. He visualizes the great mercantile establishment over which he is to preside. The ridicule of his family and of young companions cannot daunt him or blur the bright vision he sees away in the distance. He continues to nurse his vision, and behold, out of' the unknown, unexpected resources come, and soon he finds himself an office boy in a great mercantile house in the city of his dreams. He watches everything with an eagle eye; he absorbs information and ideas; he is alert, active, energetic, resourceful, and in a few months he is promoted, and then again, promoted. He attracts the attention of the head of the establishment, who calls him into his private office, tells him that he has had his eye on him for many months and that he believes he is the youth he has been looking for to manage the business. He gives him a little stock; the business prospers still further under his management, and in a few years the new manager is made a full partner in the house which he entered as an office boy. This is the flowering out of his dream, the objectifying of his vision, the matching with reality his youthful longings. His brain has been continually developing along the line of his vision, drawing to him the material to make it real.

A poor girl, the daughter of humble people in Maine who thought that to become a public singer was an unforgivable sin, could not in the beginning see any possible way to realize the dreams she held in secret, but she kept visualizing her dream, nursing her desire and doing the only thing for its realization her parents would allow—singing in a little church choir. Gradually the way opened, and one step led to another until the little Maine girl became the famous Madame Nordica, one of the world's greatest singers.

No matter, if you are a poor girl away back in the country, and see no possible way of leaving your poor old father and mother in order to prepare for your career, don't let go of your desire. Whether it be music, art, literature, business or a profession, hold to it. No matter how dark the outlook, keep on visualizing your desire and light and opportunity will come to enable you to make it a reality. Whatever the Creator has fitted you to do He will give you a chance to do, if you cling to your vision and struggle as best you can for its attainment.

Think of the Lillian Nordicas, the Lucy Stones, the Louisa Alcotts, the Mary Lyons, the Dr. Anna Howard Shaws, the thousands of women who were hedged in just as you are, by poverty or forbidding circumstances of some sort, yet succeeded in spite of everything in doing what they desired to do, in being what they longed to be. Take heart and believe that God has given you also "all implements divine to shape the way" to your soul's desire.

If you are a boy on a farm and feel that you are a born engineer, yet see no possible way to get a technical education, don't lose heart or hope. Get what books you can on your specialty. Cling to your vision. Push out in every direction that is possible to you. It may take years, but if you are true to yourself your concentration on your desire, your pushing toward it, will open a door into the light and before you know it you will be on the road to your goal.

Washington, Lincoln, Faraday, Edison—the men who have done so much, had to struggle as hard as you are struggling to attain their hearts' desires. And today, the opportunities are ten to one to what they were one hundred, or fifty, or even twenty-five years ago. The great danger in our time is not lack of chance or opportunity but of losing our vision, of letting our ambition die.

Most of us instead of treating our desires seriously, trifle with them as though they were only to be played with, as though they never could be realities. We do not believe in their divinity. We regard our hearts' longings, our souls' yearnings, as fanciful vagaries, romances of the imagination. Yet we know that every invention, every discovery or achievement that has blessed the world began in a desire, in a longing to produce or to do a certain thing, and that the persistent longing was accompanied by a struggle to make the mental picture a reality.

It is difficult for us to grasp the fact that ambition, accompanied by effort, is actually a creative power which tends to realize itself. Our minds are like that of the doubting disciple, who would not believe that his Lord had risen until he had actually thrust his finger into the side which had been pierced by a cruel spear. Only the things that we see seem real to us when, as a matter of fact, the most real things in the, world are the unseen.

We never doubt the existence of the force that brings the bud out of the seed, the foliage and the flower out of the bud, the fruits, and vegetables from the flower. It is invisible. We cannot sense it, but we know that it is mightier than anything we see. No one can see or hear or feel the force of gravity, or the forces which balance the earth and whirl it with lightning speed through space, bringing it round its orbit without a variation of the tenth of a second in a century, yet who can doubt their reality? Does any one question the mighty power of electricity because it cannot be seen or heard or smelled?

The potency of our desires of our soul longings, when backed by the effort to make them realities, is just as real as is that of any of the unseen forces in Nature's great laboratory. The great cosmic ether is packed with invisible potentialities. Whatever comes out of it to you comes in response to your call. Everything you have accomplished in life has been a result of a psychic law which, consciously or unconsciously, you have obeyed.

Do not make the mistake of thinking that the way will not open because you cannot now see any possible means of achieving that for which you long. The very intensity of your longing for a certain career, to do a certain thing, is the best evidence that you have the ability to match it, and that this ability was given you for a purpose, even to play a divine, a magnificent part in the great universal plan. The longing is merely the forerunner of achievement. It is the seed that will germinate if nurtured by effort.

If, however, you stop at sowing the seed you will get just about as much harvest as a farmer would get if he should sow his seeds without preparing the soil, without fertilizing or cultivating it or keeping down the weeds. It is the blending of the practical with the ideal that brings the harvest from the seed thought. You must keep on struggling toward your ideal. No matter how dark and forbidding the way ahead of you, just imagine you are carrying a lantern which will advance with you and give light enough for the next step. It is not necessary to see to the end of the road. All the light you need is for the next step. Faith in your vision and persistent endeavor will do the rest. If you do your part, faith in having an appointed place in the plan of the universe will bring things out better than you can plan or even imagine.

Send out your wishes, cherish your desires, force out your yearnings, your heart longings with all the intensity and persistency you can muster, and you will be surprised to see how soon they will begin to attract their affinities, how they will grow and take tangible shape, and ultimately become actual things. Fling out your desires into the cosmic ether boldly with the utmost confidence. Therein you will gather the material which shall build into reality the castle of your dreams.

The trouble with us is that we are afraid to do this. We fear that fate will mock us, cast back to us our mental visions empty of fruition. We do not understand the laws governing our thought forces any more than we understand the laws governing the universe. If we had faith in their power, our earnest thoughts and efforts would germinate and bud and flower just as does the tiny seed we put into the earth.

Think how the seed must be tended and nurtured before it will give forth the new life. See how the delicate bud has to be coaxed by the sun and air for many weeks or months before it pushes its head up through the tough sod to the light. Suppose it were afraid to make the attempt and, should say: "It is impossible for me to get out of this dark earth. There is no light here. I am so tender the slightest pressure will break me and stop my growth forever. The only way out of my prison is to push up through this tough sod, and it would take a tremendous force to do that. I would be crushed, strangled, before I got half way through."

But the sun beckons, coaxes, encourages. The bud is moved into attempting the "impossible," and behold, soon it rears its tender head above what could otherwise be considered the great enemy of its progress. And then, the dark sod, the very thing which appeared to make its future impossible, becomes its support and strength. The very struggle to get up through the soil has strengthened its fiber and fitted it to cope with the elements above, with the storms it must meet.

Just like this tender plant, you may be hemmed in by seemingly insurmountable obstacles; you may not see a ray of light through the sod of hard, forbidding circumstances.

Hold your vision and keep pushing. In your struggle you will develop strength, you will find sunshine and air, growth and life. You may be shut in by an uncongenial occupation and tempted to lose heart and give up your dreams because you can see no way to better yourself. This is just the time to cling to them, and to insist that they shall come true. Without knowing it you may be just in the middle of the sod, and if you keep pushing where you are, in season and out of season, you will come to the sunlight and the air, to freedom.

There is no human being who doesn't have some sort of a chance. If your present position cramps you; if it does not give you room to express yourself, you can make room by filling it to overflowing, by doing your work as well as it can be done, by keeping your mind steadfastly fixed on the ladder of your ascent. In your mind you make the stairs by which you ascend or descend. Nobody else can do it for you. The master key which will unlock that cruel door that keeps you back is not in the hand of fate. You are fashioning it by your thoughts.

Your next step is right where you are, in the thing you are doing today. The door to something better is always in the duty of the moment: The spirit in which you do your work, the energy which you throw into it, the determination with which you back up your ambition—these, no matter what opposes, are the forces that unlock the door to something better. If you hold to your vision and are honest, earnest and true, there is nothing that can stand in the way of its realization.

I have never known a person who was dead-in-earnest in his efforts to gain his or her heart's desire who has not finally reached the goal. No great, insistent, persistent, honest longing backed by downright hard, conscientious work ever comes back empty-handed.

Desire is at the bottom of every achievement. We are the product of our desires. What we long for, strive for, the vision we nurse, is our great life shaper, our character molder:

Very few can realize the close coordination which exists between their visions, their mind pictures, and the actual accomplishments of their career. If I were asked to name the principal cause of the majority of failures in life I should say it was the failure to understand this, to grasp the relation of thought to accomplishment. The gradual fading out of one's dreams, the losing of one's vision, may be traced to this cause.

When we first start out in life we are enthusiasts. Our vision is bright and alluring and we feel confident we are going to win out, that we shall do something distinctive, something individual, unusual. But after a few setbacks and failures we lose heart, and faith in our vision dies. Then we gradually awaken to the fact that our ambition is beginning to deteriorate. It is not quite as sharply defined as formerly. Our ideals are a trifle dimmed, our longings a trifle less insistent. We try to find reasons and excuses for our lagging efforts and waning enthusiasm.

We think it may be due to over-work—because we are tired and need a rest, or because our health is not quite up to standard—and that, by and by our former intense desire to realize our dreams will return. But the whole process is so insidious that before we realize it our fires, for lack of fuel, are quite burned out. Our grip on our vision was not strong enough. We did not half understand its mighty power, when firmly and persistently kept in mind, to help us to our goal.

What we get out of life depends very largely on fidelity to our visions. If we believe in them, we will not let them die for lack of nursing. If we really have ability to match them, and are not self-deceived by egotism, petty vanity, and conceit, then no misfortunes, no failure of plans, no discouragements, no obstacles—nothing in the world—can separate us from them. We will cling to them to our dying day.

The world stands aside for such a one who believes in his or her vision, who consecrates himself or herself without reserve to its fulfillment. People know there is something back of the dreamers who have such faith in their life dreams that they will sacrifice everything to make them come true.

How much of a grip has your vision on you? Does it clutch you with a force that nothing but death can relax, or does it hold you so lightly that you are easily separated from it, discouraged from trying to make it real?

Constant discouragements are a great temptation to abandon one's life dreams, to drop one's standards. One's vision is apt to become blurred in passing through great crises, in periods of general depression, in times of financial stress, but this is really the test of a strong character—that obstacles are not allowed to divert one from one's aim. Those who are made of the stuff that wins, hang on to their vision, even to the point of starvation, for they know that there is only one way of bringing it down to earth, and that is by clinging to it through storm and stress, in spite of every obstacle and discouragement.

Never mind what discouragements, misfortunes or failures come to you, let nobody, no combination of unfortunate circumstances, destroy your faith in your dream of what you believe you were made to do. Never mind how the actual facts seem to contradict the results you are after. No matter who may oppose you or how much others may abuse and condemn you, cling to your vision, because it is sacred. It is the God-urge in you. You have no right to allow it to fade or to become dim. Your final success will be measured by your ability to cling to your vision through discouragement. It will depend largely upon your stick-to-it-ive-ness, your bulldog tenacity. If you shrink before criticism and opposition you will demagnetize your mind and lose all the momentum which you have gained in your previous endeavor. Keep working, keep visualizing your life dream, and some unexpected way will surely open for its fulfillment.

Put out of your mind forever any thought that you can possibly fail in reaching the goal of your longing. Set your face toward it; keep looking steadfastly in the direction of your ambition, whatever it may be. Resolve never to recognize defeat, and you will, by your mental attitude, your resolution, create a tremendous force for the drawing of your own to you. If you have the grit and stamina to stick, to persevere to the end, if you persistently maintain the victorious attitude toward your vision, victory will crown your efforts.

CHAPTER V
A New Rosary

"Mary," said a young girl to a Catholic friend, "why do you carry that rosary everywhere, and what possible good does it do you to count those beads over and over?"

"Oh," answered Mary, "I never could make you understand what a comfort this rosary is to me. When I am tired out, or blue or discouraged about anything, or when I long very much for something that it seems impossible I should ever get, I take my rosary and begin to pray. Before I have gone over half of its beads, everything is changed. The tired, discouraged feeling is gone. Or if I have been asking for something I long to have, it doesn't seem nearly so far away as before. And I know that if I don't get just what I ask for, I'll get something better."

Those who are too narrow-minded or too prejudiced to see anything good in a creed which is not their own, often sneer at the Catholic custom of "saying the rosary." To them it is only "superstition," "nonsense," to repeat the same prayer over and over. These people do not understand the philosophy as well as the religion underlying this beautiful old custom. They do not know the power that inheres in the repetition of the spoken word and in the influence of the thought expressed.

Any one can prove this for himself or herself. It isn't necessary to get a rosary made of beads. You can make your own, an intangible but very real rosary, and if you say it over, not once, or twice a day, but over and over many times, and especially before retiring at night, you will be surprised at the wonderful results.

Is it a fault you wish to correct; is it a talent or gift you desire to develop and improve; is it money, or friends, an education, success in any enterprise; is it contentment, peace of mind, happiness, power to serve, power in your work? Whatever it is you desire, make it a bead in your rosary, pray for its accomplishment, think of it, work for its fulfillment and your desire will materialize.

There are many ways of praying. All our prayers are not vocalized petitions to the Almighty. They are also our inspirations, the aspirations of the soul to be and to do. Desire is prayer. The sincerest prayer may be the longing of the heart to cultivate a talent or talents. That which we dream of and struggle to attain, our efforts to make good; these are genuine prayers.

When Jane Addams, as a little girl, longed for the power to lift up other little girls and make them happy; when she dreamed of a time when she should be grown up and doing a great work in the service of humanity, she was praying. She was even then laying the foundations of Hull House, the Chicago settlement house she co-founded as a service to the poor and source of social reform activities, including women's right to vote. Her whole life from childhood up was a prayer because it was a preparation for a great and noble work.

When the child, Frances Willard, longed and dreamed in her remote Wisconsin home she was praying and building as surely as in her later years when she was the moving power of the Women's Temperance Union she brought into being, and which, among other things, advocated women's suffrage. "I always wanted to react on the world about me to my utmost ounce of power," she said in telling of her early life and aspirations. "Lying on the prairie grass and lifting my hand toward the sky, I used to say in my inmost spirit, 'What is it? What is the aim to be, O God?'"

Such noble heart yearnings are, in the truest sense, prayers. Words uttered in places of worship, if the people are repeating prayers automatically while busily looking all about, watching other people, mentally occupied in noticing what others are wearing and how they look—there is no real praying in such a performance as this. It is not heart talking. It is mere parrot talking.

"Prayer is the heart's sincere desire." What we long for and hope for we pray for by our very longing and hope. The real prayer may be struggling in the heart without words, it may be a noble desire, a heart longing which no language can express. It may be voiceless or it may not, but the true prayer always comes from the heart, and it is always answered.

A remarkable illustration of this is afforded in a story told by the English evangelical preacher and founder of Methodism, John Wesley. He was once riding through a dark wood, carrying with him a large sum of money entrusted to his safe keeping. All at once a sense of fear came over him, and dismounting from his horse, he offered up a prayer for protection. Years afterward, Wesley was called to see a dying man. This man told the preacher that at the time he had passed through the wood, so many years before, he, the robber, had been lying in wait to rob him of the money he carried. He told Wesley that he had noticed him dismounting and how, on his remounting and resuming his journey, the appearance of an armed attendant riding beside him had so filled the would-be robber with awe and a great fear that he had abandoned his purpose.

Balzac said, "When we are enabled to pray without weariness, with love, with certainty, with intelligence, we will find ourselves in instant accord with power, and like a mighty roaring wind, like a thunderbolt, our will will cut its way through all things and share the power of God."

Everybody prays, because everybody hopes and desires, has longings and yearnings which he or she hopes will be realized. In a sense the atheist, the agnostic, the unbeliever, although they may not know it, pray just as much as do believers, for every longing of the heart, every noble aspiration, is a prayer. We pray as naturally as we breathe—for the desire for a better, nobler life, a grander and higher attainment, is an unconscious prayer.

Many people mistake the very nature of prayer, and complain that it is no use to pray, because their prayers are never answered. The reason is clear, and is admirably expressed in Irving Bacheller's pithy verses on "Faith."

> "Now, don't expect too much o' God, it wouldn't be quite fair
> If fer anything ye wanted ye could only swap a prayer;
> I'd pray fer yours, an' you fer mine, an' Deacon Henry Hospur
> He wouldn't hev a thing t' do but lay abed an' prosper.
>
> "If all things come so easy, Bill, they'd hev but little worth,
> An' some one with a gift o' prayer 'u'd mebbe own the earth.
> It's the toil ye give t' git a thing—the sweat an' blood an' care—
> That makes the kind o' argument that ought to back yer prayer."

If your prayers come back to you unanswered it is because they are not backed by the conditions on which the answer to prayer depends—faith and work. You don't get the thing you pray for either because you don't really believe you will get it, or you don't back your prayer with the necessary effort, or because you fail in both requisites.

To pray for a thing and not work for it not strive and do our level best to obtain it is a mockery. To ask to be given that which we long for, but are too lazy to help get ourselves, is begging. If you think your stumbling block will be removed, or your desire realized without raising a finger to help yourself, you may pray until doomsday without ever getting an answer. Prayer without faith is of no avail. And faith without work is a barren virtue.

In the second stanza of a little poem entitled "God's Answer," Ella Wheeler Wilcox gives us the answer to the plaint of the discouraged, unsuccessful souls who cry that their prayers are not heard, and that no hand is stretched out to lead them to the heights they would attain.

> "Then answered God: 'Three things I gave to thee—
> Clear brain, brave will and strength of mind and heart,
> All implements divine to shape the way;
> Why shift the burden of the toil on Me?
> Till to the utmost he has done his part
> With all his might, let no man *dare* to pray.'"

The answer to your prayers is right inside of yourself. They are answered by your obeying the natural as well as the spiritual law of all supply. If you don't do your part in the actual working world down to the minutest detail, your prayer is bound to come back to you unanswered.

Everything in the universe has its price, a perfectly legitimate one. You can realize what you desire if you are willing to pay the price, and that is honest, earnest, persistent effort to make it yours. The Creator answers your prayer by fitting you to answer it yourself, by enabling you to put into practice the law of demand and supply, the fundamental principle on which answer to prayer is based. You must put yourself in absolute harmony with the thing you pray for. It cannot be forced. You must attract it. Answer to prayer comes only to a receptive mind in a positive condition, that is, in a condition to create, to achieve.

The law of affirmation and the law of prayer are one and the same. "Affirm that which you wish, work for it, and it will be manifest in your life." Say to yourself, "I am that which I think I am—and I can be nothing else." Affirm it confidently, with the utmost faith, without any doubt of what you affirm. But if you affirm, "I am health; I am prosperity; I am this or that," and do not believe it, you will not be helped by affirmation. You must believe what you affirm; you must constantly strive to be what you assert you are, or your affirmations are but idle breath.

There is a mysterious power in the spoken word which gets a greater hold upon us than simply passing the same word through the mind or looking at it on the printed page. What is called auto-suggestion, or self-suggestion, is one of the most active agencies employed in mind building. We can literally make our minds; thought by thought, as we can our bodies, fiber by fiber, through vigorous affirmation. The vocal expression of a thought makes greater impression upon the memory and especially influences the subconscious mind. It works like a leaven in the whole nature, putting agents in motion that establish a connection between us and our desires, the objects for which we are working. The persistent affirmation of our ability to do that which we wish to undertake in a superb, kingly fashion, is a great stimulus, a positive, creative force.

Make yourself a New Thought rosary, not of set formal prayers, but an original one whose beads shall be your heart's aspirations, your desires to *e*-volve the strong, radiant, successful happy man or woman the Creator has *in*-volved in you.

If you are unhappy, crushed by repeated failures and disappointment, suffering the pangs of thwarted ambition, put this bead in your rosary and say it over to yourself frequently:

"The being God made was never intended for this sort of life. Mary (or John)," addressing yourself by name, "God made you for success, not failure. He never made any one to be a failure. You are perverting the great object of your existence by giving way to discouragement, going about among your fellows with a long, sad, dejected face, as though you were a misfit, as though there were no place for you in this great glad world of abundance. You were made to express gladness, to go through life with a victorious attitude, like a conqueror. The image of God is in you; you must bring it out and exhibit it to the world. Don't disgrace your Maker by violating His image, by being anything but the magnificent man or woman He intended you to be."

Back up every "bead," or prayer you put in your rosary by action during the day, otherwise you might as well save yourself the trouble of stringing your beads, for

> "It's the toil ye give t' get a thing-the sweat an' blood an' care—
> That makes the kind o' argument that ought to back yer prayer:"

If you are a victim of timidity and self depreciation, afraid to say your soul is your own; if you creep about the world as though you thought you were taking up room which belonged to somebody else; if you shrink from responsibility, from everything which draws attention to yourself; if you are bashful, timid confused, tongue-tied, when you ought to, assert yourself, turn to your rosary and add another bead. Boldly assume the quality of a hero, vehemently affirm that you actually possess invincible courage, and you will be surprised at your immediate increase of strength and positiveness. Deny that you have any weakness, defect or deficiency which can handicap your career. Insist upon affirming the opposite quality, the winning quality. Say to yourself, "I am a child of the King of kings. I will no longer suffer this cowardly timidity to rule me—a prince (or princess) of heaven. I am made by the same Creator who has made all other human beings. They are my brothers and sisters. The earth and the stars and the sun are mine. I will quit this everlasting self-depreciation, this self-effacement, this cringing habit of forever appearing to apologize for being alive. It is a crime against my Maker and myself. Henceforth I shall carry myself like a prince (or princess). I will act like one, and will walk the earth as a conqueror. I will let no opportunity pass today for assuming any responsibility which will enlarge me, for expressing my opinion, for asserting myself whenever and wherever necessary.

"This specter, this shadow of self-depreciation which has held me back so long, which has darkened my path in life must go. I shall walk henceforth with my face toward the sun so that the shadows of life will fall behind me, and not across my path as before. I am going to face life with a self-respecting, victorious attitude, with a hopeful outlook, for I know that I am victory organized. Hereafter I am going to think more of myself. I am not going to put myself on the bargain counter any longer by going around as though I had a skim milk opinion of myself. No more of the poorhouse attitude of inferiority for me. I have just as much right n this earth as any potentate, as much right to hold up my head and assert myself as any monarch. I know that I was born for victory, born to conquer. I am going to win out in this great inspiring game of life."

If you feel that you lack initiative, decision; if you are a waverer, a vacillator, a putter-off of things, not a self-starter; if procrastination runs in your blood, persistently affirm that you possess the opposite qualities. Boldly assert the opposite and add the assertion to your rosary. Stoutly affirm your ability to begin things, to do them as well as they can be done, and to push them through to a complete finish. Learn to trust that there is a divine force within you which will carry you through. Never again allow yourself to harbor thoughts of your inferiority or deficiency. Resolve that you are going not only to play the heroic part in life, that you are not only going to begin work upon the duty awaiting you, but that you are going to put it through, that you are going to do things, and that you will never again allow yourself to waver, to procrastinate in the smallest matter, even if you do make mistakes now and then. Better make a mistake and forge ahead than to remain negative and inactive.

Say to yourself, "I am going to assert my manhood or womanhood and stand for something. I am going to be a force in the world and not a weakling. I was made to make my life a masterpiece and not a botch; I was created for a great end, and I am going to realize that end. There are forces inside of me which if aroused and put into action would revolutionize my life, and I am going to get control of them, to use them. I am going to find myself and use a hundred per cent, instead of a little fraction of my ability."

If you are obsessed with the idea that you are not as bright, that you have not as much ability as most other people; if you have been called dull, dense, stupid by your parents and teachers, until you have lost confidence in yourself; if you have been dwarfed by the suggestion of inferiority, either through, what others have said of you, or the thought you have held of yourself, you must change all this. You must assert your ability and hold tenaciously the ideal of the able, efficient man or woman you long to be and that it is in you to become. You must not only affirm your power to be that which you wish, you must replace the picture of your inferiority with the ideal of wholeness, of completeness, of the man or woman you have been intended you to be. Cling to this ideal of yourself, assert your superiority, and you will soon drive out the dwarfed, inferior, defective image which others, or your own false thoughts, have established in your subconsciousness. Holding the truth, the perfect ideal, in mind will give you confidence, assurance to do the thing you are capable of doing.

If you brood over the failure suggestion, if you visualize an inferior picture of yourself, you will become obsessed with the failure idea, with the thought of your inefficiency, and make it well-nigh impossible for you to succeed in any undertaking. If for any reason you have dropped into the failure habit, you will have to make a very determined effort to break away from it, or your life will indeed be a failure. If you feel this way about yourself, just add another bead to your rosary. Cut "I can't" out of your vocabulary and substitute "I can"—for they can who think they can.

Napoleon, one the greatest achievers the world has ever seen, hated the word "can't" and would never use it if it could be avoided. He did not believe in the "impossible." When he was praised for his daring and genius in crossing the Alps in the dead of winter, he said, "I deserve no credit, except for refusing to believe those who said it could not be done."

Did you ever think that every time you say "I can't" you weaken your confidence in yourself and your power to do things?' Did you ever know a person who has a great many "I cant's," and excuses in his vocabulary to accomplish very much? Some people are always using the words, "Oh, I can't do that"; "I can't afford this"; "I can't afford to go there"; "I can't undertake such a hard task, let somebody else do that." These negative assertions undermine power. Have nothing to do with them. In all questions of achievement, let your rosary deal in affirmations. Instead of "I can't," say *"I can," "I must," "I will."* Begin what you fear to undertake, and half its difficulties will vanish.

Make it a rule never to affirm of your health, your success, or yourself what you do not wish to be true. Don't say that you feel "rocky," that you are used up, played out, that you feel miserable, that you don't feel like doing anything. Never tell people of your aches and pains, for every repetition means etching the foreboding pictures of these conditions deeper and deeper into your consciousness. Instead of thus intensifying them, say to yourself, "I am health, I am vigor, I am power, I am that which I think I am." Refuse to see or to hold for an instant an imperfect, discordant image of yourself. Do not harbor a suggestion of your inferiority, physically or mentally. Always picture yourself as a great, strong, splendid man or woman, clean, true, beautiful—a sublime specimen of humanity. Do not allow yourself to harbor a thought of physical or mental weakness. Think health, power, perfection at every breath. Persist in holding the thought of yourself as you long to be, the ideal which your Creator saw ahead of you when he fashioned you.

Are you in the habit of losing your temper, of flying into a rage over trifles? Anger, whatever its cause, is temporary; insanity. To retain self-control, mental poise, equanimity, under all provocations, great or small, is an index of a fine strong character. It is a triumph of strength over weakness, of greatness over littleness. The habit of conquering ourselves is the habit of victory; it strengthens all the faculties. You can bring this great force of control to your aid. Say to yourself, "I was not intended to be passion's slave. It is unworthy of a real man, of a real woman to be the plaything of temper, or any sort of explosive tearing down passion. There is something divine in me and I will not allow my lower nature to get control."

If you are cursed with the fatal habit of indecision; if you are a weak vacillator, always taking things up for reconsideration because you are not quite sure that you have done the right thing; if you allow yourself to waver, to doubt the wisdom of your decision, you will be incapable of ever under any circumstances arriving at an intelligent conclusion.

You can cure the curse of indecision by asserting your power to see clearly, think quickly and act decisively. If you are in doubt as to what career to choose; if you hesitate in regard to what course you should take in any difficulty, which of two or three paths you should follow—whatever your problem may be—ask for light and the divine power within will come to your aid and guide you aright. Resolve every morning that you will, during that day, decide things without possibility of recall or reconsideration. First go over the matter to be decided very thoroughly and carefully. In making your decision use the best judgment at your command and then close the incident. You will secure yourself against vacillation by refusing, after it is thus closed, to wonder whether, you have done the wisest thing, by resisting every temptation to open the matter for reconsideration.

If you are suffering with the poverty disease, if your whole life has been stunted by poverty, saturated with poverty-stricken thoughts and convictions, if you have been heading towards the poverty goal, just turn about face, and put the law of abundance into operation. Face towards prosperity and success instead of poverty and failure. All, the good things you need are yours by inheritance. Claim them, expect them, work for them, pray for them, and you will realize them in your life. Make this last stanza of Ella Wheeler Wilcox's splendid little poem "Assertion" a new bead on your rosary. Repeat it frequently, and work cheerfully, confidently, courageously toward its fulfillment.

> "I am success. Though hungry, cold, ill-clad,
> I wander for awhile. I smile and say,
> 'It is but for a time—I shall be glad
> Tomorrow, for good fortune comes my way.
> God is my father, He has wealth untold,
> His wealth is mine, health, happiness and gold.'"

If you have made fatal mistakes for which you have been ostracized from society; if you are morbidly worrying over some unfortunate experience, thus making it bigger, darker and more hideous, just thrust it out of your mind, bury it, forget it, say to it, "You have no power over me; I will not allow you to destroy my peace and thwart my career. You are not the truth of my being. The reality of me is divine, and you cannot touch that. I can and I will rise above all my troubles, make good all my mistakes and errors. *I* will not be overcome. *I will* overcome."

If you are the slave of a demon habit which has blasted your hopes, blighted your happiness, thwarted your ambition, cast its shadow across your whole life, say to yourself "I will break away from this vile habit. I will be free and not a slave."

If it is drugs holding you back in life, string this bead on your rosary, "I was not made to be dominated by you, a mere weed, an extract of grain, a habit which I forged. I am done with you, once and forever. The appetite for you is destroyed. There is something divine within me which makes me perfectly able to overcome you. You have disgraced me for the last time. Never again can you humiliate me and make me despise myself. There can be only one ruler in my mental kingdom and I propose to be that one. I don't propose to allow you to ruin my life, to force me to carry in, my face the signs of my defeat, the scarlet letter of my degradation, my failure. You have humiliated, insulted me, tyrannized over me long enough, making me confess that I hadn't enough strength of mind to stand up against a single vicious, degrading habit. Now I defy you. Your power over me is at an end. The spell is broken. Hereafter I am going to walk the earth as a conqueror, a victor, not as a slave. I am going to front the world with my head up and face forward. God and one make a majority. I am, in the majority NOW."

Nothing will be of more help to you in achieving your great results than the constant daily use of your New Thought rosary. It will help you to put further and further away the things that make you weak, that make you think you are a mere puppet, at the mercy of a cruel Fate, which tosses you about in the world regardless of your own birthright, desires, and volition. You can make each bead a prayer, an affirmation, to lead you closer and closer to the life and career you desire.

Whether it be the overcoming of a vicious habit, the strengthening of some defect or deficiency, the getting away from poverty and despair, whatever you desire, you can repeat your affirmation concerning it, silently, if with others, audibly when you are alone, until it becomes a part of you. But you must be very positive, very insistent and persistent in your affirmations. No matter what fault you are trying to overcome or what good quality you are eager to acquire there must be no weakness, indecision or vacillation in your affirmations or your efforts.

And most especially, repeat the beads of your rosary which fit your greatest needs before retiring to sleep.

CHAPTER VI
Making Yourself a Prosperity Magnet

Every human being is a magnet, the attractive power of which may be developed in any desired direction. Each one can so direct this power that he can draw to himself whatever he wills.

Before your life can be really effective you must make yourself a magnet for the things that will make it so. You must learn how to attract, how to draw to yourself all that will help you to succeed in your work, that will enable you to attain your ambitions.

If poverty is holding you down, you can conquer it by making yourself a prosperity magnet. We are living in the midst of a stream of inexhaustible supply. It is one's own fault if he does not take from this stream whatever he needs.

What we get in life we get by the law of attraction. Like attracts like. Whatever you may have managed to get together in this world you have attracted by your mentality. You may say that you have earned these things, that you have bought them with your salary, the fruit of your endeavor. True, but your thought preceded your endeavor. Your mental plan went before your achievement.

The mere changing of your mental attitude will very soon begin to change conditions. Your decision to face toward prosperity hereafter, to cultivate it, to make yourself a prosperity magnet will tend to draw to you the things that will satisfy your ambition.

The text "He that hath a bountiful eye shall be blessed" (Prov. 22:9) is the expression of a fundamental truth. The pictures you make in your mind's eye, the thoughts you harbor are day by day building your outward conditions They are real forces working ceaselessly in the unseen, and the more you think and visualize favorable conditions the more you increase your power to realize them. You make yourself a magnet for the thing you desire. This is a psychological law.

If you want to become a prosperity magnet you must not only think prosperity but you must also turn your back resolutely on poverty. Begin today. Don't wait for tomorrow or next day. If you don't look, prosperous assume a prosperous appearance. Dress as far as possible like a prosperous man or woman, walk like one, act like one, think in terms of prosperity. A mental healer could not cure a cancer by holding in mind a picture of the hideous disease, with all its horrible appearances and symptoms. The healer must eliminate all this from his or her mind. He or she must see his patient whole, clean, healthy—free from all disease.

The same thing is true if you want to be prosperous: you must hold the prosperous thought, the prosperous picture in your mind. You must refuse to see or recognize poverty. You must not acknowledge it in your manner. You must erase all marks of it, not only from your mental attitude, but just as far as possible from your appearance. Even if you are not able to wear fine clothes at first, or to live in a fine house, you can radiate the hope and expectancy of the glorious inheritance which is your birthright, and everything about you will reflect this light.

Prosperity begins in the mind. You must lay its foundations in your thoughts, surround yourself with a prosperity atmosphere. In other words, you will build into your environment, into your life, whatever dwells in your mind.

We hear of some people that "they are always lucky"; "everything seems to cone their way." Things come their way because there are invisible thoughts forces radiating from their minds toward the goal they have set for themselves. Things fall in line and come our way just in proportion to the force and velocity of the thought forces we project.

Thinking better things might be called the first aid for those who want to be prosperous. To picture yourself as prosperous, living in a comfortable home, wearing good clothes, surrounded with the refinements of life, in a position to do your best work in the service of mankind, this is to put yourself into the current that runs successward.

It is a strange thing that most of us believe the Creator will help us in everything but our financial troubles. We seem to think that it is in some way almost sacrilegious to call upon Him for money to meet our needs. We may ask for comfort, for solace in our afflictions, for the assuaging of our griefs and the healing of our diseases, but to implore God to help us to pay the rent, to pay off the mortgage on the home or the farm, does not seem quite right.

Yet we know perfectly well that every mouthful of food we eat, the material for the clothing we wear and for the houses we live in every breath we breathe must come from this Divine Source, of infinite supply. If the sun were to be blotted out, or to cease to send its magic rays to the earth, in a few days there would not be a single living thing on the globe. Not a human being, not an animal could exist without it. Not a tree, not a plant, not a flower, no fruits, no vegetables, no grass, nothing green, no vegetable life, would be possible. Without the sun's energizing power all, life would cease on this planet. It would be as cold, barren and lifeless as on the moon. In a like manner, everything we have comes from the creator, and without the supply which flows from His abundance we could not live a single instant. Why should we not, then, look to this great Source for our money supply?

The truth is we were all intended to live the life abundant. Never for a moment harbor the thought that anything can come to you but prosperity, for this is your birthright; and because it is, you should demand it.

Turn your back on poverty. Make up your mind that you will never again have anything to do with it, that you will not encourage it by dwelling on and visualizing poverty suggestions. Face toward prosperity. Think of and plan for prosperous conditions; struggle toward prosperity with all your might and you will draw it to you.

Suppose you are poor and live in a humble home, just have a talk with your spouse and children, and make up your minds that you will all focus on your objective—improved conditions—that you will face the other way, toward prosperity instead of poverty. Say to yourself, "It is a shame for God's children to exhibit such a pauperized appearance. It is a reflection on my Father-Mother-God to go about among my fellows looking as though everything had gone wrong with me, as though I were disappointed with life. This is ungrateful. I can at least show gratitude for health, for the privilege of living in God's pure air and sunlight by holding up my head and walking erectly, joyously, as His child should. I am really insulting the Creator, to whom I pray, by reflecting such despair and degrading poverty in my mental attitude, thus erasing the divine image from my face. No matter how little I have, I can at least appear respectable. I can show that I respect myself by doing away as far as possible with the depressing appearance and influence of poverty."

Tidy up your little home and make it as neat and cheerful as possible. Do the same with your dress and general appearance. Keep yourself better groomed; look up brace up, brush up, struggle up. Surround yourself with an atmosphere of hopefulness and show everybody by the new light in your eyes the light of hope and expectancy of better things, that there is a change in you. Your neighbors will notice it. They will see a change in your home and your family. The change in the mental attitude of yourself and family, through facing toward the light instead of darkness, toward hope instead of despair, will make a tremendous change in your whole outlook on life.

In this way you are making yourself a prosperity magnet, you are radiating thought waves of hope, of ambition, of determination. Your new mental attitude is expressed in an erect carriage, in squared, thrown back shoulders, in a neat, clean appearance—even though the clothing be old and threadbare—in a winning, forceful, magnetic countenance. You are thus establishing the conditions of success. The positive prosperity thought flows out like a wireless current and connects itself with similar thought currents. Hold the prosperity conviction, work steadily toward your object; see opportunity and success in your vista, determine to be somebody, hold firmly to the resolve, and your mentality will direct the invisible magnet of your personality to lift you higher and higher, to attract toward you others who will help you in the direction in which you are moving.

If you want a better position, more salary, money to pay off debts, or to get what you need, whatever it may be, cling with all the power of your mind to the thing you are trying to get, and never for a moment doubt you will get it.

As long as you keep yourself saturated with the poverty conviction you cannot rise out of poverty. You must think yourself out of it. "The Lord is my Shepherd, and I *cannot* want." Hold that thought firmly and steadfastly in your mind. Believe it. Live up to it.

Abundance will never flow through pinched, doubting, poverty thoughts, any more than clear, crystal water can flow freely through foul, grease-clogged pipes. A right view-point must be your mental plumber to keep the connection open and free. Things of a kind attract one another. The poverty thought attracts more poverty, the fear thought more fear, the worry thought more worry, the anxiety thought more anxiety. On the other hand, the faith thought, trust thought, and the confidence thought attract things like themselves.

Poverty is a mental disease, and you carry the antidote to its poison in your mind. The prosperity thought is the natural antidote for the poverty germ. It kills it. The poverty thought cannot exist in the mind at the same moment with the prosperity thought. One will drive out the other. It rests with you which one you will harbor and encourage.

The trouble with us is that we have been in the habit of looking for a material supply when our first supply must be mental. We keep the supply avenues open or we close them with our thoughts, our convictions. We materialize poverty by our doubting thoughts, by our fears of it. We are just beginning to find that we get out of this world what we think into it and work out of it, that our thought plan precedes its material realization just as the architect's plan precedes the building.

Remember that prosperity cannot flow into your life while your mind is filled with poverty thoughts and convictions. We go in the direction of our thought and our convictions. By no law can you expect to get that which you do not believe you will get. Prosperity can not come to you if, you are all the time driving it away from you by your poverty thought.

You must think in a positive determined way that you are going to succeed in whatever you desire to do or to be before you can expect success. That is the first condition by which you make yourself a magnet for the thing you are after. It doesn't matter whether it is work or money, a better position or health, or whatever else it is, your thoughts about it must be positive, clean cut, decisive, persistent. No weak, wobbly, "*Perhaps* I may get it," or "*Maybe* it will come, *sometime*," or "I *wonder* if *I* shall *get* this," or "if *I* can *do* that" sort of thought will ever help you to get anything in this world.

When young John Wanamaker started with a pushcart to deliver his first sale of clothing, he turned on a positive current toward a merchant princeship. As he passed big clothing stores he pictured himself as a great merchant, owner of a much bigger establishment than any of those he saw, and he did not neutralize or weaken this thought current by all sorts of doubts or fears as to the possibility of reaching the goal of his ambition.

Most people think too much about blindly forcing themselves ahead. They do not realize that they can, by the power of thought, make themselves magnets to draw to them the things that will help them to get on. Wanamaker attracted to himself the forces that make a merchant prince. Every step he took was forward, to match the vision of his advance with its reality:

Marshall Field projected himself mentally out of a little country store into a clerkship in Chicago. Then he thought and worked himself out of this clerkship into a partnership. Still thinking and climbing upward, he next visualized himself at the head of the greatest merchandising establishment in America, if not in the world. His mind always ran ahead. He was always picturing himself a little higher up, a little further on, always visualizing a larger business, and so making himself a magnet for the things he sought.

If John Wanamaker had been satisfied with himself at the start he would have remained in his first little store in Philadelphia, and thus cut off all possibility of becoming what he is—one of the greatest merchants the world has ever seen. If Marshall Field had stopped thinking himself higher up when the man he worked for in the little Pittsfield store predicted that he never would succeed as a merchant, he never would have been heard from But that man did not stop Marshall Field from thinking himself ahead. "On to Chicago, the City of Opportunity," he said to himself, and on and up he went until the little country merchant who predicted his failure was a Lilliputian by comparison.

The story of each of these men is, so far as the success principle is concerned, the story of every person who has ever succeeded in his undertakings. They may not have been conscious of the law underlying their methods, but they worked in unison with it, and hence succeeded.

The same thing is true of Andrew Carnegie, and of all the millionaires and self-made men and women among us who have raised themselves from poor boys to the ownership of colossal fortunes, or to commanding positions in some phase of the world's activities.

Any one who makes the accumulation of a fortune his or her chief goal, and who has grit, determination, willpower and sufficient faith in himself or herself to stick to his or her purpose, will get there. But sadly, long before many who have chosen such a goal have reached it, they will have dwarfed their ambitions and shriveled their souls.

To get away from poverty is one thing; to set one's heart on money as the ultimate good is another—and quite different—thing. There is a whole world of difference between so saturating one's mind with the thought of money and its acquisition that there is no room for any other aspiration, and the constant dwelling on the hopeless poverty thought, the incessant picturing yourself as a pauper until you are so convinced of poverty's hold on you that you destroy the very ability which should help you to get away from it.

People who are down and out financially are down and out mentally. They are suffering from a mental disease of discouragement and loss of hope. There ought to be institutions conducted by government experts for the treatment of these poverty sufferers, for they are just as much in need of it as are those in our hospitals. They need advice from mental experts. They have lost their way on the life path, and need to be shown the way back. They need to be turned about mentally, so that they will face the light instead of the darkness. They should be shown that they are stopping up their prosperity pipes, cutting off their source of supply by their pinching, poverty-stricken, limiting thought. Their whole mental attitude points toward failure, toward poverty, and by a natural law their outward conditions conform with the pictures they hold in mind.

What a revelation would come into your life if you will only eliminate from your mind for a single year the poverty thought; if you would erase from your mind poverty pictures and all the suggestions of grinding want that sadden and discourage; if, instead of expecting poverty, and all that the idea implies, you would go through one year expecting just the opposite—prosperity—visualizing, talking prosperity, thinking prosperity, acting as though you expected to be, as though you *were*, prosperous! Just this radical change of thought, this transposition of mental attitude; the persistent holding of the prosperous viewpoint for a year would not only change your whole outlook on life, but would revolutionize your material conditions.

Your ambition would grow; your new way of looking at life would give an upward tendency to your surroundings. Everything would take on a different appearance. There would be a new light in your face; expectancy of better things would give a glow of cheerfulness to your countenance. There would be a light in your eyes which never was there before. Working in the spirit of hope and expectancy of better things instead of that of discouragement and the fears of even greater poverty, you would forge ahead in a way that would astonish yourself. We have not yet tapped the possibilities of any part of the world's human resources.

Every inhabitant of the earth today is treading on secrets which would emancipate humanity from drudgery and allow it to live happily, instead of merely to mostly eke out a wretched subsistence as he it has done up to the present. Hitherto, in the great majority of cases, we have barely been existing on the husks of things.

Now we are beginning to taste the kernel, because we are coming into a knowledge of the powers locked up within ourselves. Here and there, people are mastering the law of opulence.

They are demonstrating that they can make themselves prosperity magnets, by thinking and working in conformity with the law of opulence, of abundance.

It is monstrous that so many of God's children are starving right on the shores past which the stream of inexhaustible plenty flows, a stream laden with all the rich things of the universe. There is no excuse for the horrible misery and suffering that exist in our midst. There is no reason why the children of the King of kings should be harassed and tortured, driven into premature graves by poverty, for the Creator has produced enough to make every one of His children rich, to give them an abundance of all they need. There is no necessity for those who have inherited all the good things of the earth to remain poor.

The very structure of the human machine indicates that it was intended for the best, that it was planned for comforts, for luxuries, and not for poverty-stricken conditions. If we could only realize the far-reaching influence of always expecting the best to come to us, always expecting opulence, success, we would never allow ourselves to be dominated by the dark pictures of poverty and failure.

If every one of you reading these words who is suffering from the limitations and humiliations imposed by a grinding poverty would proceed to establish the prosperity habit along the lines suggested; if you would, by continually holding the prosperous thought, convince your subconscious self that you were made to be successful, that prosperity belongs to you; that it was never intended that you should live in poverty-stricken conditions, then you will have struck the very basic principle of prosperity.

Hold this victorious attitude toward life, and you will overcome all unfavorable conditions.

CHAPTER VII
The Suggestion of Inferiority

In olden times criminals, fugitives from justice, and slaves were branded. The words, "I am a fugitive," "I am a thief," or others indicating their crime or their inferior status were seared on some part of the body with a red hot iron.

In Rome robbers were branded on the forehead with a degrading letter. Laborers in mines, convicts, and gladiators were also branded. In Greece slaves were sometimes branded with a favorite poetical passage of their master. In France the branding iron used on slaves and criminals often took the form of the fleur-de-lis. In England deserters from the army were marked with the letter D, and vagabonds, robbers and brawlers were branded in some way to advertise their disgrace.

The barbarous custom of branding human beings with the badge of crime or inferiority persisted in America even after it had been discontinued in the mother country. Hawthorne's *The Scarlet Letter* gives us a vivid picture of the suffering inflicted on the moral delinquent by Puritan moralists in Colonial days. The tragic heroine, Hester Prynn, is never allowed to forget her misdeed. The sinister scarlet letter with which she is branded proclaims her shame to every one she meets.

The mere idea of this stamping human beings with an indelible badge of disgrace, of inferiority, shocks us moderns. Yet in truth, we do not hesitate to mark people today with the scarlet letter of outlawry, the brand of ostracism. Even now, in some of our penal institutions, we continue to put the criminal badge on our prisoners by clothing them in stripes, thus perpetually keeping before them the suggestion that they are criminals, outlaws, apart from their kind.

There are certain inalienable rights which human beings inherit from their Maker, rights which no fellow being, no human law or authority is justified in taking away. No matter what offense a person may commit against society we have no right to degrade him or her below the level of a human being; we have no right so to bombard that person with the suggestion of degradation, of inferiority, that we are almost certain to make that person less a man or woman; to lower that individual's estimate of himself or herself to such a degree that we rob him or her of the power even to attempt to regain his or her self-respect and any position in society. We have no right to insist that those who work for us shall wear a badge of inferiority. We have no right to thrust the suggestion of inferiority perpetually into the mind of any human being.

One of the greatest injuries we can inflict on any one is to convince that person that he or she is a nobody, that he or she has no possibilities and will never amount to anything. The suggestion of inferiority is responsible for more blighted ambitions, more stunted lives, more failures, more misery and unhappiness than almost any other single cause. Just as the, constant dripping of water will wear away stone, so the constant iteration of a statement will cause its acceptance by the average person. Even though the facts may be opposed to it, a constant suggestion presented to the mind impresses us in spite of ourselves and tends to a conviction of its truth.

When the weight of the Civil War as nearly crushing Lincoln, when it was the fashion to denounce and criticize and condemn him, when he was being caricatured as a hideous monster in the jingo press all over the world, one day, walking the floor in the White House, he was overheard saying to himself, "Abe Lincoln, are you a dog or are you a man?" During these dark days it would appear that Lincoln sometimes had a doubt as to whether he was really the man his closest friends knew him to be, or the caricature an antagonistic press pictured him.

The curse of the inferiority suggestion not only tends to destroy our faith in ourselves, but it often makes even the innocent take on the appearance of guilt. When Capt. Alfred Dreyfus, a French military officer, was convicted, through a foul conspiracy based on anti-Semitism, of the crime of treason against France, he showed outwardly all the manifestations of guilt. When stripped, in the presence of a vast multitude, in a public square in Paris, of all his insignia of rank as an officer in the army of France, the epaulettes and buttons being cut from his uniform and his sword broken, although conscious of his innocence of the crime imputed to him, he actually looked like the guilty thing he was accused of being. All but a very few close friends in the vast concourse that witnessed his public disgrace believed that even his appearance corroborated his guilt. The brain of the unfortunate Dreyfus was a wireless receiving station for the hatred, the contempt of millions of people who believed they were looking at a vile traitor who had sold valuable military secrets to Germany.

Many young employees, especially if they are at all sensitive, are irreparably injured by nagging, fault-finding, employers, who are constantly reminding them of their shortcomings, scolding them for every trivial mistake, and never giving them a word of praise or encouragement, no matter how creditable their work, or how well they deserve it.

Enthusiasm is the very soul of success and one cannot be enthusiastic about one's work, one cannot take continued pride in it, if he or she is constantly being told that it is no good, that it is in fact disgracefully bad, that he or she should be ashamed of himself or herself, and that he or she ought to quit if he or she can't, do better. This fault-finding and continual suggestion of inferiority has ruined many a life.

Young writers, for instance, often gets a serious setback in their early efforts because of a severe criticism, an unqualified condemnation of their first book by a reviewer, or the return of their manuscript with an editor's sneering suggestion that the aspiring writer made a mistake in his or her calling. Harsh critics, editors and book reviewers have deterred many young writers from developing their talent. The fear of further criticism or humiliation, of being called foolish, dull or stupid, has blighted in the bud the career of many talented people who under encouragement might have done splendid work. If an individual is of a sensitive nature even though he or she really has great ability, such rebuffs often so dishearten the individual that he or she never has the confidence to try again.

The perpetual suggestion of inferiority holds more people back from doing what they are capable of than almost anything else. In the Old World—China, Japan, India, in England and other European countries, for example—who can measure the harm it has done in the form of "caste." Think what superb men and women have been held down all their lives, kept in menial positions, because they were reared in the belief that once a servant always a servant; that because their parents were menials they must also be menials.

What splendid brains and fine personalities we see serving in hotels, restaurants and private households in Europe—often much superior to the proprietors themselves. Saturated with the idea that the child must follow in the parent's footsteps, though they may be infinitely superior in natural ability to those they serve, these individuals remain waiters or waitresses, butlers, coachmen, maids, gardeners or humble employees of some sort. No matter what talents they possess they are held in leash by the ingrained conviction of generations that the accident of birth has decided their position in life. They are convinced that the barriers established by heredity and by caste, an outworn feudal system, are insurmountable.

How delightfully the gentle humorist Barrie satirizes this Old World condition in his play, *The Admirable Crichton*. How skillfully he portrays the clever and resourceful butler, Crichton, who in the crucible of a great emergency proves himself a born leader, a man head and shoulders above the noble lord, his master.

When the yacht carrying the master and his family, Crichton and some other servants, is wrecked, they escape with their lives to a desert island. In their desperate plight the barriers of caste are broken down, and master and man change places. Removed from an artificial environment, where hereditary rank and wealth determine the status of the man, Nature unmistakably asserts herself, and Crichton, by the tacit consent of all, becomes leader. By the force of his inborn ability he controls the situation. He commands, the others obey. Yet when they are rescued by a passing ship and brought back to England, old conditions at once resume their sway. Crichton, without a murmur, or thought of change, falls back to his former menial position, and all goes on as before.

While we Americans laugh at, or severely criticize and denounce, the snobbishness of class distinctions in other countries, we are guilty of similar snobbishness, especially in regard to one section of our fellow-Americans—the black people. No matter how highly educated, how able, how refined or charming a man or a woman, if he or she has but a drop of Negro blood, we brand him or her with the stigma of race inferiority.

I always feel sympathy for the black people who must suffer keenly from the discrimination against their race. They have seen white people avoiding them everywhere; refusing to sit down beside them in public places, in churches, on trains and cars, everywhere they can possibly avoid it. In the South they were once not permitted to ride in the same trains with whites, and in other parts of the country, while they were allowed travel on the ordinary day coaches, they were not allowed on the Pullman cars, except as waiters and porters. Our hotels, private schools, public places, and even many of our churches, have practiced similar discrimination The churches pretend to draw no color lines, but by their attitude most of them have practically done so.

Everywhere they turn in this land of ours where we boast that every man is "born free and equal," black people are embarrassed, placed at a disadvantage. In all sorts of ways white people are constantly humiliating them, reminding them that they belong to an inferior race, and they take their places according to the valuation of those born to more favorable conditions. This constant suggestion of inferiority has done much to keep black people back, because it has added tremendously to their sense of real or fancied inferiority and has been a discouragement to their efforts to make themselves the equals of those who look down upon them.

We cannot help being influenced by other people's opinion of us. It makes us, according to its nature, think more or less of ourselves; of our ability. We are similarly, affected by our environment. We unconsciously take on the superiority or inferiority of our surroundings.

Employees who work in cheap, shoddy stores or factories soon become tagged all over with the marks of inferiority, the cheap John methods employed in the establishments in which they work and, spend their days.

If the employees in a store like Tiffany's or Altman's, for example, were to be mixed up with those of some of the cheap, shoddy New York stores, it would not take much discernment to pick out the worker in the superior environment from the one in the inferior. To spend one's best years selling cheap, shoddy merchandise will inevitably leave its mark on those who do so. Even though we may struggle against it, we are unconsciously dyed by the quality of our occupation, the character of the concerns for which we work.

In making your life choice, avoid as you would poison shoddy, fakery concerns which have no standing in their community. Keep away from occupations that have, a demoralizing tendency. Every suggestion of inferiority is contagious, and helps to swerve life from its possibilities. Every influence in our environment is a suggestion which becomes a part of us. If we live with people who lack ambition, who are slovenly, slipshod, or with people of loose morals, of low flying ideals, we tend to reflect their qualities. If we mingle much with those who use slangy, vulgar, incorrect English, people who are not careful about their manners or their expression, these things will reappear in our own conversation and manners. If we read inferior books, or associate with perpetual failures, with people who botch their work and botch their lives our own standards will suffer from the contagion.

It does not matter whether inferiority relates to manner, to work, to conversation, to companions, to thought habits—wherever it occurs, its tendency is to pull down all standards and to cut down the average of achievement. We are all living sensitive plates on which the example, the thoughts and suggestions of others, our own thoughts and habits, our associations and surroundings indelibly etch themselves.

I wish I could burn it into the consciousness of each of you who wants to make a success of life, that you cannot do so while you associate yourself with inferiority and harbor a low estimate of yourself. Get away from both. Have nothing to do with them. If you are a victim of the inferiority suggestion, deny the suggestion, drive it from your mind as the greatest enemy of your welfare.

You can only do what you think you can. If you hold in mind a cheap, discreditable picture of yourself; if you doubt your efficiency you are shackled, you are not free to express yourself: You erect a barrier between yourself and the power that achieves.

The mere mental acknowledgment or feeling that you are weak, inefficient, is contagious.

It is sensed by other people and their thought is added to yours in undermining your self-confidence, which is the bulwark of achievement. No matter what others say or think of you, always hold in mind a lofty ideal of yourself, a picture of your own efficiency Never allow yourself to doubt your ability to do what you undertake. You can not be inferior, because you are made in God's image You can, if you will, make a masterpiece of your life, because it is part of His plan that you should.

CHAPTER VIII
Where Your Supply Is

We never can get more out of ourselves than we expect. If we expect large things, demand them; if we hold the large mental attitude toward our work, toward life, we shall get much greater results than if we depreciate, ourselves and look for only little things. Before you can hope to win out in any undertaking, therefore, you must be able to say "I" positively, with the force of conviction. You must polarize your mind to the positive attitude. This is the attitude that creates, that produces results in the world of matter as well as in the realm of spirit.

Positive people are forceful, because they have faith in themselves. They form their opinions without the aid of others and are not afraid to stand for what they think. They do not hesitate to differ with others. They are not a "mush of concession," like those who subscribe to what everyone they meet says, thinks or believes. They make statements with positiveness, without hesitation.

The Bible would never have gained such a dominating place in our lives had it referred to authorities to substantiate its statements, had it tried to prove its doctrines. Much of its supremacy has come from its tremendous positiveness, its vigorous affirmation of facts.

You will find nothing negative or wishy-washy in the Great Book. Its assertions are imperious, positive, dogmatic. It is one perpetual hammering, driving home of truths, of great fundamental facts. The Biblical writers speak with assurance and authority because of their profound conviction of the truths they utter. They do not argue or plead. They affirm. There is no appeal. As has been well said of the Bible, "It never appeals to readers for confirmation. It states. Every line breathes dominance, superiority and confidence."

We find the same dominant qualities, the same positiveness in great achievers. They deal in affirmations. They throw themselves with intense conviction into whatever they attempt. They continually, both mentally and vocally, assert their power to do it, and the result is a natural corollary; they succeed in what they attempt.

The difference between the positive and the negative mind, the one that can "assert the I" with vigor and the one that cannot, is the difference between success and failure.

The positive person keys his or her life to the "I can" note, the negative person to the "I can't."

The positive person denies the limitations of environment, of resources, of opportunities. He or she not only believes, but *knows*, that infinite bounty surrounds us—and that he or she can make it his or her own. The negative person, on the other hand, will not fight against environment, but will yield to it without a struggle. He or she sees limitations and difficulties everywhere—and the obstacles are "insurmountable."

But for the positive, dominant qualities in humanity, we would still be living in caves and eating our food raw.

It is the positive, forceful person who overcomes. Obstacles do not frighten, or turn such people from their purpose. They are to them but the apparatus in the gymnasium which give them additional strength and reinforce their determination to achieve. They know that they can command infinite supply, that the great forces of the universe are working for them, and that they have only to direct them. They know that it is their birthright to conquer; that the Creator put him here for that very purpose—to overcome, to grow, to ascend, to be godlike.

Everyone has sufficient positive power to guide and direct their own life if they will only use and develop that power. If we do not use, we lose. If you do not think and act for yourself, if you do not assert yourself and push your own way, the forces about you will take command and push you.

Every one in this world is either a pusher or pushed. When you are pushed, however, you go downhill; when you push yourself, you go up-hill.

If you ever expect to do anything to justify your existence, quit looking for some outside agent which will move your life train. Your power is coiled up right inside of you. There is where your engine is. The name of that engine is "I." Use the great force at your command. Get up steam and forge ahead. You will never get very far by any other means. You are only losing time in trying to get any power outside of yourself, in pulls or influence, to move you forward.

Develop and use your machinery, and no power on earth can hold you back from the goal you set for yourself.

Say to yourself, "It is my duty to make good, to obey that inner urge, that ambition prod which ever bids me up and on. I am resolved to not allow anything to interfere with the free and untrammeled exercise of my physical and mental faculties. I will unfold all the possibilities that have been infolded in the ego, the I of me. I am determined henceforth to make the most of the stuff that has been given me."

Every day has a splendid possible prize awaiting every human being, a prize which no money can buy.

It can be obtained only at the price of splendid effort and self-assertion. We are too timid, too fearful of results even to attempt what we long to do. And we are top easy with ourselves, too willing to drift with the tide of our mods. Every person who has ever achieved grandly has been a stern schoolmaster to himself or herself. They have incessantly affirmed their ideal and held themselves unwaveringly to its realization.

By cultivating the positive we drive out the negative. This is a psychological law. It is to "empty by filling." Affirmation is always more potent than negation.

"Refuse to express a passion," said philosopher and psychologist William James, "and it dies. Count to ten before venting your anger and its occasion seems ridiculous. Whistling to keep up courage is no mere figure of speech. On the other hand, sit all day in a moping posture, sigh, and reply to everything with a dismal voice, and your melancholy lingers. There is no more valuable precept in moral education than this, as all of us who have experienced know. If we wish to conquer undesirable emotional tendencies in ourselves we must assiduously, and in the first instance cold-bloodedly, go through the outward movements of those contrary dispositions which we wish to cultivate. Smooth the brow, brighten the eye, contract the dorsal rather than the ventral aspect of the frame, and speak in a major key, pass the genial compliment and your heart must indeed be frigid if it does not gradually thaw."

Few of us realize the tremendous force there is in the vigorous incessant affirmation of conditions which we long to establish. United with the visualizing of the man or woman we yearn to be or the thing we are determined to achieve, it becomes an irresistible power in shaping events. Act the part, affirm the possession, the assured realization of the thing desired, and it will tend to materialize. This is a fundamental law of creation.

There is nothing more helpful in building a strong positive character than bracing yourself up by having searching, heart to heart talks with yourself. In this way, better perhaps than in any other, you can take stock of your mental assets and improve yourself all along the line.

The habit of vigorous self-affirmation is the habit of victory. But remember that action must follow on the heels of resolution or you will never go any farther. Affirmation and resolution without prompt endeavor for realization are worse than useless. It is the man of action, of continued and repeated action, the man who never acknowledges defeat who ultimately wins out.

During our Civil War the Southern generals said it didn't do any good to beat Grant, because he never knew when he was beaten and, consequently, wouldn't stay beaten.

The first step toward a happy, successful life is to get control of the supply that is ready to flow in answer to our demand. This you can do by forming the habit of affirming that the best will come to you, that only the things that are good for you can come into your life. Don't let yourself slip into the foolish habit of anticipating trouble, misfortune, sickness, disaster, accidents. To anticipate or expect such things is to affirm their reality and draw them, to you. The habit of anticipating them will get them into the habit of "arriving." You will thus be drawn into a current of circumstance corresponding to the character of your negative thought.

Put yourself into a positive, success and happiness attitude the first thing every morning by taking time, even if only a few minutes, to say to yourself, "Happiness is my birthright. I was made to exult in life, not to go about with a long, sad, dejected face as though it had been a bitter disappointment, as though I were a misfit in the world.

I was made to radiate joy and gladness and to go through life as a conqueror. If I am indeed a child of the Creator (and I know that I am), it is a positive insult to Him to go through the world as though I were a beggar, a slave. I bear the image of the King of kings, and it is my business to make all people see the likeness. It is my duty to prove my divine heritage by radiating royal selfhood."

If you get up in the morning feeling negative, blue and discouraged; if you don't feel like working at anything, just go off alone and have a good heart to heart talk with yourself something like this:

"Now, look here, young man (or young woman), none of this: you are going to do a grand day's work today: you are going to get right out of this condition; you have had enough of it. If you are a real man (or woman) you will rise above your mood and wring victory out of this day, even though it looks so unpromising.

"It does not matter what comes or what goes, what happens or what does not happen there is one thing I am sure of, and that is, I am going to be positive, creative, to get the most possible out of today; I am not going to allow anything to rob me of my happiness, or of my right to *live this day through from beginning to end*, and not merely to exist.

"I do not care what comes, I shall not allow, any annoyance, any happening, any circumstance which may cross my path to rob me of my power and peace of mind. I will not be unhappy today, no matter what occurs. I am going to enjoy it to its fullest capacity. This shall be a complete day in my life. I shall not allow the enemies of my happiness to mar it. No misfortune in the past, nothing which has happened to me in days gone by, which has been disagreeable or tragic, no enemies of my efficiency, shall be guests in my spirit's sacred enclosure today. Only happy thoughts, joy thoughts, friend thoughts shall find entertainment in my soul this day. No negative thoughts, none of my enemies shall gain admittance to scrawl their hideous autographs on the walls of my mind. There shall be *'no admit-*

tance' today, except to the friends of my best moods. I will tear down all dark, sable pictures and hang in their place pictures of joy and gladness, of things which will encourage, cheer, and increase my power. Everything which ever handicapped my life, which has made me uncomfortable and unhappy, shall be expelled from my mental kingdom this day and every coming day."

I know of no practice which will do more for one's growth and life-enlargement than the habit of rising above one's moods and discouragements through perpetual affirmation of one's self-determination, the affirmation of one's "I." If you make a resolve like this every morning and live up to it during the day, you cannot help being positive, productive, creative.

The positive mind repels all thought enemies that would hinder progress. Doubt, fear, despair, worry, these have no place in the creative brain. They are products of the negative mind. The person who would bend circumstances to his or her will can not afford to harbor them.

Hold negative, despondent, discouraged thoughts and your surroundings will be negative, unpropitious. Hold positive, confident, hopeful, cheerful thoughts and a congenial environment will manifest itself.

It is wonderful what right thinking can accomplish. The insistent and persistent holding of the positive thought, the assurance thought, the self-confidence, the self-faith thought, the determined effort to think and act for oneself, to direct one's own forces, will gradually change a negative non-productive "I" into a positive, creative one.

I have known very timid, sensitive people who scarcely dared to say their, souls were their own before others, but who so cured their habit of self-effacement and so strengthened their weak self-confidence by constant audible affirmation of their own "I" strength, that in a very few months they had largely overcome this weakness.

Fear is negative; courage is positive, affirmative. If we would make our lives effective, we must root out all of the things which keep us in discord, all negative elements, and give ourselves over to the power, of affirmation.

We radiate our faith, our confidence in ourselves or our doubts, and distrust. Others catch the contagion of our opinion of ourselves. Many people have ruined their lives effort depreciating it and sending out to those about them the negative vibration of their inferiority.

Whatever you do, don't set up in your own mind and in that of others a picture of yourself as a weak, ineffective, negative personality. People do not realize the harm they do by making uncomplimentary and unfavorable remarks about themselves. It does not matter what it may be, the assertion of anything unfavorable to us or unlike what we wish to be is injurious. How often we hear men and women say: "I never can remember anything. I am always forgetting umbrellas and packages. I never can remember names or faces," and similar negative, depreciatory remarks. It never occurs to them that by making such statements as these they are strengthening their defects, weakening their "I". They are not aware that by impressing these unfortunate images of themselves upon their mental mirror they are seriously injuring their, self-confidence, their ultimate chance of being what they would like to be or of getting what they desire.

The worst enemy, as well as the best friend, every human being ever has is inside of him or her. Sadly, the very mental attitude of the majority of people is utterly antagonistic to their advancements.

A really brainy, professional man whom I meet quite often is a striking example of the baneful effects of the negative self-depreciatory thought. He wanted to do something big in his line, but he has had only mediocre success, and in consequence has so soured on life that he seems to have lost the power to enjoy himself. The truth is that the early contracted habit of self-castigation and unfavorable comparison with others who were more fortunate at the start has stayed by him through the years and practically disqualified him of real enjoyment or for making the most of his talents.

Another negative character of this type is the person who is forever recalling his or her lack of opportunities. Such people never tire of referring to the fact that they were handicapped at their very birth by a slovenly, slipshod father or mother, and that all through life they have been, placed at a great disadvantage compared with others. They believe, and constantly affirm, that they are unlucky, that they have never been at the right spot at the right time, that no matter how hard they works they feel a mysterious something holding him back. Some malignant fate, or destiny, they complain, is always tripping them up, thwarting their every efforts, overturning their best-laid plans. Through this "something's" machinations, although they has worked harder than anybody else they know, they and their family have remained in poverty, while their associates have become prosperous.

The cause of these people's failure is not far to seek. It is plain that they started wrong and has been going wrong ever since. They have been talking failure all their lives, affirming hard times, poverty, ill luck, and disappointment. They have been sowing thistles and all sorts of ill weeds in their garden, and now they wonder why their harvests have been so stingy, so blighted and over-shadowed by weeds.

The only soil in which our good-seed thoughts can truly flourish is that of mental harmony. In this fruitful ground lies the secret of all efficiency and happiness. Self-affirmations, *accompanied by corresponding acts*, in other words, are the true success seeds sown in our human gardens. Our present reaping is dependent entirely on our past sowing. What we are enjoying or suffering today is the result of yesterday's sowing. We are reaping weeds, thistles, thorns, or beautiful flowers and luscious fruit, according to the seeds we have sown.

In a similar way, our future reaping depends on the seeds we are currently sowing. Their character determines what our future harvests shall be.

When you long for something that it is perfectly legitimate for you to have, sow your affirmation seed in perfect confidence that it will bloom in reality. Do not wait for an opportunity, make your opportunity. You will see that the power of self-affirmation will work miracles for you.

Most people seem to think that if they were only in an ideal environment, without worry or anxiety regarding the living-getting problem, if they were free from pain and in vigorous health, they would then be perfectly happy. But, as a matter of fact, we are not half so dependent for happiness upon environment, upon circumstances, as we imagine we are. False ambition, envy and jealousy are responsible for much of our uneasiness, our restlessness and discontent.

Our minds are so intent upon what other people have and are doing that we do not get a tithe of the enjoyment and satisfaction out of our own work, out of our own possessions, that they should afford us. We think so much about what others have and spend so much time wondering why we cannot have similar-things that we do not see the beauty, loveliness and sweetness in our own environment. We question and envy when we should affirm and realize. We neglect the most potent means within our grasp—the miracle-working power of affirmation. The supply will come in answer to our demand.

Every one of us has an inalienable right to be comfortable, prosperous, free from anxiety—in short, to be happy. We were not intended to be worrying machines. The fundamental principle of the human constitution is based on harmony, and when we are in harmonious relations with the ourselves and the universe, we attain the maximum of efficiency, of power, of usefulness for ourselves. It is then that we get the maximum of enjoyment and happiness out of life.

Is it not worth while to get into such relations?

Is it not foolish to remain in discord, when by the simple process of affirmation—affirmation of the "I am"—linked with faith and effort, we can transform ourselves and our environment?

CHAPTER IX
You Are Headed Toward Your Ideal

We tend to become like what we admire, sympathize with and persistently hold in mind. Whatever we hold in our minds, dwell upon, contemplate, whatever is dominant in our motives, will stand out in our flesh so that the world can read it.

"The contemplation of perfection is always uplifting." Nothing so strengthens the mind, enlarges manhood, or womanhood, widens the thought, as the constant effort to measure up to high ideals. The struggle to better our best, to make our highest moments permanent, the continual reaching of the mind to the things above and beyond, the steady pursuit of the ideal, which constantly advances as we pursue, is what has led the race up from savagery to twentieth century civilization.

Without an ideal there is no growth; and where there is no growth there is retrogression. Without a vision the people perish. Nothing in the universe is static. None of us stands still. We are all traveling in, some direction, either forward or backward. Everything depends on the ideal.

A high and beautiful ideal, that should be our pole star, the highest, brightest light we know. A recent writer says: "My advice to all those just starting to travel life's turnpike is, 'Don't start until you have your ideal; then don't stop until you get it.'"

Of course we all have ideals of some kind when we are young; but how many of us keep them even till middle age? What young man or woman has entered into active life without an ideal of what he or she is going to do, and how the world is going to be bettered by him or her?

But do they hold these ideals throughout the years, with the strength of conviction that overcomes all difficulties, or do they abandon them with the first discouragement and settle down into a commonplace existence with interest in nothing above the material?

To youth, naturally, come glorious ideals, not only of what one's own life is to be, but of what life in general should be, the ideal man, the ideal woman, the ideal social system—and with all these is a vague desire or intention to help toward their fulfillment. But too often the result of disappointment in the effort to better conditions is, first, to give up the hope of realizing the ideal, and then to abandon the ideal itself. Here is where the great danger of retrogression comes in. Unless the ideal be held with a tenacity that no failure or disappointment can relax, it is, apt to fade away after the first ardor of youth is past.

One of the greatest aids to the preservation of the youthful ideal in all its freshness and beauty is to recall frequently, daily, the moral heroes who first gave you a glimpse of your possibilities and aroused your ambition. Read the special books, or particular chapters which fired you to emulate some noble character. Renew yourself mentally by visualizing the life and work of men and women who have wrought nobly for humanity. Think of the Washingtons, the Franklins, the Lincolns, the Emersons, the Ruskins, the Florence Nightingales, the Jane Addams, the Susan B. Anthonys, the Frances Willards, and you will be strengthened to resist the debasing influence of the fierce competition for wealth and preferment, even for mere subsistence, which in so many instances pushes out of sight the aspirations and ideals of youth. Keep constantly in mind the grand characters whose achievements aroused you to noble thoughts and endeavor in the springtime of life and your standards will never drop. Character always develops according to the pattern within us. No artist could paint the face of Christ with the model of Judas before his or her mental vision. No great character can ever be built with low, groveling ideals in the mind.

The constant struggle to measure up to a high ideal is the only force in heaven or on earth that can make a life great, beautiful and fruitful. If we would ever accomplish anything of worth, if we would ever accomplish the work we were here to do, we must live up to our ideal.

With eyes fixed on this ideal, we must work with heart and hand and brain; with a faith that never grows dim, with a resolution that never wavers, with a patience that is akin to genius, we must persevere unto the end; for, as we advance, our ideal as steadily moves upward.

Wrapped up in every human being there are divine energies which, if given proper direction, will develop the ideal from stage to stage. Who sees a sculptor at work upon a block of marble sees what appears to be only a mechanical performance. But, out of sight in the sculptor's brain, there is a quiet presence we do not perceive; and every movement of the hand is impelled by that shining thought within the brain. That presence is the ideal. Without it, the sculptor would be a mason; through it, the sculptor becomes an artist.

"The ideal is the real." By it we shape our lives as the sculptor shapes the image from the rough marble. External means alone will not accomplish this. You must lay hold of eternal principles, of the everlasting verities, or you never can approach your ideal. Your first advance toward it lies in what you are doing now, in what you are thinking.

We will not carve out the ideal that haunts our souls, on some far-off height, in some distant scene, or fabled land, where longing without endeavor is magically satisfied, but as Carlyle has said, "here and now in this poor, mean Actual, here or nowhere is thy ideal!"

"Your circumstances may be uncongenial," says James Allen, "but they shall not long remain so if you but perceive an Ideal and strive to reach it. You cannot travel within and stand still without."

The great curse of the average person is commonness—the lack of aspiring ideals. There are thousands of farmers who never get above cattle and wheat, of doctors who never become superior to prescriptions and diseases, of lawyers who never wholly subordinate their briefs. The ideals of the masses rarely rise out of mediocrity. Most of us live in the basement of our lives, while the upper stories are all unused. Millions of human beings never get out of the kitchen of their existence. We need aspiration and great thought-models to lift us.

God has whispered into the ear of all existence, "Look up." There is potential celestial gravitation in every mortal. There is a spiritual hunger in humanity which, if fed and nourished, will lead to the up building and developing of great souls—which must be aroused before there can be any great progress in individual uplift.

In a factory where mariners' compasses are made before the needles are magnetized, they will lie in any position, but when once touched by the mighty magnet, once electrified by that mysterious power, they ever afterwards point only in one direction. Our lives lie equally listless, purposeless, until touched by some magnet, after which, if we nourish its aspirations, it always points to the north star of our hopes and ideals.

The aspiration that is not translated into active effort will die; just as any power or function that is not used will atrophy or disappear. Great things will not grow either in material or mental soil without care and nourishment. Only weeds, briers, and noxious plants thrive easily.

We rise or fall by our ideals, by our pursuit or our disregard of them. And sadly, the majority of us make bungling work of our living. Everywhere we see those who are making a splendid *living*, but a very poor *life*; succeeding in their vocations but failing as people, swerving from their own highest ideals for the sake of making a little more money—dwarfing the best thing in them for a superficial material advantage, selling the birthright of the soul's ideal for a mess of pottage.

Is there any reason or intelligence people continuing to turn their abilities, their energies, all there is in them, into dollars after they have many times more of these than they can ever use for living and betterment? Is the gift of life so cheap, so meaningless, of so little importance, that we can afford to spend time on things that do not endure—upon unnecessary, material things which so soon pass away, to the neglect of those that endure? We know that life is our great opportunity to acquit ourselves like worthy individuals who make a difference, who contribute in some way. Yet it is too often into the transient things that we pour the full force of our energies, all the while sighing and wishing that we could achieve, our ideals. We sacrifice much to gain wealth, but practically nothing to realize the outreach of our souls.

The ideal is indeed the "pearl of great price," in the balance with which "all that a person hath" besides is as nothing. The true successes of the world have always been those of high ideals, to which they were ever loyal—those said "this one thing I do," and have put the whole strength of their lives into their effort to realize their ideal.

If from the start you listen to and obey that something within which urges you to find the road that leads up higher; if, you listen, to and obey the voice which bids you look up and not down, which ever calls you on and up, no matter what its outward seeming, your life can not be a failure. The really successful men and women are those who by the nobility of their example contribute to the uplift, the happiness, the enlargement of life, to the wisdom of the world—not those who have merely piled up selfish dollars. A rich personality enriches everybody who comes in contact with it. Everybody who touches a noble life feels ennobled thereby.

Phillips Brooks said: "The ideal life of full completion haunts us all. We feel the thing we ought to be beating beneath the thing we are. God hides some ideal in every human soul. At some time in each person's life, each feels a trembling, fearful longing to do some great good thing. Life finds its noblest spring of excellence in its hidden impulse to do one's best."

Substitute the finer for the cheaper goal. Today and every day, hold to your high ideal despite the stress and turmoil of modern daily living. In such measure, you will hasten the day when such an ideal will be the inspiration and the power that moves you . . . and your world.

CHAPTER X
Education Under Difficulties

"I am poor, unknown, and friendless," thought Ti Yin of Quono, Si, "and it is more than twelve hundred miles to Peking, where the great civil-service examination will be held a month hence; but what is a walk of twelve hundred miles to a healthy youth with ambition for a government office, and in China who ever heard of poverty and lack of influence standing in the way of merit, learning, and justice?

"From earliest childhood I have studied diligently and have improved every opportunity to increase my store of learning. I feel that I am worthily prepared, and who will say that I may not hope to take the first degree, or possibly the second degree of Tszin S. S.? I sometimes think that I should not presume too much if I should try to get the third degree of Han Lin, or even, perhaps, that of Chung Yuen, highest of all and honored throughout the Empire. I will go and do my best. The richest youth can do no more."

Long and weary was the journey, but the young aspirant, although poorly clad, gaunt from hunger, and footsore from his month's tramp, was received with as much consideration as the wealthiest competitor. He remained long enough to hand in a full set of essays; but he had spent his last penny, and was forced to leave before the awards were made, too tired and sick to give more than passing thought to what he had come to consider a waste of time and effort. So despondent had he become that he had almost determined to commit suicide.

"What is the matter?" asked a kind-hearted waiter at a little inn where Ti stopped for a few minutes' rest. "Your sorrowful looks would add gloom to a funeral."

"Ah!" exclaimed Ti Yin, with a sigh. "I have studied for years for the civil-service examination, and have undergone great hardship to attend it, only to find myself forced to withdraw before the decision, for lack of money, and probably without having won a degree, so unfitted was I from hunger to do myself even scanty justice."

"Never mind," said the waiter. "I will tell the innkeeper, who is a kind man, and he may find a way to aid you."

"Yes," said the landlord, when he had heard the story. "You shall be my assistant clerk until you can earn enough to proceed homeward in tolerable comfort. So cheer up! Things are bad, but not so bad as they might be."

"It is one of the strangest things that ever happened," Ti heard a guest remark a few days later. "When the highest degree of Chung Yuen was awarded at the examination, nearly a mouth ago, no one appeared to claim it, so the Emperor dispatched his special herald to Quong Si, the home of the successful candidate, but he could not be found there, and the Emperor feels very anxious for his safety."

"But what name, sir?" asked the astonished restaurant clerk, in tones which attracted the attention of all.

"What concern is that of yours, you young intruder?" asked one of the aristocratic guests. "You seem, to have a brotherly sympathy for the Emperors anxiety."

"Ti Yin is the name of our new Imperial Councillor" said another guest, a little more civil than his fellows. "Do you claim the honor of his acquaintance?"

Without replaying, the young clerk withdrew modestly, made himself as presentable as possible with scanty means; excused his departure to the innkeeper, and hastened to report to the Department of Ceremonies.

"You cannot enter here," said the guard.

"But I have important business to attend to," said Ti, "and must have immediate audience with his Majesty, the Emperor."

"Begone!" shouted the guard, as he drove the ragged stranger from the gate. "This is no place for vagrants."

Ti Yin soon returned and renewed his request for an audience, but was arrested and imprisoned as a dangerous character. He remained in confinement for some time, while without the whole Empire was in a ferment over the strange disappearance of the new "Chung Yuen," who had not been seen during the month which had elapsed since the examination.

"General!" exclaimed one of the prison guards, addressing the jailer. "I beg you to liberate this inoffensive stranger and allow him to go his way in peace. For," he added, "my heart goes out to this man who I feel sure, is more sinned against than sinning. I will pledge my life that he is not one to do evil."

"Well," said the jailer, after inquiring carefully into the matter, "I am willing to order his release; but first he must needs receive the corporal punishment due on account of his conviction for vagrancy and disturbing the peace."

"Have I not borne humiliation enough?" cried Ti when he heard of this. "Tell your jailer that I, Ti Yin, am here basely confined, and that I command him to appear before me and in person loose these fetters from my limbs."

"Oh! My master . . ." began the kind-hearted guard, as he knelt and clasped the knees of his distinguished charge. But at that moment the doors of the prison were thrown open, and his words were drowned by a laugh from the President of the Board of Ceremonies, who had just returned from an unsuccessful search for Ti Yin and was overcome by the sight of an officer upon his knees before a prisoner.

"What is the meaning of all this?" he asked in surprise. But when he had heard the story, he hurriedly descended from his chair of state.

"Mayest thou, O master, live a thousand years!" he exclaimed.

"Imagine the picture!" exclaims a writer in *Harper's Magazine.* "The still manacled prisoner; the kneeling officers; the crowd of awe-struck onlookers; the death-like silence in that gloomy prison-room! Could there be imagined a greater tribute to knowledge and education than was there expressed? The physical power of a mighty nation doing homage to the intellectual power of an individual. Although trite, still is true the proverb that 'knowledge is power.'"

"May I remove these disgraceful fetters from the limbs they profane?" at length asked a thoughtful member of the President's suite.

"No!" said Ti Yin, proudly and firmly. "He who put them on, and he alone, has the right to remove them."

The jailer fell upon his knees, unlocked the manacles, and besought forgiveness for bringing disgrace upon so illustrious and noble a man.

"Rise," said Ti Yin, and sternly added: "Never again act hastily in matters pertaining to the duties of your office, or render less willing aid to those appearing poor and helpless than to those whom you know to be both rich and powerful. It is the greatest wrong of all. The tears of the helpless and oppressed shall be garnered in heaven, and poured out in fiery vengeance upon the oppressor's head, and her ears will refuse to listen to impious prayer. Go in peace."

It is hardly necessary to add that Ti Yin, second in rank to the Emperor, proved a wise and efficient Imperial Councillor.

"Those who live," said Victor Hugo, "are those who struggle; are those whose high resolves fill soul and eyes; who, urged by noble destiny, ascend the slopes."

"I once knew a little colored boy whose father and mother died when be was but six years old," said Frederick Douglass, addressing a colored school not long before he died. "He was a slave and had no one to care for him. He slept on a dirt floor in a hovel, and in cold weather he would crawl into a meal bag, head foremost, and leave his feet in the ashes to keep them warm. Often he would roast an ear of corn and eat it to satisfy his hunger, and many times he has crawled under the barn or stable and secured eggs which he would roast in the fire and eat.

"That boy did not wear pantaloons, as you do, but a tow-linen shirt. Schools were unknown to him, and he learned to spell from an old Webster's spelling-book, and to read and write from posters on cellar and barn doors, while boys and men would help him. He would then preach and speak, and soon became well known. He became a presidential elector, United States Marshal, United States Recorder, United States Diplomat, and accumulated some wealth. He wore broadcloth, and didn't have to divide crumbs with the dogs under the table. That boy was Frederick Douglass."

"What was possible for me, is possible for you. Don't think because you are colored, you can't accomplish anything. Strive earnestly to add to your knowledge. So long as you remain in ignorance, so long will you fail to command the respect of your fellow-men."

"I learned grammar when I was a private soldier on the pay of sixpence a day," writes British journalist, reformer, and member or Parliament William Cobbett. "The edge of my berth, or that of the guard-bed, was my seat to study in; my knapsack was my book-ease; a bit of board lying on my lap was my writing-table, and the task did not demand anything like a year of my life. I had no money to purchase candle or oil; in winter, it was rarely that I could get any evening light but that of the fire, and only my turn even at that. To buy a pen or a sheet of paper, I was compelled to forego some portion of my food, though in a state of half-starvation. I had no moment of time that I could call my own; and I had to read and write amidst the talking, laughing, singing, whistling, and bawling of at least half a score of the most thoughtless of men. I remember, and well I may, that upon one occasion I had, after all absolutely necessary expenses, on a Friday, made shift to have a half-penny in reserve, which I had destined for the purchase of a red-herring in the morning; but when I pulled off my clothes at night, so hungry then as to be hardly able to endure life, I found that I had lost my half-penny. I buried my head under the miserable sheet and rug, and cried like a child.

"If I," said he, "under such circumstances, could encounter and overcome this task, is there, can there be in the whole world, a youth to find any excuse for its non-performance?"

Could there be a more striking example of the pursuit of knowledge under difficulties?

One pleasant day in 1858, the young law student Henry Fawcett and his father went hunting together. A flock of partridges flew over a fence where the father had no right to shoot; as he was moving forward, they flew back toward his son. The father, so eager to bring down a bird that he did not think of his son's danger, fired. Several shots entered Henry's breast, and one went through each glass of a pair of spectacles he wore. In an instant he was blind for life.

But within ten minutes from the time of the accident, which deprived him of eyesight forever, this boy of iron nerve had determined that even blindness should not swerve him from his purpose.

"Will you read the newspaper to me?" were his first words to his sister when they carried him home.

Obliged to abandon law, young Henry said to his father, "Never mind, father, blindness shall not interfere with my success in life," when his father reproached himself for carelessly destroying all his son's prospects of advancement.

Henry began the study of Political Economy with a zeal rarely equaled; meanwhile having friends read to him, in his moments of leisure, the works of Milton, Burke, Wordsworth, all of George Eliot's novels, and a wide course of general literature, for he was determined that his blindness should not limit the breadth of his culture.

He became Professor of Political Economy at the University of Cambridge, a member of Parliament, and an unusually successful Postmaster General of England, as well as the author of several able books.

Helen Keller, made such marvelous progress in her studies under the care of her friend, companion, and teacher, Miss Sullivan, that she was able to enter the regular classes at The Cambridge School for young ladies. The object of her friends in placing her among seeing and speaking girls was to develop her powers of self-guidance in greater degree than could have been possible under private tuition.

Mr. Arthur Gilman, the director of the school, wished, when Miss Keller was first brought to him, to find out how great had been her progress in the different subjects which she had studied. To this end he gave her some of the preliminary Harvard examination papers— the same papers which were presented to candidates at Harvard and Radcliffe colleges. Though she had never had any preparation for college examinations, in fact had never had examinations of any sort, she passed the papers submitted with great credit. The time allowed for each paper was precisely the same as that given at regular examinations, but the questions had of course to be read and interpreted to Miss Keller, which made the time left for answering them considerably less. The answers were typewritten in clear, precise English, and with very few mistakes, either in spelling, punctuation, or subject-matter. The Harvard examiners to whom they were submitted agreed that, judged by the same standard by which they are accustomed to judge all papers, Miss Keller passed in every subject tried. These subjects were English, French, German, and history. Thus she passed five hours of Radcliffe's elementary examinations—at the uncommonly early age of sixteen, after only nine years of conscious development!

At the Cambridge School, Miss Keller studied Latin, history, and arithmetic with the regular classes. Miss Sullivan was with her constantly at school, and the two friends lived together at Howells House on Concord Avenue, one of the home buildings connected with the school. Miss Keller, a tall, bright-faced girl of sixteen, told her visitors, with evident pleasure, that she was preparing for Radcliffe—which she, indeed, did attend and graduate from in 1904 with honors.

Helen Keller was born in Alabama, June 27, 1880, her father being a former Confederate officer, and later a United States Marshal. At about eighteen months old, she lost all sense but that of touch. As a result, no attempt at education was made for the first seven years of her apparently hopeless life. In 1887, Miss Annie M. Sullivan went to Alabama and became her instructor.

She is affected by the mental condition of those about her, and can tell immediately on meeting a person whether that person is happy or unhappy—having become became apt in interpreting the speech of others by feeling their lips, and now is able to communicate with any one within reach of her sensitive finger-tips. She bursts into speech the moment she is introduced to a stranger, her evident wish being to get from the new personality all that is interesting in it.

Those finger-tips, resting lightly on the lips of acquaintances and friends, carry to Helen Keller's mind the messages from the world in which she lives unseeing and unhearing. Those fingers keep her in touch with the intellectual life of the world. She reads German,

French, and English with her fingers resting on the raised letters of the books which have been published for her. She seems almost to have gray brain-matter in her finger-tips.

If it has been possible for this girl—deaf, mute, and blind—to make such wonderful progress in her education, and, at the age of sixteen, to be prepared to pass the Harvard College examinations, what might not those who are blessed with all their faculties accomplish, even if only possessing ordinary ability, if they could only realize the value of the gifts they have, instead of waiting and longing for genius to help them along!

Years ago an English lady, who had a deaf and mute daughter, read in the newspaper one morning that a professor, A. Graham Bell, in America, had invented a system of visible speech by which it was possible for the deaf and mute to learn to speak. She told her husband that she was going to America. He laughed at her folly, for they were poor. Besides, what could she do with such a complicated system to assist her child? But no impossibilities could dissuade her from her purpose. To America she went, found Professor Bell, learned the system, returned to England, and not only taught her daughter to speak and relieved her from a life of silence, but taught many other English deaf-mutes to speak, thus bringing gladness, intelligence, and beauty into many a silent life.

"A young man," begins Sir Robert Kane, telling of the career of James Watt, the man who brought the steam engine to its full development and coined the term "horsepower," "wanting to sell spectacles in London, petitions the corporation to allow him to open a little shop without paying the fees of freedom, and he is refused. He goes to Glasgow, and the corporation refuses him there. He makes the acquaintance of some members of the University, who find him very intelligent, and permit him to open his shop within their walls. He does not sell spectacles and magic lanterns enough to occupy all his time; he occupies himself at intervals in taking apart and remaking all the machines he can obtain. He finds there are books on mechanics written in foreign languages; he borrows a dictionary, and in his leisure hours learns those languages to read those books. The professors, as well as the students of the University, wonder at him, and are fond of dropping into his little room in the evenings to tell him what they are doing, and to look at the queer instruments he constructs. A machine in the University collection wants repairing and he is employed. He makes it a new machine. The steam-engine is constructed later, and the giant mind of Watt stands out before the world, the author of the industrial supremacy of his country, the herald of a new force in civilization. But Watt was educated! Where was he educated? At his own workshop and in the best manner. Watt learned Latin when he wanted it for his business. He learned French and German; but these things were tools, not ends. He used them to promote his engineering plans as he used lathes and levers."

"All the inventions and improvements of recent times, if measured by their effects upon the condition of society, sink into insignificance when compared with the extraordinary results which have followed the employment of steam as a mechanical agent. To one individual, the illustrious James Watt, the merit and honor of having first rendered it extensively available for that purpose are pre-eminently due."

"Ashamed to ask my father to instruct me," he wrote famed British astronomer James Ferguson, "I used, when he and my brother were abroad, to take the Catechism and study the lesson he was teaching my brother; and when any difficulty occurred I went to a neighboring old woman, who gave me such help as enabled me to read tolerably well before my father had thought of teaching me." This was when the little chap, too shy to ask his father to teach him, was six years old.

"Some time after," he goes on to say, "father was agreeably surprised to find me reading by myself, and all my further instruction, after he taught me to write, consisted of three months at the Keith grammar school."

It was after this that he saw the wonderful mystery of the lever, which sent him to the study of science after having learned the alphabet.

"In the evenings, when my work was over," he says, "I went into a field with a blanket about me, lay down on my back, and stretched a thread with small beads upon it at arenas length between my eyes and the stars, sliding the beads upon it till they hid such and such stars from my eyes, in order to take their apparent distances from each other; and then laying the thread down on a paper, I marked the stars thereon by the beads, according to their respective positions, having a candle by me."

Lincoln's father could neither read nor write. The Bible and *Pilgrim's Progress* were the only books the family possessed until they moved into Illinois, where young Abe cleared the trees and split rails for their little farm. He thought himself rich when able to add to their library Shakespeare, *Robinson Crusoe*, and *The Life of Washington*.

He asked to be made postmaster, for the sake of reading all the papers that came to town. He read the aforementioned books along with *Life of Franklin*, *Life of Henry Clay*, and Aesop's "Fables" over and over again, until he could almost repeat them by heart; but he never read a novel. His education came from the newspapers, from the few books he could obtain, and from his contact with people and things. After he read a book he would write out an analysis of it.

What a grand sight to see this long, lank, back-woods student lying before the fire in a log-cabin without floor or windows, after everybody else was abed, devouring books which he had walked many miles in the wilderness to borrow, but could not afford to buy!

There is scarcely a person in America today who does not have better opportunities than Abraham Lincoln, if each person would show the same enthusiasm.

Thomas Erskine, whom Lord Campbell pronounced the greatest advocate and most consummate forensic orator that ever lived, began his legal career under many discouragements. Though be had a sublime self-confidence, which was itself almost a sure prophecy of success, yet he fought the battle of life for many years up hill and against many obstacles. His father's means having been exhausted in educating his two older brothers—he was obliged to start in life with but little training and a scanty stock of classical learning. While pursuing his law studies, he found it hard, even with the strictest economy, to keep the wolf from the door. For several years he lived very economically, and was declared by Jeremy Bentham to be "so shabbily dressed as was quite remarkable." Conscious, all the time, of powers that fitted him to adorn a larger sphere, he chafed against the iron circumstances that hemmed him in. A chance conversation led to his being employed as counsel in an important case. The effect produced by his speech was prodigious. He won a verdict for his client, and by a single bound, overleaping all barriers, passed from want to abundance, from the castle of Giant Despair to the Delectable Mountains. Entering Westminster Hall that morning a pauper, he left it prospectively a rich man. As he marched along the hall after the judges bad risen, retainer fees rained upon him. From that time his business rapidly increased, until his annual income amounted to 12,000 pounds.

The power of a resolute purpose was illustrated in the Hebrew Professor at Cambridge, England, Dr. Lee. Educated at a charity school, he was so dull that the master could scarcely endure the sight of him. He was apprenticed to a carpenter, but spent every leisure hour reading. He was so curious to know what the Latin quotations meant which he met that he bought a Latin Grammar, rose early, and sat up late, that he might learn the language.

Once, while working in a church, he noticed a Greek Testament, which he was so curious to learn to read that he sold his Latin books and bought a Greek Grammar and Lexicon. After he learned Greek, he sold his Greek books and bought Hebrew. After he learned Hebrew, he sold those books and bought books in the Chaldee and Syriac languages. But the strain of his overwork nearly ruined his health and his eyes. His chest of carpenter's tools was burned, and want stared his family in the face. He sold his books to buy bread. Too poor to buy more carpenter's tools, the great linguist began to teach children their letters; but he was so deficient in elementary branches that he had to learn them as he went along.

His reputation as the learned carpenter soon attracted attention, and he got the mastership of a charity school. From this he went onward and upward. No obstacle could daunt him, no opposition stop him. He was elected Professor of Hebrew and Arabic in Queen's College, Cambridge. He became a very noted scholar, and translated the Bible into several Asiatic dialects.

Half a century ago, the girls working in the Lowell mills gave one of the finest examples ever seen of "plain living and high thinking." One of those girls wore out Watts' *Improvement of the Mind* by carrying it about in her working-dress pocket; others studied German in the evening, though their hours of labor were from daylight till half-past seven at night; they organized Improvement Circles, and published a magazine or two. They were high-minded and refined, not afraid of drudgery, but determined to make their way to something beyond it. And most succeeded in their hopes. They earned their education; they became teachers, writers, artists; some married men of wealth and standing—and many of them went on to hold important positions in society.

Miss Lucy Larcom, whose lovely *New England Girlhood* every girl should read, tells us that when she was working in a Lowell cotton factory at the age of thirteen or fourteen years, she obtained permission to tend some frames that stood directly in front of the windows looking off on the beautiful Merrimac River; and she made her window-seat into a small library of poetry—pasting its sides all over with newspaper clippings. These she could look at and even learn by heart without interrupting her work.

A century ago a poor boy was blacking boots for the Oxford University students. By untiring energy, he raised himself above his difficulties, step by step, until he became one of the greatest of preachers: George Whitefield.

Though English writer Harriet Martineau was a poor girl, she was bound to use every minute of her spare time for self-improvement, which she did—eventually writing two famous collections of stories explaining the principles of economics to the layperson.

She says: "I had a book in my pocket, a book under my pillow, and in my lap as I sat at meals. I devoured all Shakespeare sitting on a footstool and reading by the firelight. I made shirts, but it was with Goldsmith, Thomson, or Milton open on my lap under my work, or hidden by the table, that I might learn pages and cantos by heart."

Dr. Rittenhouse was a joiner. His thirst for learning was intense. He passed his nights in study, and committed to memory the few books he could lay his hands on. He covered the fences, the barn-doors, and loose shingles with diagrams. He mended the clocks of the poor, and repaired the rude machinery of the town. Alone and unaided he became an accurate surveyor—determining several state boundary lines and part of the Mason-Dixon line with the use of his own instruments—and by tireless study placed himself among the great mathematicians of the world.

A glover's apprentice in Glasgow, Scotland, Elihu Burritt was too poor to afford even a candle or a fire; he studied in the street by the light of the shop windows, and when the shops closed he would climb a lamp post, hold his book in one hand and hold on to the lamp post with the other. This poor boy, with less chance than almost any boy in America, in spite of his poverty and hardships which would have disheartened most boys, became the most eminent scholar of his country.

"That boy will beat me one day," said an old painter as he watched a little fellow named Michelangelo making drawings of pot and brushes, easel and stool, and other articles in the studio. The barefoot boy did persevere until he had overcome every difficulty and become the greatest master of art the world has known. Yet we find by his correspondence, now in the British Museum, that when he was at work on his colossal bronze statue of Pope Julius II., he was so poor that he could not have his younger brother come to visit him at Bologna, because he had but one bed in which he and three of his assistants slept together.

Among the companions of English portrait painter Sir Joshua Reynolds, while he was studying his art at Rome, was a fellow-pupil of the name of Astley. They made an excursion, with some others, on a sultry day, and all except Astley took off their coats. After several taunts he was persuaded to do the same, and displayed on the back of his waistcoat a foaming waterfall. Distress had compelled him to patch his clothes with one of his own landscapes.

Bartolomé Estéban Murillo's mother had marked her boy for a priest, but nature had already laid her hand upon him and marked him for her own. His mother was shocked on returning from church one day to find the child had taken down the sacred family picture, "Jesus and the Lamb," and had painted his own hat on the Savior's head, and had changed the lamb to a dog.

The poor boy's home was broken up, and he started out on foot and alone to seek his fortune. All he had was courage and determination to make something of himself. He not only became a famous religious and portrait artist, but a man of great character. He was too great for the little hates and jealousies which characterized his profession, and was always a friend to the poor and unfortunate.

Horace Mann, founder of the common-school system of Massachusetts, was a remarkable example of a resolute soul pushing his way up through every obstacle to a definite goal. A college education was the dream of his youth. He was obliged to braid straw to earn his school books, but could only go to school eight or ten weeks in the year; yet his unbounded thirst for knowledge overcame all obstacles, and we soon find him in Brown University.

He was very, very poor, and most boys would have given up before they would have economized as did this resolute youth. "Work," he said, "has always been to me what water is to a fish." "If the children of Israel," he wrote home, "were pressed for 'gear' half as hard as I have been, I don't wonder they worshiped the golden calf. It's a long, long time since my last ninepence bid good-by to its brethren. I believe in the rugged nursing of toil, but she nursed me too much."

Mann eventually succeeded John Quincy Adams in Congress, where Henry Wilson said of him, "He made one of the most brilliant speeches for liberty that ever fell from human lips in our own or any other country." He was nominated for Governor of Massachusetts, but on the same day was elected President of Antioch College. He accepted the presidency, and filled it with marked zeal and ability until his death.

The young German boy, Jean Paul Richter, thought it a great boon to be allowed to copy books he never expected to be able to buy, from his good pastor. He copied, every bit of time he could get, for four long years, until he had quite a fine library of his own. Determined to go to college at Leipzig, he had no money and no friends there, yet he hoped to get a chance to teach. But alas! many other poor boys were there for the same purpose. He was not only very poor and scantily dressed, but he was very timid and did not know what to do. He wrote his mother, "I cannot freeze, but where shall I get wood without money." The poor mother was also in debt, yet she managed, as mothers always do, to get a little now and then for her boy. He wrote her that if she would send him $8 he would ask for no more. Young Jean Paul was all this time writing a book, "Eulogy of Stupidity," which his young enthusiasm had magnified into a fortune. He sent it to a publisher, but waited and waited months in vain. It was returned, finally, and poor Paul, discouraged, tried to get another publisher.

He spent six months writing another book, "Greenland." He had gained courage with defeat, and now went personally with his precious roll to every publisher in Leipzig, but all refused it. He sent it to Vass of Berlin. One day, when he was hungry and cold, for he had no fire, a letter came from Vass offering him $70 for the manuscript. It was a great day for the struggling boy of nineteen. But his second and third volumes were not wanted. Publishers finally refused all he wrote. He must give up college or starve. He had found fame a hard ladder to climb. He could not pay his board and rent and could not starve, so he stole away in the night and went to his mother. But his Leipzig boarding mistress followed him on foot clear to his home. He found a friend to go surety for his debt, put a little desk in his mother's room where she and all her children lived and did all their work, and where she, by spinning far into the night, earned bread for the dear ones—but where they nearly starved.

But Richter wrote: "What is poverty that man should whine under it? It is but like the pain of piercing the ears of a maiden and you hang precious jewels in the wound." At length the disheartened, though ever cheerful youth made a hit in his novel, *The Invisible Lodge*.

He got $226 for it, and hastened to his mother with $70. It was a proud day. Everybody talked about the wonderful novel and the poor boy was on the road to fame.

Letters of congratulation poured in from the great. One admirer sent $50 in Prussian money. He was invited to Court to visit such men as Goethe and Schiller. Now thirty-four, he wrote his mother: "I have lived twenty years in Weimar in a few days. I am happy, wholly happy, not merely beyond all expectation, but beyond all description." His mother died, and he found in the house the paper on which she had kept the record of her scanty earnings by spinning into the midnight hours. He carried it next his heart as long as he lived. *Titan*, Richter's masterpiece, took the literary world by storm, and was a great success. One hundred volumes and a noble, manly life were Richter's legacy to the world.

A student named Borysik recently passed the final examinations at Warsaw University, qualifying him to practice as a Doctor of Medicine in Russia. He was born in 1822, and his early education had a view to the medical profession, but lack of money prevented his going further than the preparatory school. He then worked twenty years, tutoring in order to save money enough to continue his studies; at the end of which period he presented himself at the Warsaw Medical Academy and passed the entrance examinations with honor. The Polish Revolution broke out and he, at the age of forty-one, threw himself into the warfare with all the ardor of a youth. With the suppression of the revolt he was exiled to Siberia, where he put in thirty-two years of hard labor in the silver mines.

In 1896 he was pardoned fully and returned to Warsaw, where, in spite of his age and the hardships he had undergone, he enthusiastically took up his studies where he bad left them off in 1863.

After a two years' course this remarkable man, at the age of seventy-five, graduated with honors and began to practice in Warsaw.

Unfortunately, for many, when they think of education and pursuit of one's career, the association of the word "genius" often slips into their thinking if they're not careful. They think that the those who best profit from learning are those who are in fact unleashing latent genius.

But nothing of the sort is intended, here. In fact, in pursuit of one's career, genius ought not be a concern. And in the attainment of success, it's not a prerequisite.

Indeed, often a school will graduate or a family rear two children—one said to be a great genius, the other almost a dunce. Yet how often do we see the bright child sink and die poor, obscure, and wretched, while the so-called dull one plods a slow but sure way up the hill of life, to fame and honor?

Does it not seem strange that in later years, one often hears so little of the smart children at one's school, as they fall behind in the race of life because they do not feel the need of hard work in their cases; while, with no other hope, the "dunce" rises slowly but surely as a natural result of tireless industry.

Mr. Wiseman, in English writer Anna Barbauld's story, on his return from a summer vacation received a new pupil with the following letter:

> SIR.—I send this by my son Samuel, whom I place under your care, hoping that you may be able to make something of him. He is now eleven, yet can do nothing but read, and that very poorly. We have made various attempts to teach him the ordinary branches, but without success. If he has any genius at all, it has not yet shown itself. But I trust to your experience and skill to discover what he is fit for and to instruct him accordingly.
>
> Your Obedient Servant, HUMPHREY ACRES.

"A pretty subject they have sent us," said Mr. Wiseman to his assistant. "A boy with a genius for nothing at all. But perhaps my friend Mr. Acres thinks a boy ought to show a genius for a thing before he knows anything about it."

Samuel Acres stood, with downcast eyes, as if he expected a whipping.

"Come hither," said Mr. Wiseman.

"Stand by me and do not be afraid. How old are you?"

"Eleven last May, sir."

"A well-grown boy for your age. You love play, I daresay?"

"Yes, sir," replied Samuel.

"Are you a good hand at marbles?"

"Pretty good, sir."

"You can spin a top and drive a hoop, I suppose?"

"Yes, sir."

"Can you write?"

"I learned a little, sir," said the boy; "but I left it off again."

"And why so?"

"Because I could not make the letters."

"No? Why, how do you think other boys do? Have they more fingers than you?"

"No, sir."

"Are you not able to hold a pen as well as a marble?" Samuel was silent.

"Let me look at your hand," said Mr. Wiseman. "I see nothing here to hinder you from writing as well as any boy in the school. You can read, I suppose?"

"Yes, sir."

"Tell me, then, what is written over the school-room door."

Samuel, with some hesitation, read, "Whatever man has done, man may do."

"How did you learn to read, was it not by taking pains?"

"Yes, sir."

"Well, taking more pains will aid you to read better. Do you know anything of arithmetic?"

"I began addition, sir, but did not go on with it."

"Why so?"

"I could not do it, sir."

"How many marbles can you buy for two cents?"

"Twelve new ones, sir."

"And how many for one cent?"

"Six."

"And how many for four cents?"

"Twenty four."

"If you were to have two cents a day, how many would you have in a week?"

"Fourteen cents."

"But if you paid out four cents how many would you have left?"

Samuel studied for a while, and then said, "Ten cents."

"Right; why, here you have been practicing the four great rules of arithmetic—addition, subtraction, multiplication, and division. I see what you are fit for. I shall set you about nothing but what you are able to do; but you must do it. We have no 'I can't' here."

Samuel went away, glad that his examination was over, but with more confidence in his powers than he ever felt before. The next day he began to study in the belief that he could learn.

In the school there was a spirit of "I'll try" manifested on all sides, and Samuel worked so well and made such unmistakable progress that his teacher soon sent the following letter to Humphrey Acres:

> Sir:—I now think it right to give you some information concerning your son.
>
> You, perhaps, expected it sooner; but I always wish to avoid hasty judgments. You mentioned in your letter that you had not discovered which way his genius pointed. If by genius you meant

such a decided hour of mind to any one pursuit as will lead him to excel with little or no labor or instruction, I must say that I have not met with such a quality in more than three or four boys in my life, and your son is certainly not among the number. But if you mean only the ability to do some of those things which the greater part of mankind can do when properly taught, I can affirm that I find in him no peculiar deficiency, and whether yon choose to bring him up to a trade or some practical profession, I see no reason to doubt that he may in time become sufficiently qualified for it.

It is my favorite maxim, sir, that everything most valuable in this life may generally be acquired by taking pains. Your son has already lost much time in the fruitless expectation of finding out what he would take up of his own accord. Believe me, sir few boys will take up anything of their own accord but a top or a marble. I will take care while he is with me that he loses no more time this way, but is employed about things that are fit for him, not doubting that we shall find him fit for them. I am, sir,

Yours respectfully,
Solon Wiseman.

In due time a profession was chosen for Samuel, which seemed to suit his temperament and talents, but for which he had no particular turn, having never thought at all about it. He made a respectable figure in it, and went through the world with credit and usefulness, though without a genius.

"Nobody thought when Grant was a boy," said one of his old school-mates, "that, he would amount to much; he was only middling in his studies, and used to spend a great deal of time in reading the life of Napoleon, which interfered considerably with his school duties, until his teacher put the book into the stove."

A man of such ordinary appearance as Ulysses S. Grant never before occupied such a prominent place in the world's thought. He showed not the least sign of genius to the casual observer. "His genius," said Senator Richard Yates of Illinois, "is neither ostentatious nor dramatic, but it is the genius of accomplishment. When his work is done, there it is, done; and there is the man, except for the work, ordinary as before."

As a boy at home, he was distinguished for nothing save fearlessness, slowness of comprehension, and a certain invincible pertinacity of will. At West Point, he occupied only a medium position in his class, and gave little promise of eminence. As a captain in the Mexican war he showed only average ability.

On his farm near St. Louis, he had hard work to support himself and family. As a business man, subsequently, he was not successful; but, when the Civil War broke out, every power in his nature came into play, and he went quietly to his work, doing that which first came to hand, without complaining of any want of appreciation on the part of the public. Yet he rose from one position to another, until he held the very destiny of the nation in his hand. He brought the war to a triumphant close, was chosen President, was re-elected, and was considered the best specimen of an American hero by all the crowned heads of the Old World.

But General Grant with all his honors thick upon him was nothing more than a good man of common-sense, with a level head, a patient, plodding mind, a true heart, and a heroic, fearless, persistent purpose and will. He never tried to do anything which he did not know how to do, and when he began a work, he stuck to it until he accomplished his object if it should take "all summer."

This man, who was graduated from West Point twenty-first in a class of thirty-nine, kept everlastingly at it, finally superseding McLellan and conquering Lee, each of whom was second in his class.

There is, perhaps, no mistaken notion more common than that of supposing that, in the pursuits of life, extraordinary talents are necessary to the one who would achieve more than ordinary success. To minds that lack energy, it seems impossible to believe that those who have made themselves a place in history and whose influence has been felt through ages, have so often been those of ordinary intellectual caliber—not possessed of a comprehensive grasp of the wholeness of things which embraces all their bearings and relations and which places one in advance of the philosophy of his or her age.

Success depends less on the general superiority of one's intellectual powers, than on one's peculiar adaptation to the work in hand. A moderate talent well applied will achieve more useful results, and impress mankind more than minds of the highest order, whose temper is too fine for the mechanical parts of a profession. The astonishing variety of talents, which some people display, is purchased at the dear price of comparative feebleness in every part. The highest reputation in every department of human exertion is reserved for minds of one faculty, where no rival powers divide the empire of the soul, and where there is no variety of pursuits to distract and perplex its energies.

How foolish it is not to struggle to make the most of oneself because one suspects that one may not have the ability to make a Lincoln, a Grant, or Bronte, an Austen. As well might the mustard seed, the apple seed, the grape seed, the kernel of wheat, or the flower seed, refuse to unfold its leaves and to become what it was intended to be because it cannot hope to grow into the stalwart oak or lofty pine.

The violet is as grand a creation as the California pine which rears its head hundreds of feet above the modest flower.

Every soul is a seed, and in fact *it does not know itself what manner of tree it shall become, or what manner of fruit it shall bear until it begins blossoming.*

The great duty of the soul seed is to keep in the sunlight, where the rain and the dews shall moisten it, and expand its budding powers into leaf, into fiber, into flower and fruit. It is not to blame for the kind of seed it may be, but it is to blame for keeping away the sunlight, the dew, and the rain which alone can unfold its possibilities.

It is equally foolish and unkind to teach that one can become *anything* he or she likes. As well tell the mustard seed that it has the possibilities of an oak coiled within itself. We can never exceed the limits set in the germ of our lives, but we can prevent our lives from being dwarfed, one-sided, or half-developed. It our business so much to determine what we shall be, as to grow into what we were intended for. And along the way, to remember that circumstances have rarely favored greatness. A lowly beginning is no bar to a great career.

Only lack of enthusiasm is.

CHAPTER XI
Misfit Occupations

"My father wanted me to be a minister," said Ole Bull, "and I thought I must do as he wished. But when I was eight years old, he bought me a new violin to study under a teacher, for be said that a minister ought to know a little about music.

"That night I could not sleep; I rose in the night to get a peep at the precious violin. It was so red," he added, telling the story years afterward, "and the pretty pearl screws did smile at me so, I pinched the strings just a little with my fingers, and it smiled at me ever more and more. I took up the bow and looked at it; it said to me it would be pleased to have me try it across the strings. So I did try it just a very, very little, and it did sing to me so sweetly. At first I did play so soft. I forgot that it was midnight and everybody asleep, but presently I heard something crack, and the next minute I felt my father's whip across my shoulders. My little red violin dropped on the floor and was broken. I did weep very much for it, but it did no good. They did have a doctor to it the next day, but it never recovered its health."

His father determined that Ole should study for the ministry, so he hired a pious tutor who used to kneel down and pray before whipping the boy. One morning at half-past four, as the tutor was dragging

Ole and his brothers out of bed, Ole sprang upon him and gave him a good beating, encouraged by the smaller boys who shouted, "Don't give it up, Ole, give it to him with all your might."

The father becoming convinced that theology was not Ole's forte, sent him, at the age of eighteen, to the university, and as he left home begged him not to yield to his passion for music, and forbade him playing at all. But Ole could not resist, and sometimes played for days, scarcely sparing time to eat and sleep, thus incurring his father's displeasure and becoming a wanderer. At Paris he had the misfortune to be robbed by one who pretended to be a friend.

In Venice, later, unknown, he worked day after day in an upper room composing a concerto, and played on his violin at night at his window.

One night, when Malibran was engaged to sing, she suddenly refused, having learned that De Beriot, whom she loved, was to receive, for singing with her, a smaller sum than herself. So it happened that Ole Bull was roused from his bed and urged to play to the disappointed audience, his playing at the window having been heard by an appreciative critic and reported to the manager of the theater.

This was the opportunity of his life, and, rushing to the theater, he won fame in a single night. The house shook with applause after the first piece. It was his boyhood of unconscious training for this opportunity, which made him equal to the occasion, instead of ridiculous, as he would have been, without it.

Your talent is your call. "What can you do?" is the interrogation of the century. 'Tis better adorn your own than seek another's place.

A young broom-maker thought that he had a call to be a preacher, and applied to his Presbytery for a license, which, after an official examination, it was thought best to refuse.

The decision was made known to the candidate by the oldest minister, who said with great deliberation: "My young friend, the

Lord requires every man to glorify Him in some particular calling, some in one and some in another, according to the talents He hath committed unto them; and the Presbytery are of the opinion that the Lord desires that you should glorify Him by making brooms."

When misfortunes happen, they may be paving the way for great successes. Our failure may be due to our superiority. Milton, for example, failed as a teacher of small boys, and Dr. Marion Sims as keeper of a country store.

It is said that P. T. Barnum had tried fourteen different occupations before he found out what nature had best fitted him for—a showman.

The Queen of Sheba once presented Solomon two garlands of flowers, one real, and the other so natural appearing that even the wise man could not distinguish between them. A bee, however, came to his aid, for it immediately flew to the real flowers. The instinct of this little insect was wiser than the wisdom of Solomon. The moral: One's bent often leads it straight to one's natural occupation, which often thwarts the wisdom of one's elders.

Galileo was sent to the University at Pisa at seventeen, with the strict injunction not to neglect medical studies for the allurements of philosophy or literature. But when he was eighteen he discovered the great principle of the pendulum by observing a lamp left swinging in the cathedral. The republic of Venice appointed him Professor of Mathematics at Padua, a position which he held for eighteen years. He was so popular and fascinating that his immense audiences would frequently have to adjourn to the open air for room. Imagine mathematics made so charming! Like Gladstone, he had the rare faculty of making figures eloquent. What a loss it would have been to the world had he become a physician!

There is a tradition that Tennyson's first poems were published at the instigation of his father's coachman. His grandfather had previously given the lad ten shillings for writing an elegy on his grandmother. As he handed it to the youth, he said, "There, that's the first money you ever earned by your poetry, and take my word for it, it will be your last."

Had 1st Baron Erskine remained in the navy, he would probably never have been heard from. When elected to Parliament, his lofty spirit was chilled by the cold sarcasm and contemptuous indifference of Pitt, whom he was expected to annihilate. But he was again shorn of his magic power, and his eloquent tongue faltered from a consciousness of being out of his place. At length, he found his place as one of Britain's most famous jurists.

When Leland Stanford was a boy, his father told him he could have all the timber on their land. The lad contracted with the railroad to buy it, hired wood-choppers, and cleared twenty-five hundred dollars by the bargain. His instincts were for business; but he ignored all this, studied law, and settled in a lonely part of Washington, Wisconsin. He had not the slightest adaptability for law. Fortunately he was burned out, lost everything, and returned to his brothers in California. He then returned to a business life—his early choice—and laid the foundation of his immense fortune and benefactions.

Franklin was so disgusted with his work cutting wicks for his father, who was a tallow chandler and soap boiler in Boston, that he determined to run away to sea as one of his brothers had done. He did run away to Philadelphia, later, as all the world knows.

Dickens was one of the greatest of English novelists; but it was his failure to become an actor which caused him, in the first place, to turn his attention to literature.

Peter Cooper was only thirty-five years old when he bought a glue factory, and had been in business for himself nine years, having made six changes of occupation in that time. Starting as a carriage-maker, the occupations of woolen-shearer, inventor, cabinet-maker, and grocer were followed in quick succession, each an improvement on the one before, until his right place was firmly established in the glue factory. He became richer than most people do who make so many changes in their career.

Scottish explorer David Livingstone studied for three years with the sole aim of being a missionary to China. It was only because his hopes were crushed by the opium war, which made it impossible to enter China, that he thought of going to Africa, where he became the means of opening up a whole continent to Christianity and civilization—discovering, as a medical missionary, the Zambezi River and Victoria Falls.

There was once a boy in the Isle of Wight whose whole soul was absorbed with the sights and sounds of the sea, whose mind was filled with dreams of its romance and adventure. His parents insisted that he should become a tailor, and apprenticed him to a worthy tradesman in the village of Niton. One day it was reported in the workshop that a squadron of men-of-war was off the island. The lad threw aside his needles, leaped from the shop board, and mingled with the crowd that had assembled to gaze upon the stately spectacle. His old sympathies kindled immediately into fresh life. He jumped into a boat, rowed off to the admiral's ship, offered himself as a volunteer, and was accepted. That boy was afterwards Admiral Hobson, who broke the boom of Vigo.

Robert Clive, as a boy, was wild and reckless. Nobody could control or tame him. He was the terror of the shopkeepers of the town. His father regarded him as a vagrant, and shipped him off to die of fever in Madras. He exchanged his pen for a sword, became a great soldier and statesman, and saved for the British their possessions in India. Long after the English nation was wild with enthusiasm over his name, his father continued to refuse to believe that "Bob Clive" would ever come to anything but a gibbet.

Grant's failure as a subaltern made him commander-in-chief.

When extracts from James Russell Lowell's poem at Harvard were shown his father at Rome, instead of being pleased, the latter said: "James promised me when I left home that he would give up poetry and stick to books. I had hoped that he had become less flighty."

The lover of art almost shudders at what the world would have lost had English landscape painter Joseph Turner shaved chins in Maiden Lane; had French landscape painter Claude Lorraine continued a pastry cook; had Michelangelo not persisted in disobeying his parents.

Half the world is out of place and tortured with the consciousness of unfulfilled destiny. How many thousands of round men and women are today misunderstood, persecuted, maligned, struggling in obscurity and failure to release themselves from the square holes into which they have been wedged by circumstances or mistakes of themselves or of parents who misunderstood them!

Civilization will mark its highest tide when every person finds his and her place and fills it.

Those out of place may manage to get a living, but they will have lost the buoyancy, energy, and enthusiasm which are as natural to a person as his or her breath.

Those who are out of place may well be industrious, but they work mechanically and without heart. It is to support themselves and family, not because they cannot help it.

Those who are out of place are constantly looking at their watches and thinking of their salary. The end of the work day does not come two hours before they have already realized it.

Those *in* their place are happy, joyous, cheerful, energetic. The days are all too short for them. All their powers give their consent to their work—say "Yes" to their occupation. They are the men and women who respect themselves and are happy because all their powers are at play in their natural, sphere.

People and animals and vegetation are all very much dependent upon the soil in which they are located, upon the climate and surroundings. The same tree that is fat and spongy in a swamp, grows hard and noble on the hillside. Acorns from the same oak planted in different parts of the world will retain the oak-identity, but will produce a great variety of oaks. The timber in some localities would be entirely unfit for use in ships, for example, because the enervating climate would rob it of its tenacity and stamina.

When the late O. S. Fowler was lecturing in Peoria, Illinois, at the hotel where be was stopping he noticed a young man employed as a porter, who appeared to have more than ordinary ability. He called him to his room, gave him an examination, told him that with an education he would become an excellent criminal lawyer. The young man, taking his advice, studied law, and became known as Chicago's leading criminal lawyer.

When we see so many misfits in the world—a minister who would have made a successful physician, a dry-goods clerk who would have made a successful civil engineer—we realize that personal judgment is often at fault in the selection of a place in life. Every one has some ambition. If you depend on your own judgment and choose wrongly, after a few years of perseverance you will sees your mistake. If you do not rectify it, however, you may become discouraged and so lose all chance of success.

There is no sadder sight than a human being out of place. I have seen a fish cast out of the sea by a huge wave, and left high and dry on the beach. Helplessly it beat the sand with its fins, but could make no headway. It floundered about, exerting itself to no purpose, exhausting its energy, until happily, another wave broke over it. Then, the moment its fins felt the water, the creature darted forward briskly, joyously, without apparent effort, back to its native place. The instant it was in its element its fins meant something, life was a precious boon.

Many young people get into situations by accident or from necessity, which are not along the line of their bent, which, however, yield them the means of living, and they often are afraid to sever the connection and start lower down along the line of their inclination. This is a dangerous situation, for none of us can do our best work until we get in the right place. We must pull with, not against, the current of nature.

Numerous people are trying to make their living by the exercise of faculties which they know are not their strongest ones. In other words, their vocations do not coincide with their bent, but they hesitate to change, simply because they have been brought up to think they must stick to what they have begun, and make the best of it.

We should not stick to a thing if were are convinced that we are in the wrong place and that there is a possibility of satisfying our inclinations elsewhere. No one should stick to a thing when a change is possible, when they are conscious that they are getting their living by their weakness instead of their strength.

We should not stick to a thing when to do so will tie us forever to commonness or mediocrity, when a larger, fuller expression of life is possible.

No one should stick to a thing when in doing so he or she finds that it will cramp his or her better life and handicap his or her career.

So, now comes the question: How *am* I to know my right place in life? The answer is simply this, know yourself.

Individual happiness and success, indeed, the welfare of the whole fabric of society, depend upon the answer that you make to the questions "What can I do best? In what capacity can I best serve others and develop to the utmost my highest powers?" These searching questions must be answered thoughtlessly. You owe yourself the best opportunity possible for expansion and expression, and nothing else will call out your possibilities, or make you so manly or womanly, as the healthy exercise of all your powers in a congenial occupation.

If you pursue a vocation for any other reason but that you love it, that your whole soul is in it, that it your meat, your drink, your life, you may suspect that you are out of your place.

If you have to be driven to your task, if you hate it, if you want to get away from it, if it is drudgery to you, if you watch the clock, or long for the sun to go down that you may be free from your bondage, you may be sure you have made mistake. You will not reach a great success in life if you are not in love with your occupation, if you faculties do not give their complete consent. If there is a protest anywhere in your nature against what you are doing, there is something wrong. The thing you were made to do will give you pleasure, harmony, satisfaction, contentment. If you attempt anything else, you will get incompleteness, unhappiness, disappointment.

Choose your career along the lines of your strongest qualities. You may fail completely in the effort to become a Marshall Field, a John Wannamaker, or an Andrew Carnegie, and yet make a brilliant lawyer, a great engineer or inventor or doctor, or any number of other professions, simply because you lack some quality absolutely indispensable to the success of a business person, but not some other field of endeavor.

It requires a great deal of judgment to choose a career, as inclination is not the only factor. Nature may have endowed you with a special ability in some line and yet there may be physical reasons why you are not likely to succeed in it. Someone with a very delicate constitution, for instance, not matter what that person's ambition may be, would have scarcely a possibility of succeeding in a career that demands tremendous physical stamina and rugged strength.

Do not be discouraged because you have not been able to determine upon your career earlier in your life. While one person may know at fifteen what he or she wants to do in life, another may not know until he or she is thirty, or even older.

The trouble is we mistakenly measure people by years. There may be a quarter of a century's difference between two people born on the same day. Years have little to do with age. When one person comes to maturity, another may be just getting a start. The fiftieth milestone may in reality mean only the thirtieth to one person, and be practically the seventieth to another.

I know a man who was in great distress, almost driven to despair, in fact, for years, because he could not decide what he could do best. In fact, he went to several different kinds of business and was successful in them, and still there was a silent protest in him all the time against what he was doing, and he never felt all his faculties and powers were pulling together in his work. He felt there was something wrong, that he ought not to carry this interrogation point before him all the time, but he seemed powerless to get into the right place. He was so troubled by his doubt, and uncertainty, and inability to decide, that he almost gave up in despair, and nearly decided to make the best of an uncongenial choice—make as much of a success of it as possible, and let it go at that. But his uncertainty continued, and it was not until he as past forty-five years of age that he found his niche, that he got a complete and unconditional consent of all his faculties to his choice. Then he felt a thrill of power, a tonic of enthusiasm, such as he had never dreamed of before, and in a very few years he accomplished more than he had been able to do in all his previous life—simply because he was in his place. He not only got the full consent of all the forces within him to his choice, but also they seemed to act with redoubled strength, with renewed energy, and he felt a power which had been wholly wanting in the previous years.

Do not jump to the conclusion that you have no special aptitude running in your blood, no bent in your make-up, simply because you have not yet been able to decide just the best thing for you. Some of the most successful men and women in the world have not discovered themselves until middle life, or even later, but they have been conscientious men and women; they have been all the time feeling for the light and groping their was as best they could in the dark, always following what little light they got.

The important thing is to always look for the light, to follow it, to listen for the voice that bids you up and on—to never lose sight of the finger beckoning you, and which will lead if you will follow.

Look for the inclination. If an inclination for some particular line runs in the blood, you may be sure it is only a question of time in finding out what it is.

In truth, each of us is a sphinx—an unsolved riddle, an agent from our creator, with sealed orders which we have not yet read ourselves in full.

When we find our place, we will know it. We will feel at home, enthusiastic and contented.

When we are in our element, we exert our powers as by instinct. A caged eagle is conscious of inferiority, of loss of power. He knows that his wings were intended for soaring, and feels a perpetual humiliation while imprisoned. But open the cage and let his proud wings feel the air once more, and he will mount and mount until he becomes but a speck between the earth and the sun. So caged minds never feel their power until they are free, until their wings touch the air, then they aspire and soar towards their natural goal.

We cannot carve ourselves into anything we please, unless it is what we are intended for.

If we attempt otherwise, the result will be a botch—or a lifelong arduous labor or tugging disappointment.

A farmer boy, mistaking the zeal of his conversion for a call to preach, is still farming in the pulpit. A good shoemaker is doing bad cobbling in the legislature. A fine mechanic, fired by some lecturer who made him dissatisfied with his humble lot by telling him that "where there's a will, there's a way," and "labor conquers all things," that "nothing is impossible to him that wills," and that "a man can do what he thinks he can," and many other half-truths, abandons his trade to study law, for which he has not the slightest adaptability.

Everything in nature is naturally beautiful, and each thing is necessary in its place. One flower does not envy another. Every blossom is a sacred censer, swinging its perfume out on the air without jealousy of any other flower, or of the mighty trees above it. Its great mission is to throw out just as much sweetness and beauty as possible.

When you have found your orbit, you will feel satisfied in it. You will feel that all your powers are pulling; your purpose is tugging away at all your faculties. You will not feel humiliated because you are a farmer or a cook or a school-teacher or a housewife. You will not apologize because your not this or that. You will have found your place, and your are satisfied—and the consciousness of fulfilling your natural destiny makes you a power. The violet is as perfect and as necessary as the pine which towers hundreds of feet above.

Do not ask yourself whether you will be the next Webster, Lincoln, Grant, Nightingale, Bronte, Susan B. Anthony, or Marie Curie. Ask what yourself what you are best fitted for. Then you will find a place just as important as any filled by these others.

Find *your* place and fill it.

"Be what nature intended you for," said Sydney Smith, "and you will succeed; be anything else, and you will be ten thousand times worse than nothing."

Never allow yourself to think that Fate is against you, or that destiny has decided your future. Think of yourself as always on the up-grade, and feel that abundance of all that is good will be yours.

Expect delightful things to come to you and pleasant things to happen. If you build air-castles, build beautiful ones. Never mind the things which are past, do not hunt for things which are lost, and do not waste time over lost opportunities or lost prospects.

Be a magnet to draw all that is beautiful, pleasant and desirable out of your today. Cut off the past, and do not touch the morrow until it comes, but extract every possibility from the present. Remember that destructive, tearing-down thoughts will drive away from you your magnetic attraction for abundance by thinking of limitation, poverty, and failure. Think positive, creative, happy thoughts, and your harvest of good things will never fail.

CHAPTER XII
"This One Thing I Do"

As important as willpower is, without regard to direction it is simply constancy, firmness, perseverance. It should be obvious that everything depends upon right direction and motives.

"I have come here to read," said Dickens, when asked to attend social gatherings in Boston. "The people expect me to do my best, and how can I do it, if I am all the time on the go? My time is not my own when I am preparing to read, any more than it is when I am writing a novel; and I can as well do one as the other without concentrating all my power on it till it is done."

Zoologist and geologist, Louis Agassiz, when once invited to lecture in Portland, Maine, replied that be was very sorry, but he was just then busy with some researches that left him no time to make money.

Those who succeed have a program: they fix their course and adhere to it; lay their plans, and execute them; go straight to the goal. They are not pushed this side and that every time a difficulty is thrust in their way. If they can't go over it, they go through it.

What a sublime spectacle is that of one going straight to one's goal, cutting his or her way through difficulties, and surmounting obstacles which dishearten others as though they were stepping-stones!

To attain your career, you must devote yourself to one overmastering purpose, one unwavering aim, with an exclusiveness of application, a blindness of attachment to the occupation or profession which will make you forget, for the time being, that any other career could possibly be desirable.

Those who make the great failures in life are the aimless, the purposeless, the indifferent, the blundering, the shiftless, the half-hearted. There is no trend of purpose running through their work, unifying their efforts, and giving direction or meaning to their lives.

It has been truly said that "great minds have purposes, others have wishes," and that "the most successful people are those who have but one object and pursue it with great persistence."

"The great art," says Goethe, "is to judiciously limit and isolate one's self."

That whole long string of habits—attention, method, patience, self-control, and the others, so essential to success—can be rolled up and balled, as it were, in the word, "concentration."

The way that stretches into the future, that seems dark and forbidding to the world, is often illumined to the individual by an inner light which others cannot see. But the soul sees it and is confident, joyful, even when others are turbulent and sad. The soul sees victory in its apparent defeat; it sees joy in the gloom, light in the darkness. A power stronger than their own, and outside themselves, holds a singularly focused person in his or her orbit just as the stars are held in their courses.

Every person with an idea, with an overmastering purpose, usually has a minority of one—only one person who believes it. Himself or herself! But nature herself is the greatest umpire in these circumstances, where only the most determined and directed can survive.

Bismarck adopted it as the purpose of his life to snatch Germany from Austrian oppression, and to gather round Prussia in a North German Confederation, all the states whose thought, religion, manners, and interests were in harmony with those of Prussia. "To attain this end" he once said in conversation, "I would brave all dangers—exile, the scaffold itself. What matter if they hang me, provided the rope with which I am hung binds this now Germany firmly to the Prussian throne?"

German unity was engraven upon his heart. What cared this Herculean despot for the Diet that was chosen year after year simply to vote down every measure he proposed? He simply defied and sent every Diet home. He could play the game alone. To make Germany the greatest power in Europe was his all-absorbing purpose, and also to make William of Prussia a greater potentate than Napoleon or Alexander. It mattered not what stood in his way, whether people, Diet, or nation, all must bend to his mighty will.

If you give yourself wholly to an idea, you are certain to, accomplish something; and, if you have ability and common sense, your attainment will be assured.

Cyrus W. Field said: "It has been a long and hard struggle to lay the Atlantic cable—nearly thirteen years of anxious watching and ceaseless toil. Often has my heart been ready to sink. I have sometimes almost accused myself of madness for sacrificing all my home comforts for what might after all prove a dream. I have seen my companions one after another fall by my side, and feared that I, too, might not live to see the end. I have often prayed that I might not taste of death till this work was accomplished. That prayer is now answered."

Mr. Vanderbilt paid his cook a salary of $10,000 a year, because he understood the art of cooking to perfection. As a well-known humorist spoke of this situation in his funny way, "If Monsieur Sauce-agravi could cook tolerably well, and shoot a little, and speak three languages tolerably well, and keep books fairly, and could telegraph a little—and so on with a dozen other things—he wouldn't get ten thousand a year for it."

Nothing had been heard from Dr. Livingstone for three years, and it was feared he was lost in the jungles of Africa or had met some terrible death. If alive, he was supposed to be somewhere in that vast region indicated in our geographies by a large blank. Newspapers and clergymen throughout the civilized world were asking that a relief expedition be sent in search of the great explorer and missionary.

"Come to Paris on important business," James Gordon Bennett telegraphed to a young man in Madrid who was there corresponding for the New York *Herald*. Within an hour this "ever-ready" man was on his way. Arriving at Paris, he went straight to Mr. Bennett, though it was late at night, saying he was ready for anything wanted of him.

"Where do you think Livingstone is?" asked Mr. Bennett.

"Really, sir, I have no idea."

"Well, I think he is alive, and I am afraid he may be in want, so you are to go to him. Take whatever you need for yourself and for him: go as you please; but find Livingstone. Draw 1,000 pounds now, and as much more as you need later; but find Livingstone."

John Rowlands, the young man thus commissioned to one of the greatest undertakings in history, had lived for ten years in his youth in a poor-house in Wales, from which he managed to escape at the age of thirteen, and ship as a cabin-boy on a steamer which landed him at New Orleans. He early changed his name to Henry M. Stanley, and by sheer energy and force of character pushed his way upward until we find him the most trusted correspondent of one of the greatest newspapers.

The story of the wonderful expedition, of the fighting, of the wasting disease which killed so many of his men, and of his conquest of obstacles which seemed insurmountable is as fascinating as a romance.

After terrible discouragement, he wrote in his journal, "No living man shall stop me, only death can prevent me. But death; not even this: I shall not die—I will not die—I cannot die. Something tells me I shall find him—write it larger—FIND HIM, FIND HIM. Even the words are inspiring."

And find Livingstone he did.

No one can succeed who does not have a fixed and resolute purpose in their mind, and an unwavering faith that they can carry that purpose out.

"There is no secret about amassing wealth," said Vanderbilt. "All that you have to do is to attend to business and go ahead, except one thing, and that is, never tell what you are going to do until you have done it."

English essayist and writer William Hazlitt was accustomed to stick a wafer on his forehead when he began to write. When his housekeeper saw that wafer she dared not disturb him, even if a prince called to see him. What were princes to him when he was communing with gods and angels!

It is no uncommon thing to see a person of considerable talent surpassed in commercial life by another of apparently greater inferiority—for no other reason than this: that while the one devotes whole energy and undivided thought to the object of his or her life, the other is diverted by many irreconcilable tastes, and grudgingly gives but half a mind to the business on which depend all his and her worldly prospects.

The most successful people have been those of one dominant idea.

Find some new want of society—some fertile source of profit or honor—some *terra incognita* of business, whose virgin soil is yet unbroken, and there stick and grow. "Specialties" are the open sesame to wealth.

Shun that rapidity that leads to superficiality. Welcome that habit of concentration which takes us to the root of things.

It is the single aim that wins.

Bonaparte once said of himself: "When my resolution is taken, all is forgotten except what will make it succeed."

Look at a ship, becalmed without a pilot, with sluggish sails flapping against the mast, swayed alternately by wind and tide, ever in motion, and yet never nearer its destined port. Just such is the irresolute person. Every breeze that blows makes such a one its sport, and every turn of the tide of fortune drags such a person helplessly along in its current.

But see the same ship with all its sails bent, a prosperous wind urging it on, the pilot at the helm, the seamen ready, each at his appointed post of duty, and the rude ocean yields to its prow, and flings up its spray unheeded and harmless on its sides.

"One without a purpose is no one," says Carlyle.

We waste our time doing too many things, reading too many books, seeing too many people, talking too much.

"Mental shiftlessness" is the cause of many a failure. The world is full of unsuccessful people who spend their lives letting empty buckets down into empty wells.

Is it anything surprising that those who aim at nothing, accomplish nothing?

From the beginning of his career Johns Hopkins declared that he had a mission from God to increase his store, and that the golden flood which poured into his coffers did not belong to the hundreds who sought to borrow or beg it from him. They called him an "old miser," "old skinflint," "mean," "stingy," and every opprobrious epithet they could think of. But it was all the same to him, for he had a grander use and purpose for his millions than feeding professional beggars. Four millions were given to endow a free hospital in Baltimore. Three millions were given to endow the Johns Hopkins University, near Baltimore. He left in all nine millions for these institutions. As a result, the unfortunates were without money and were sick had a place to go, where they would be tenderly cared for—and those seeking an education would be most liberally assisted. Think of the thousands down to the end of time who will reap the benefits of Johns Hopkins' carrying out the magnificent purpose he had planned early in his business career.

Everyone needs the inspiration of a great mission to lift him or her above the pettiness and cheapness which are the bane of ordinary lives. Some great undertaking with an element of heroism and moral sublimity in it, the very contemplation of which quickens the blood and fires the soul and awakens an ever-present sense of the dignity and significance of life—a sublime purpose.

Walter Scott spared no pains and considered no labor burdensome which helped him in his purpose. He studiously avoided making acquaintances who would rob him of his time and divert his mind from its object. Amusements were shunned with the same intention, and sleep was retrenched in order that the morning might be devoted to study. He furnishes a suggestive instance of the possibility of doubling life by doubling the work while life lasts.

A one-talent person who concentrates his or her powers upon one unwavering aim accomplishes more than the ten-talent person who scatters energies and never quite knows what he or she can do best.

A definite purpose is like the sides of a cannon or barrel of a rifle, which give aim and direction to the projectile. Without these barriers to concentrate the expanding powder, it would simply flash without moving the ball. How many a miserable failure might have been a great triumph; how many dwarfs might have been giants; how many a "mute inglorious Milton" has died with all their music in them? How many a scholar has sipped of many arts, but drunk of none, from just this lack of a definite aim!

The mind is naturally a vagrant, prone to wander into all sorts of by-ways unless kept steadily and resolutely to its purpose. The mental reservoir of most people is like a leaky dam which we sometimes see in the country, where the greater part of the water flows out without going over the wheel and doing the work of the mill. The habit of mind-wandering, of worrying about his and that, crowding the thoughts with petty anxieties and jealousies, is like a little leak in our mental reservoir, which is constantly sapping our reserve power and lessening the chances of our success. The great thing is to learn the secret of running all of the water over the wheel of the mill and not allowing any of it to go through the holes in the dam.

To succeed in pursuit of your career, then, you must concentrate all the powers of your mind upon one definite goal and have a tenacity of decision which means death or victory. Every other inclination which tempts you from this unswerving purpose must be repressed.

Of course, I do not mean to suggest in any of this that one should work at one thing every minute. We should have sidetracks on which we can "switch off" now and then, provided the sidetracks all lead to the same terminus with the main line. It is just that one must not be on side-tracks all one's life.

Your purpose may not be very definite at first, but like a river which starts in a series of ill-defined pools or streams, if all your aims are in the right direction they will finally run together, and, swollen by hundreds of side rills, merge into a mighty stream of purpose and sweep you on to the ocean of success.

PURSUIT

CHAPTER XIII
Enthusiasm

"Rub-a-dub-dub, rub-a-dub-dub, rub-a-dub-dub-dub-dub," sounded through the keen Alpine air; and cheerily from behind the drum looked forth the fresh, rosy face of a boy but ten years old, so bright and pretty and buoyant among the grim, scarred visages of the army of veterans. When the cutting wind whirled a shower of snow in his face, he dashed it away with a jolly laugh, and awoke the echoes with a lively rattle of his drum, till it seemed as if the huge, beetling rocks, the icicles, and the pinnacles of snow around were all singing in the reverberating chorus.

"Bravo, *petit tambour!*" (little drummer), exclaimed "Fighting Macdonald," one of the bravest of Napoleon's marshals.

"Rub-a-dub-dub, rub-a-dub-dub, rub-a-dub-dub-dub-dub," rattled the drummer, with redoubled zeal and a bright, optimistic air that spread a contagion of hope and ambition through the division.

"Long live our General!" shouted a hoarse voice, and from mouth to mouth a cheer rolled like distant thunder along the towering mountains.

But hark! What undertone is that, so tremulous yet so rustling, so faint yet so oppressive, so mysterious in its muffled whisper like the sound of viewless wings, yet so ominous in its husky menace of coming doom? It is not well to shout among the Alps, lest the drifted snow swoop downward on its storm-wings to punish the intruder.

Scarcely had the echo died away, when the second noise, so different in kind from the echo—a strange, uncanny murmur—seemed to moan and wail far up the mountain side. Nearer and nearer it swelled, add louder and harsher it grew, until all the air shuddered in the deep, hoarse roar.

"On your faces, lads! down, for your lives!" shouted Macdonald. "It's an avalanche!"

Down thundered the ruin, sweeping the narrow path, bearing along heaps of boulders and gravel, uprooting bushes and trees and great blocks of pale blue ice. Darkness as of midnight followed for a moment—the darkness of the grave to many a soldier, caught in the whirl-wind rush.

"Where's our Pierre? Where's our little drummer!" were the first words that broke the awful stillness when the avalanche had come to rest in the valleys, and its echoes had died among the hills.

Where indeed?

A cry of grief burst from many a veteran who had looked unmoved into the muzzles of a line of leveled muskets.

"Rub-a-dub-dub, rub-a-dub-dub, rub-a-dub-dub-dub-dub, dub-dub," came the faint roll of a drum beating the charge from far below.

"What courage! What enthusiasm!" exclaimed an old grenadier, with tears in his eyes. "We must save him, lads, or he'll freeze to death down there! He must be saved!"

"He shall be saved!" broke in the deep voice of Macdonald, as he threw off his cloak on the very brink of the precipice.

"No, no, General!" cried the grenadiers. "You mustn't run such a risk as that. Let one of us go instead; your life is worth more than all of ours put together."

"My soldiers are my children," said Macdonald, quietly, "and no father grudges his own life to save his son."

Down, down by a rope they lowered their General until he disappeared in the cold, black depth below.

"Pierre!" he shouted as loud as he could. "Where are you, my boy?"

"Here, General," came a weak voice from a huge mound of snow whose softness alone had saved the little fellow.

"All right now, brave boy," said Macdonald, as he pulled the half-buried drummer out. "Put your arms round my neck and hold tight; we'll have you out of this in a minute."

But the stiffened fingers of the boy had lost their strength; and, even when the General clasped the tiny arms about his neck, their hold gave way at once.

The numbing cold of that dismal place would soon make Macdonald as powerless as the boy. What could be done?

Tearing off his sash and knotting one end to the rope, he bound Pierre and himself together. Then he signaled upward, and soon they were on the cliff above. Forgetting all risk of an avalanche, the soldiers gave cheer after cheer, and the echoes joined until it seemed as if the hills shared in the rejoicing. "We've been under fire and snow together," said the General, tenderly chafing the cold hands of the boy, "and nothing shall part us as long as we live."

In an hour Pierre felt as well as ever; and, when the order was given to advance, his "rub-a-dub-dub, rub-a-dub-dub, rub-a-dub-dub-dub-dub," rolled from the drum with redoubled determination and zeal. All through that fearful winter "Passage of the Splugen"—more terrible in many ways than Napoleon's feat of crossing the Alps in summer—the little drummer's enthusiasm proved an inspiration and encouragement to officers and men alike.

What may not even a boy do when his whole heart is in his work?

"I would give my skin for the architect's design of that building!" exclaimed Christopher Wren, as he gazed at the Louvre in Paris, whither he had gone to get ideas for the restoration of St. Paul's Cathedral in London. His enthusiasm seemed to possess him. When he died, the following epitaph was placed on his tombstone: "Underneath is laid the builder of this church and city, Christopher Wren, who lived more than ninety years, not for himself, but for the public good. Reader, if you seek his monument, look around!"

And those who do look around will soon find that the finest architecture in England is the work of Christopher Wren.

Nearly all the great improvements, discoveries, inventions, and achievements which have elevated and blessed humanity have been the triumphs of enthusiasm.

What is enthusiasm but a passionate belief in what seems to be a high and holy aim—an unselfish devotion to some noble cause—a consecration of heart and mind and soul to the attainment of a great object? What is it but an earnest effort to attain the heights of spiritual and intellectual endeavor! What is it but the life, the force, the power, which makes individuals capable of enduring much and waiting long, in the conviction that ultimately the thing they have at heart will be accomplished. It is easy to ridicule this boundless hope, this all-embracing faith, to sneer at visionaries, and laugh at their dreams. *But are not all individuals enthusiasts who, at the risk of their heart's blood and the sacrifice of much that is very dear, incessantly labor to purify and better the world?*

When 16th Century potter, Bernard Palissy, saw in a show-window an imported enameled cup which no one in his country knew how to duplicate, he could not rest until he had discovered the secret of its manufacture. Toiling in the face of poverty and failure to discover the secret of the white enamel, was so intoxicated with enthusiasm that men thought him a fool. God's fool he was, with a great hope in his heart for which he gladly suffered the loss of all things.

"Cranks, my son?" asked writer/journalist Robert J. Burdette. "The world is full of them. What would we do were it not for the cranks? How slowly the tired old world would move, did not the cranks keep it rushing along! Columbus was a crank on the subject of discovery and circumnavigation, and at last he met the fate of most cranks—was thrown into prison, and died in poverty and disgrace. Greatly venerated now? Oh, yes, Telemachus, we usually esteem a crank most profoundly after we starve him to death.

"Harvey was a crank on the subject of the circulation of the blood; Galileo was an astronomical crank; Fulton was a crank on the subject of steam navigation; Morse was a telegraph crank; all the abolitionists were cranks; John Bunyan was a crank. Any man who doesn't think as you do, my son, is a crank.

"And by and by the crank you despise will have his name in every man's mouth, and a half-completed monument to his memory crumbling down in a dozen cities, while nobody outside of your native village will know that you ever lived. Deal gently with the crank, my boy. Of course, some cranks are crankier than others, but do you be very slow to sneer at a man because he knows only one thing and you can't understand him. A crank, Telemachus, is a thing that turns something, it makes the wheels go round, it insures progress. True, it turns the same wheel all the time, and it can't do anything else, but that's what keeps the ship going ahead.

"The thing that goes in for variety, versatility, that changes its position a hundred times a day, that is no crank; that is the weather-vane, my son. What? You nevertheless thank heaven you are not a crank? Don't do that, my son. Maybe you couldn't be a crank if you would. Heaven is not very particular when it wants a weather-vane; almost any man will do for that. But when it wants a crank, my boy, it looks about very carefully for the best man in the community. Before you thank Heaven that you are not a crank, examine yourself carefully, and see what is the great deficiency that debars you from such an election."

It is this *solid faith in one's mission*—the rooted belief that it is the one thing to which one has been called—this enthusiasm, that marks the successful career.

Jame's Watt's whole heart was buried in his engine "I can think of nothing else," he says, "but I cannot let my family starve."

Raphael's enthusiasm inspired every artist in Italy.

Turner could not bear to sell a favorite painting. It was a portion of his being; to part with it was the rendering up, the blotting out of that space of his life spent in its creation. He was always dejected and melancholy after such a transaction. "I lost one of my children this week," he would sadly exclaim, and that with tears in his eyes.

From the baking of a loaf of bread for the family to the law-making of a statesman for a nation, there must enter in this vivifying element that electrifies and makes potent every effort. Just as soon as this dies away, no matter what success has been attained in the past, a season of dry rot sets in, and the end is death to further accomplishment.

The foreman of a bootblack shop in Madison Square, Now York, is a continual source of surprise to the customers, but his conduct justifies his employer's confidence. He never allows a customer to go away unless he is satisfied that his boots have been polished in the best manner possible. He is ever full of enthusiasm, and works at the end of a busy day with as much energy as at the beginning. His humor never lags, and his muscles never tire.

"It is a lesson in enthusiasm; watch that fellow," said a spectator; "he is the only man I ever saw who always seems to love to work."

There is a wide range of skill in the blacking of boots, from that which covers them with a coarse, fibrous, lusterless paste to that which changes them to polished ebony. I have seen an artistic zeal and pride in this same foreman's work which would have redeemed many an ambitious canvas from ignoble mediocrity.

The clerks in a large mercantile house ridiculed a young companion who began as an office boy, for doing so many things which did not belong to him to do. They laughed at his enthusiasm and interest in the business, saying that there was no sense in it and that he would never get a cent for it. Not long afterwards, he was selected from all the employees and taken into the firm as a partner, and became in time manager of one of the largest concerns in the country.

The most irresistible charm life is bubbling enthusiasm. It sees no darkness ahead—no defile that has no outlet—it forgets that there is such a thing as failure in the world, and believes that mankind has been waiting all these centuries for its bearer to come and be the liberator of truth and energy and beauty.

Carnot was chairman of the Committee of Public Safety during the French Revolution, and directed the operations of fourteen armies, which turned back the invaders who rushed down from the Alps and Pyrenees. As a proof and explanation of his great military genius, it is told of his boyhood that he was taken to the theater to witness the representation of a battle scene. At one stage of the play he saw that the attacking party was exposed to the sweep of a battery, and he startled the audience by crying out to the commanding officer to change his position or his men would be shot.

Enthusiasm faces the sun, its shadows fall behind it. The heart rules enthusiasm; the head, caution.

It is enthusiasm which cuts the Gordian knot hesitation cannot untie.

The simple, innocent Maid of Orleans with her sacred sword and consecrated banner, and her belief in her great mission, sent a thrill of enthusiasm through the whole French army, which neither King nor previous leader had been able to produce. Her zeal carried everything before it, and made hers a name of dread to the English army. Charles VII, who had not dared to appear on the scene of action until inspired by this simple girl, boldly set out for Rheims, where, Joan told him, he would be crowned; and, although the intervening country was in the hands of the English, every city-gate opened to them as they advanced. The coronation occurred as she had said it would.

It was enthusiasm that sent Union General Philip Sheridan dashing down the Shenandoah Valley, to utterly rout Early and his rebel host.

Courage recognizes the danger and meets it with a serene front. Confidence in one's powers, the thought of the prize to be won, the love of glory and reputation, a knowledge of the means at our disposal, and a faith in fortune are the considerations which strengthen courage, and if they are marshaled in battle array and led by enthusiasm, the fears which hovered over our path will be routed like flocks of evil-boding birds.

It is this most potent factor that is present in all accomplishment which is of value. Does a speaker thrill you with the magic of an eloquence that seems to carry you out of your ordinary self, and sometimes to lead your very convictions captive? Be assured that it is because the speech is vitalized with the enthusiasm of an earnest belief which knows no doubt or hesitation. Enthusiasm enters into every invention, every masterpiece of painting or sculpture, every great poem, essay, or novel that holds the world breathless with admiration.

It is a spiritual power. It has its birth among the higher potencies. You never find it in those people who are groveling in the dirt. In its very nature it is uplifting.

Earnest, practical, and patriotic, Henry Clay needed little assistance from books to teach him what to say. When speaking in the Senate he forgot himself as completely as if he were a father pleading for his children. On one occasion in appealing to the President of the Senate, he became so oblivious of everybody and everything but his subject, that he left his place on the floor of the Senate Chamber, and by gradual steps came down to the chair of the Vice-President, where he stood appealing to him as if none but the latter and himself were present, leaving behind him all his colleagues, who were watching him and listening to him in silent but wondering admiration.

It was enthusiasm that led Patrick Henry to utter those patriotic words so familiar to every boy and girl, and the same element made Webster defend right rather than a selfish desire.

Arouse yourself! Wake up! To dream is an acceptable habit during the night, but a ruinous one after sunrise.

"Those who succeed must always in mind or imagination live, move, think, and act as if they had gained that success, or they never will gain it," wrote the great motivational author, Prentice Mulford.

A certain bishop once said to Garrick, the famous actor, "How is it, Mr. Garrick, that you can, by your acting, persuade people that a made-up story is true, while I have difficulty in making them believe the real truth?"

"Is it note my lord," said Garrick, "that you preach the truth as if you did not believe it, while I act that which is not true as if I did believe it?"

"Men are nothing," exclaimed Montaigne, "until they are excited." Dickens says he was haunted, possessed, spirit-driven, by the plots and characters in his stories which would not let him sleep or rest until he had committed them to paper. On one sketch he shut himself up for a month, and when he came out he looked haggard as a murderer. His characters haunted him day and night.

Ole Bull showed a great passion for music at an early age, according to one of his biographers. Nothing could restrain the enthusiastic lad, and music nearly crazed him. Near his home on the island of

Valestrand, a cave is still pointed out as the place where young Ole practiced on the violin. He passed nights and days in his practice. The weird sounds that came from the cave filled the rustics with astonishment and alarm. They thought the fairies were holding carnival. In that solitary dwelling place he secured the wonderful mastery over the violin which marked all his public career. He had undoubted talent, but it was his enthusiasm, his magnetism and industry, that bore away all barriers. The sympathy that existed between him and his violin bewitched an audience. He talked to it, petted it, caressed it, and breathed his soul into it. The violin responded to his caresses, and with it the great artist swayed the multitude, as forests are swayed by the tempest. He played into it as if he were indifferent to all else, toyed with it, laid his head upon it, and held it as if he were afraid it would escape him. Whatever he willed it, that it became, and his enthusiasm was irresistible.

Those who respects their work so highly (and do it so reverently) that they care little what the world thinks of it, are those about whom the world comes at last to think a great deal.

Disraeli considered enthusiasm an incomparable faculty, a divine gift, which enabled a statesman to command the world.

Gladstone's intense earnestness and enthusiasm were a continual inspiration to his associates.

The power of Phillips Brooks, at which men wondered, lay in his tremendous earnestness.

Do not be afraid of enthusiasm. Let people call you an enthusiast with an inflection of pity or half contempt in the voice. If a thing seems to you worth working for at all, if it appears to you of moment enough to challenge any effort, then put into what you do all the enthusiasm of which you are capable, regardless of criticism. He laughs best who laughs last. It is never the half-hearted, the coldly critical, the doubting and fearing, that accomplish the most.

Enthusiasm will steady the heart and strengthen the will; it will give force to the thought, and nerve the hand until what was only a possibility becomes a reality.

Just as the lover sees in the object of his or her affections a hundred virtues and charms invisible to all other eyes, so those with enthusiasm have their powers of perception heightened and their vision magnified, until they see beauty and charms others cannot discern which compensate for drudgery, privations, hardships, and even persecution.

> No matter what the object is, whether business, pleasure, or the fine arts, whoever pursues it to any purpose must do so con amore.
>
> —*Melmoth.*

CHAPTER XIV
Doing Everything to a Finish

"Oh, that is good enough!" exclaimed a workman to a careful companion. "It looks just as well now as if you clinched the nails and set the screws a little tighter, and takes less time. Who is going to know the difference?"

"I know it myself," replied the other quietly, "and that is enough. It would not last long."

"Then we should have another job," chuckled the first. "What is the use of being so particular? Nobody is nowadays, and nobody will thank you."

"Can't help that," was the answer; "I believe in honest work, and if I didn't do it, I'd feel ashamed of myself. Why, man, it is just the same as stealing to take a job, slight it, and then get the same pay as if it was done right. No, sir. I want to respect myself, whether anybody else does or not."

"Well," replied his companion, "all I've got to say is you are a fool. The world don't wag that way, and you'll get left if you carry out a plan of that kind. Get the most money for the least work is my rule, and I make money, twice as much as you do."

"That may be," replied the other resolutely; "and you can go on making it, while I do good jobs and get less pay, perhaps; but I'll like myself better, and that's more important to me than the money."

The withdrawal of the best of one's self from the work to be done is sure to bring final disaster. Those who have made the most money, the artists who have won the greatest fame, the writers who have gained the world's ear, never "made things do" in their careers. They were not satisfied with just doing without regard to the quality of their work, even though that work were done for others and not half paid for. They recognized the fact that the effect upon themselves of careless accomplishment was far more harmful for their future than any possible present material good to be derived from such action.

Everyone should be taught that there is a great reward, a feeling of satisfaction and contentment, associated with everything that is completely finished. The discipline of being exact is uplifting.

"The man whose eyes are nailed," says Emerson, "not on the nature of his act, but on the wages, whether it be money, or office, or fame, is almost equally low." Not only is this true, but it is hardly an exaggeration to add that the person who scamps his or her work is very apt to become a scamp.

That a man or woman who, knowingly, does a poor job when receiving pay for a good one, is as much a thief as if abstracting money from another's pocketbook, is a truth that does not appear to strike home in many cases. This carelessness, this disregard for the rights of others, grows out of the failure to recognize the law of human kinship; and also from a failure to understand clearly that those who refuse to do their duty really hurt themselves and shadows their own soul, in a way for which nothing gained for the moment can at all compensate.

"I tell you what, Billy Gray," exclaimed a mechanic when reprimanded for slovenly work by a merchant-prince of Boston; "I shan't stand such words from *you*. Why, I can remember when you were nothing but a drummer in a regiment!"

"An so I was," replied Mr. Gray; "so I was a drummer; but didn't I drum *well*, eh I—didn't I drum *well?*"

Work that is not finished is not work at all; it is merely a botch. We often see this habit of incompleteness in a child, and it often increases with age. All about the house, everywhere, there are half-finished things. Children often become tired of things which they begin with enthusiasm; but there is a great difference in them about finishing what they undertake. A boy, for instance, will start out in the morning with great enthusiasm to dig his garden over; but after a few minutes his zeal has evaporated and he wants to go fishing. He soon becomes tired of this, and thinks he will make a boat. No sooner does he get a saw and knife and a few pieces of board about him than he makes up his mind that what he really wanted to do after all was to play ball, and this, in turn, must give way to something else.

"How is it that you do so much?" asked one, in astonishment at the efforts and success of a great man. "Why, I do but one thing at a time, and try to finish it once for all."

For nine years the young sculptor Thorwaldsen nearly starved in Italy. No one would buy his pieces of sculpture, though every one praised them. Homesick, poor, discouraged, he decided to go back to Copenhagen to his old vocation, wood-carving, as no one wanted statues, however beautiful, unless the maker was famous. By a mistake in his passport he was detained one day, when to his astonishment Mr. Thomas Hope, an English banker, entered his studio and asked the price of his model in marble, Jason. He had made one before, and had broken it to pieces because no one would buy it.

"Six hundred Syneiis" (twelve hundred dollars), he said, not daring to hope the stranger would buy it. "That is not enough, you should ask eight hundred," said the banker, and at once bought it.

This was the turning point in the youth's life. In two years he was professor in the Royal Academy. Such was his love of excellence that he made thirty models of his Venus before he was satisfied. He threw away the first, and worked a long time on the second. The Academy of his native city, Copenhagen, sent him five hundred dollars as an expression of appreciation for his work.

Twenty-three years before, he had left Copenhagen a poor, unknown lad. He returned, at the urgent request of the King, as the greatest living sculptor, and was created Counselor of State.

He had plenty of friends when he no longer needed them, but no one would help him in all the years when he was nearly starving. (The world is always ready to help those who have conquered their obstacles and shown their ability to live without help, but it will sometimes let aspiring talent starve.) Walter Scott came to pay his respects, and Mendelssohn became his friend, and would play for him in his studio while he worked. He loved his work so that he would refuse to dine with the King when busy.

It is the thing which we can do better than any one else, however trivial it may be, which commands success.

When Samuel F. B. Morse was a young painter studying in London—he was originally a portrait artist and only afterwards became famous as the man who developed in full the electric telegraph—he made a drawing from a small cast of the Farnese Hercules, intending to offer it to Benjamin West as an example of his work. He spent a long time on it, being anxious for a favorable opinion, and thought he had made it perfect. After giving it a critical examination, Mr. West handed it back, saying, "Very well, sir, very well; go on and finish it."

"But it is finished," said the young artist.

Mr. Morse saw the defects that Mr. West pointed out, and devoted another week to remedying them. When he carried the work back to the master, the latter was evidently much pleased with it, and lavished praises on the work; but he handed it back as before, with the same request that Morse should finish it. The young man by this time was nearly discouraged. "Is it not yet finished?" he asked.

Again he took it home, determined to perfect it, but showed it to West again with the same result. It still needed finishing. "I cannot finish it," said Mr. Morse in despair. "Well, I have tried you long enough," said Mr. West; "you have learned more by this than you would have accomplished by half a dozen unfinished drawings in double the time. Finish one picture, sir, and you are a painter."

Southern planters visiting Newport before the Civil War would frequently pass in their drives an odd-looking man building a stone wall by the roadside. Aside from his strange costume, there was something which attracted attention in the earnest but rapid examination which he gave to each stone before laying it upon the wall.

"Are you hunting for possible gold nuggets in that rock?" asked an amused planter one day, "Or what do you expect to find?"

"I am looking for its individuality," replied the laborer, a man by the name of Charles Cornell. "Every stone, like every human being, has certain peculiarities which adapt it thoroughly for certain purposes, but less perfectly for others. He who would build a wall as it should be, must get acquainted with every stone he handles, and place it just where it was intended to go."

The Southerner, a college graduate, strongly opposed this view of the matter, and carelessly misquoted a passage from Locke in support of his position. The mason politely, but confidently corrected his opponent's mistake, and showed that the quotation was really in his favor. Had the rocks spoken, the planter would not have been more astonished; but he had begun the controversy, and he did not wish to yield in the presence of the ladies in the carriage, so he tried again and again to vanquish the modest workman by arguments which seemed to him unanswerable. But he might just as well have tried to push back the ocean which washed the beach; from the deep of a well-stored mind, heaving with the feeling of an honest heart, roiled waves of logic, which were irresistible.

Charles Cornell might have had a rough exterior, but he was as much of a man as he could make himself by using every moment of leisure and throwing all the force of his being into the work of self-improvement, and his personality was to that of the pampered, educated child of wealth before him as is the mountain breeze to the dry leaf. Others who accosted him in ridicule, learned to speak to him with profound respect, and to ask his opinion on important questions.

Although always a laborer, he was economical; and, when he died at the age of about eighty, it was found that his savings, with accumulated interest, aggregated a handsome fortune, while his store of mental and moral wealth was phenomenal for one who had worked hard at his trade.

It is difficult to estimate the influence upon a life of the early formed habit of doing everything to a finish, not leaving it half done, or pretty nearly done, but completely done. Nature completes every little leaf, even every little rib, its edges and stem, as exactly and perfectly as though it were the only, leaf to be made that year. Even the flower that blooms in the mountain dell, where no human eye will ever behold it, is made with the same perfection and exactness of form and outline, with the same delicate shade of color, with the same completeness of beauty, as though it were intended for royalty in the queen's garden. "Perfection to the finish," is a motto which every person should adopt.

One of the maxims of Rothschild should be placed in every schoolroom: "Do without fail that which you determine to do."

Strafford, the great minister of Charles I., took for his motto the one word "Thorough." Ben Jonson in one of his plays makes a character say, "When I once take the humor of a thing, I am like your tailor's needle, I go through with it."

It is no disgrace to be a shoemaker, but it is a disgrace for a shoemaker to make bad shoes.

Once two rival smiths discovered a mighty boulder, under which, they had been told, was a treasure hidden by a crafty miser. They hastened away, each to his shop, to weld an iron crowbar. One, consumed by avarice, gave his work small time and careless blows, that his bar might be finished first—as indeed it was. Running forth to the boulder, he began forthwith to pry, but such was the folly of his lustful haste that he snapped his lever at a weak, poorly welded joint. Crazed with rage, he returned at once to his forge to mend the break. In the meantime the other smith came to the rock with a bar that was carefully made. Proceeding with reason and a proper diligence, he lifted the stone, and, taking the treasure, went his way rejoicing.

George Eliot, in *Middlemarch*, was drawing a picture from life, when she noted that the gradual and disastrous collapse of Mr. Viney's prosperity dated from the time when he began to use the cheap dyes recommended by his sham-religious brother-in-law, which were soon found to rot the silks for which he had once been famous.

The Athenian architects of the Parthenon finished the upper side of the matchless frieze as perfectly as the lower side, because the goddess Minerva saw that side. An old sculptor said of his carvings, whose backs were to be out of all possible inspection, "But the gods will see."

Every one of the five thousand statues in the cathedral of Milan is wrought as if God's eye were on the sculptor.

The works that have challenged the world's admiration for ages have been the result of unwearied toil. Michelangelo, who, if any man, had a right to rely on genius only, said of himself that all was due to study.

"During the nine years that I was his wife," said the widow of the great 18th Century English portrait and historical painter Opie, "I never saw him satisfied with one of his productions; and often, very often, have I seen him enter my sitting-room and, throwing himself in an agony of despondence on the sofa, exclaim, 'I never, never shall be a painter as long as I live!'" It was this noble despair, which is never felt by vulgar artists, this pursuit of an ideal which, like the horizon, ever flew before him, that spurred Opie to higher and yet higher efforts, till he filled one of the highest niches in the artistic temple of his country.

Dr. Wayland took two years to compose his famous sermon on foreign missions; but it is a masterpiece, worth a ton of ordinary sermons.

Balzac, the great French novelist, sometimes worked a week on a single page. He wrote forty novels before he secured the attention of the public. Then he began to take still greater pains with everything he wrote; writing and rewriting, correcting and recorrecting, polishing and repolishing, until he had made each work a masterpiece. He demanded as many as a dozen different proofs from his printer, and made so many corrections and additions that these sometimes cost more than the original composition.

French naturalist George Buffon's *Studies of Nature* cost him fifty years of labor, and he recopied it eighteen times before he sent it to the printer. He composed in a singular manner, writing on large sheets of paper, on which, as in a ledger, five distinct columns were ruled. In the first column he wrote down his thoughts; in the second, he corrected, enlarged, and pruned; and so on until he had reached the fifth column, within which he finally wrote the result of his labors. But even after this, he would recompose a sentence twenty times, and once devoted fourteen hours to finding the proper word with which to round off a period.

Everything must have a beginning, a middle, and an end; and the beginnings in art are seldom equal to the endings. Nearly all novel writers, for instance, have written a score or more of unsuccessful novels before they have written a successful one; and most painters have painted a score of poor pictures before they have painted a good one. These are their practice pieces, the work of their prentice hands; and when they once get their hands well in, performance becomes easy, noble conceptions come naturally, and success is certain.

The peasant boy Jean Francois Millet got his first inspiration for painting from the pictures in the old family Bible. Contrary to most fathers, his father told him, "Draw what you like; choose what you please; follow your own fancy." He earned his living at first painting sign-boards. Starvation stared him in the face, and he bad to give six drawings for a pair of shoes and one picture for a bed. During the terrible Revolution of 1818, Millet refused to degrade his noble art for money and still put his best work on pictures—his grandmother, when he was young, used to exhort him to "paint for eternity"—even when he knew he would be obliged to sell them for a song. But his celebrated "Angelus" was sold for one hundred and twenty-five thousand dollars.

A few years ago, a high granite block was built in Boston, and when it was completed it was considered one of the best blocks in the city. To all appearance it was as lasting as the granite of which it was built; tenants were numerous. The builders had the utmost faith in it. They could "pile it full of pig lead." But, alas, before it was half stocked with goods it went down, filling the street with stone, bricks, broken timbers, and bales of goods; and several persons were killed.

We saw the block when completed; we saw it in ruins. Why did it fall? Down in the cellar were a few feet of an old wall, and to save a few dollars it was left, and when the enormous weight of the structure began to bear upon it, it could not stand the pressure, and the entire block fell in ruins. A hundred or two hundred dollars' worth of work saved in the foundation was over a hundred thousand dollars' loss in the end, and that was but a trifle in comparison with the lives, sacrificed which no money could replace.

As is true in edifice building, in character building no one can afford to afford to cheat himself or herself in the foundation.

If a conqueror going through a country should leave a fort here and there, which he found it especially hard to take, and push on, would not the entrenched enemy be likely to harass him later? "Skipped points" in one's work and business training are sure to give endless trouble and mortification.

"There is a science in doing little things just right," said a business man. "I had two office boys whose main duty was to bring me notes or cards that were sent to me, or to fetch things that I wanted to use. One of these boys, when sent for a book or anything heavy, would walk rapidly by my desk and toss it indefinitely toward me. If it happened to miss me and land on the desk, he seemed to think it was all right. If it fell on the floor, he always managed to fall over it in his eagerness to pick it up. If he had a letter or a card to deliver he would come up to the desk and stand there scanning it with minute care. This being concluded, he would flip it airily in my direction and depart.

"The other boy always came and went so that I could hardly hear him. If he brought a book, ink-stand, or box of letters, he would set it down quietly at one side of the desk. Letters and cards were always laid, not tossed, right where my eye would fall on them directly. If there were any doubt in his mind whether he ought to lay a letter on my desk or deliver it to some other person in the office, he always did his thinking before he came near me, and did not stand annoyingly at my elbow studying the letter. That boy understood the science of little things. When New Year's day came, he got ten dollars. The other boy was discharged."

Canon Farrar says that young Englishmen complained bitterly because German clerks were getting their places. A wealthy member of Parliament had told him that if he advertised for a clerk who knew enough of foreign languages to conduct a wide business correspondence, he could find plenty of German youths who were competent. They had come to England, and worked for nothing in order to learn English. They could often speak and write three or four languages, whereas the English applicants really knew nothing but English. He said, also, that when six o'clock came every English clerk would jump from his seat the moment the clock struck, shut his book with a bang, hurry it into his desk, and be off in a moment to his gymnasium or his bicycle, while the German clerks would quietly wait and finish whatever they were doing before they left.

The trouble is that we live too fast—everyone is either a pusher or pushed. Everyone we meet seems to be trying to catch a train. Everything is done in a feverish spirit. Students are rushed through school and forced through college. Few take time to do anything properly. More than twenty ways of spelling "Cyrus" were found on Harvard examination papers at one time—such as, "Cyreus," "Cyrous," "Cuyus," "Soyrus." "Too" was misspelled by seventy per cent of those who used it—in a narrative. "Which" and "whose" were spelled in fifty or a hundred different ways, as "whitch," "whtch," "whish," "wich," and "who's," "hoose," "whouse." "Scholar" was rendered in over two hundred ways; for example, "skollar," "scholare," "skooler." Some wrote "bruther" for "brother," "bimeby" for "by and by," "dorter" for "daughter," and "puy" for "pie."

But beware: While it is of the greatest importance to learn to do everything well, yet there is another half to this great truth which is also of importance in this rapid age. Some people magnify the importance of the principle that if a thing is worth doing at all, it is worth doing well, and they waste a great deal of time upon trifles, instead of putting their work where it will tell. In other words, they do not discriminate between important and unimportant things. They do one thing as well as another, and their painstaking in unessential things is painful. Such people usually do not advance very far in life. Their time is all swallowed up in infinite painstaking upon unimportant matters. There is a great difference between doing important things well and that unfortunate habit of "perpetual fussiness" about the manner of doing every little thing. The habit of splitting hairs over non-essentials is almost as unfortunate as the habit of "slouchiness" or "slighting" one's work.

Common sense is the best guide.

Washington Irving tells of a Dutchman who, having to leap a ditch, went back three miles that he might have a good run, and found himself so completely out of breath when he arrived at the ditch that he was obliged to sit down on the wrong side to rest.

Carefully choose what you have a bent for; but, when started, let "this one thing I do" be your motto. "Keep everlastingly at it." Remember what Macaulay said, "The world generally gives its admiration, not to the person who does what nobody else ever attempts to do, but to the person who does best what multitudes do well."

Be thorough. Know the top and bottom; inside and outside; cause, cost, and effect; and both ends of everything you are required to handle.

The world does not demand that you be a lawyer, minister, doctor, farmer, scientist, or merchant. It does not dictate what you shall do, but it does require that you be a master in whatever you undertake. If you complete to the best in your line, the world will applaud you, and all doors will fly open to you.

Do not be as half-trained masons and carpenters, who throw buildings together to sell, which sometimes fortunately fall before they are occupied. Or half-trained medical, who students perform bungling operations and butcher their patients, because they are not willing to take time for thorough preparation. Or half-trained lawyers, who stumble through their cases and make their clients pay for experience which the law school should have given. Or half-trained clergymen, who bungle away in the pulpit and disgust their intelligent and cultured parishioners.

Do not be as those who are willing to stumble through life half prepared for their work, and then blame society because they are a failure.

In whatever endeavor you pursue, you should feel that the universe is not complete without your work feeling done.

CHAPTER XV
The Help Yourself Society

"We must move our nest at once!" exclaimed four little larks in terror, when their mother came home; "we overheard the farmer say that he would get his neighbors to help cut the grain in this field."

"Oh, there is no danger yet," said the mother, "we can rest easy." But when she returned the next night the young ones were all excited again. "The farmer was very angry because his neighbors didn't come to help him," said the larks, "and declared he would get his relatives to help him tomorrow."

"There is no danger yet," replied the mother. That evening the little birds were very cheerful.

"No news?" asked the mother. "Nothing important," was the reply; "the farmer was angry because his relatives didn't come to help him and declared that he would out the grain himself."

"We must leave our nest tonight!" exclaimed the old bird. "When a man decides to do a thing himself, and to do it *at once*, you may be pretty sure the thing will be done."

Help yourself, and all the world will help you. Prove that you can do without folks, and they will beg to give you a lift.

"Note that gas jet on the city street battling with the storm and darkness. There! it is gone. No, you are mistaken; for see, it flashes out again more brilliantly than ever. The flame is fed from within."

Everyone should join that most excellent club, called the "Help Yourself Society."

Bismarck was returning home with a friend after a pleasant day's tramp, and they had to cross a shallow stream. Bismarck got across all right on some convenient stones, but his companion, who was less careful, waded into the water and soon found that he was sinking into the quicksand. He made frantic efforts to release himself, but in vain. Then he wept, raved, stretched out his hands imploringly to Bismarck, and finally gave himself up as lost. Bismarck came to his rescue in a very strange way. He seized his gun, loaded it, pulled back the hammer, and, putting on a most ferocious look, took careful aim at his friend. In his excitement and terror the poor fellow made a determined spring and gained the bank. Bismarck laughed heartily, threw down his gun, and assured his friend that his intention had been to save his life by compelling him to put forth one mighty effort.

"How do you teach your pupils to paint?" asked some one of the artist Opie. "As you teach puppies to swim," was the reply. "By chucking them in."

There is sound truth in Aesop's old fable of "Jupiter and the Wagoner," where a teamster, whose wheel has got fast in the mud, is pictured by the Greek moralist as shouting to Jupiter for aid, upon which the king of the gods, looking down from his Olympian throne, bids the indolent clown cease his supplications and put his own shoulder to the wheel. Fortune always smiles on those who roll up their sleeves and put their shoulders to the wheel.

"The elevator has stopped running; Use the stairs," was the sign which confronted a man who wished to go to the top of a large building in New York. He uttered an exclamation of impatience, mounted five flights of stairs and stopped to rest.

"An elevator is a very handy thing," he soliloquized; "but, after all, I've never found any elevators in life; I've had to climb to every place worth reaching. And now I think it over, I wish it were so with everybody, for then no one would rise any higher than he deserves to go. I shall use the elevator when I can, to save walking up and down stairs in such a building as this, but I'm glad that we have to climb to rise in the world."

"Send us a man who can swim," wrote a western church committee. "The last minister we had was drowned in trying to get across a swollen stream to keep an appointment, and we don't want any more ministers who can't swim."

When P. T. Barnum was thirteen years old he made his first visit to New York, driving a herd of cattle from Bethel to the old Bull's Head Tavern. The great city turned his head completely. He lost all his money, got into several scrapes, and went back to Bethel in disgrace and disgust. When he was fourteen, his father died, bequeathing nothing but a lot of debts to the family. Penniless, and not too well clothed, Phineas started out in the world for himself. So poor was he, that he had to borrow shoes to wear at his father's funeral. He found work in a store near his native village, at six dollars a month. In 1827, he opened an eating-house in Brooklyn. The next year he returned to Bethel with one hundred and twenty dollars capital, and started a fruit and candy shop. Soon after he was of age he published a newspaper, the *Herald of Freedom*. In 1834, he went back to New York, but met with little success. The next year, however, he seemed to find his true work. For one thousand dollars he purchased Joyce Heth, an elderly black woman, who was said to be one hundred and sixty years old, and to have been a nurse of George Washington. It is doubtful if Barnum investigated the correctness of these claims closely. He exhibited her all over the country, and made considerable money, until the old woman died, and his income was out off.

But he had found his bent in the show business, and engaged with a traveling circus. In 1841, he purchased the American Museum at Broadway and Ann Street, without a dollar of capital. "What will you pay for it with?" asked a friend. "Brass," he replied. By shrewd advertising devices Barnum attracted crowds to his museum, which, by great economy, he paid for in one year.

While abroad exhibiting Tom Thumb, he engaged the famous Jenny Lind, who was then setting all Europe wild with her marvelous singing. He agreed to give her $150,000 and all expenses of herself and servants for one hundred and fifty concerts in America. He deposited in London $187,000 to insure fulfillment of his share of this great contract. He had advertised Jenny Lind so shrewdly that her reception in New York was such as had scarcely been given to royalty itself. The receipts for her first concert in Castle Garden were nearly $18,000.

Mr. Barnum generously insisted on giving the great songstress, over and above the contract price: one-half of the receipts above $5,500 at each concert. The contract was broken, however, after ninety-five concerts had been given. The total receipts amounted to $712,161, of which Jenny Lind received $176,675, and Mr. Barnum $535,486.

Notwithstanding Mr. Barnum's great prosperity, he became involved in the Jerome Clock Company, which failed and swept away his whole fortune. He was not the man to be discouraged, however, for he had met and overcome too many difficulties to be disheartened. He paid all his debts and began again. He traveled through Europe, lecturing and collecting curiosities.

He returned to the old American Museum, which he conducted on a scale grander than ever. He ransacked the world for animals for his menagerie. He found a bride for Tom Thumb, and the dwarfish couple attracted great attention. In 1865, however, he again came to grief: the American Museum was totally destroyed by fire. Nothing daunted, he started another museum on Broadway, but after three years this met the same fate. He retired from business, and began lecturing on "Business Success," "Temperance," etc. (Once in great danger of becoming a drunkard, but he saw the inevitable ruin it would bring upon him, and by indomitable will-power he became a total abstainer. He traveled extensively in the cause of temperance, and delivered hundreds of lectures, all at his own expense. He was prompted by a generous desire to warn others of the fate he had so narrowly escaped.)

Later he organized what has become famous as "The Greatest Show on Earth," which today has a world-wide reputation. He purchased Jumbo, the largest elephant that had ever been seen, from the Royal Zoological Gardens in London for $10,000, and brought him to America, notwithstanding the great opposition of the royal family and the press of England. After being seen by hundreds of thousands of people, Jumbo was killed in a railroad accident in 1885, while endeavoring to save another elephant from harm.

But as always, Barnum went on, exemplifying the motto of the ancient crest of a pick-axe: "Either I will find a way or make one."

What a great lesson John Bunyan has taught us when in that dark, dingy, filthy prison, he wrote *Pilgrim's Progress*, accomplishing such results that a whole world was influenced! No Oxford or Cambridge graduate or professor, no literary man of England, no great scholar with all the advantages of libraries and helps from liberal learning, with all the assistance of high culture, had ever accomplished so much as this poor, despised, unknown, ignorant tinker, in a jail, with only two books at his disposal: the Bible and Fox's *Book of Martyrs*.

Bunyan was determined not to lose his time just because be was in prison; he would not sit down and bemoan his lot and curse his persecutors; he would not wait for an opportunity to do great things, but would use even the mean chances of a prisoner.

He was responsible only for the opportunities he did have, and he was bound to make the most of them—to make the most out of his two books and his own experience. In one way the prison was a great help to him: he was thrown upon his own resources; he could not consult libraries, nor seek advice from others; a great necessity confronted him; he was forced to self-help. All his props had been knocked out from under him; he was compelled to develop his own muscles, to stand upon his own feet.

He delved in the Bible, and found in its precious depths pearls which he had never dreamed of before. What richness! what beauty! the very prison seemed to him transformed into a palace. In the depths of his own mind he discovered, too, vast treasures which he had never found in commentaries, in books, or in helps.

He found his imagination such a storehouse as he had never dreamed of before. It seemed to him that the real world, after all, was within, not without; that the true world was the subjective world; his very body seemed to him composed of living thoughts. The more he contemplated, the more he delved and mined in the depths of his own nature, the grander and more beautiful did the inward world appear to him. Instead of a dearth of material for his writings, he was deluged with a flood of imagery of the rarest beauty. He found, after all, that real being is within, not without.

The steam engine was of little value until it emerged from the state of theory, and was taken in hand by practical mechanics. What a story of patient, laborious investigation, of difficulties encountered and overcome by heroic industry, could be told of this wonderful machine! It has been called a monument of the power of self-help in man. Its history includes the biography of Savary, the Cornish miner; of Newcomen, the Dartmouth blacksmith; of Cawley, the glazier; of Potter, the engine boy; of Smeaton, the engineer; and, towering above all, of the laborious, patient, never-tiring James Watt, the maker of mathematical instruments.

Sir Richard Arkwright, whose 18th Century construction of a spinning machine led to the development of cotton mills and the factory system, never saw the inside of a schoolhouse until he was twenty years of age.

Daniel Webster wrote to his grandson: "You can never learn without your own efforts. All the teachers in the world can never make a scholar of you, if you do not apply yourself with all your might."

It is not the person of the greatest natural vigor and capacity who achieves the highest results, but the one who employs his or her powers with the greatest industry and the most carefully disciplined skill—the skill that comer, by labor, application, and experience. Many men in his time knew far more than Watt; but none labored so assiduously to turn all that he did know to useful, practical purposes.

Success is in the student, not in the university; greatness is in the individual, not in the library; power is in the person, not in his or her crutches. A determined person will make great opportunities, even out of the commonest and meanest situations.

If we are not superior to our education, not larger than our crutches or our helps, if we are not greater than the means of our culture, which are but the sign-boards pointing the way to success, we will never reach greatness. Not learning, not culture alone, not helps and opportunities, but personal power and sterling integrity, make one find one's place in life.

A parent can give a child money, influence, and a good position; can buy the child a partnership in a prosperous money-making establishment. A parent can do all that, but the parent cannot make a success of the child. The child must do that himself or herself.

Those who work by proxy are apt to find themselves in the position of Miles Standish, who sent his friend John Alden to propose marriage for him to Priscilla. Everybody knows that John, not Miles, married the Puritan maiden. In a like manner, those who depend on someone else to work out the problem of success for them are taking big chances; for the other person, in all probability, will be the successful one.

Luck is waiting for something to turn up; labor, on the other hand, with keen eye and strong will, will turn something up. Luck lies in bed and wishes the postman would bring him news of a legacy; labor turns out at six o'clock, and, with busy pen or ringing hammer, lays a foundation for a competence. Luck whines; labor whistles. Luck relies on charms; labor depends on character. Luck slips down to indigence; labor strides upward to independence.

But how, then, is success to be attained? How shall we realize those burning dreams which set our hearts astir with eagerness, and move our brains with ceaseless action? True, yonder shine the Golden Gates which open into the our hoped-for Enchanted Land. But so often difficulties or hostile terrors intervene between the attainment of our dreams and ourselves. How shall we run the race? How shall we fight the battle? Whither shall we turn for aid, advice, or consolation?

To biography. Every great and good life is rich in necessary warning, in hopeful promise. Most illustrious individuals have owed the inspiration which spurred them on to excellence to the perusal of what others have suffered and achieved.

Napoleon, at school at Brionne, wrote his mother, "With my sword by my side and Homer in my pocket, I hope to carve my way through the world."

In the weighty pages of biography you shall see how others have endured and, enduring, triumphed; how through doubt, and danger, and suffering, the strong heart has worked its way to its goal at last; how the faltering brain and craven soul have gone down in life's battle, unheeded and unknown.

Those who begin with crutches will generally end with crutches. Help from within always strengthens, but help from without invariably enfeebles its recipient. Trust yourself.

Those who run perpetually to others for advice become at length those with no *self* within them, believe in no self within them, and go as a supplicant to others—entreating of them, one after another, to lend them theirs.

Not lack of schools and teachers, nor want of books and friends; not the most despised rank or calling; not poverty nor ill health nor deafness nor blindness; not hunger, cold, weariness, care, nor sickness of heart have been able to keep the determined individual in this life from self-education.

What is it that you want to learn and cannot?

Is it writing? Remember Sir James Murray, the lexicographer and editor of the *Oxford English Dictionary*, who made a pen for himself out of a stem of heather, sharpening it in the fire, and for a copy-book used a worn-out wool card.

Is it English grammar? Remember William Cobbett, British journalist and reformer, who learned it while he was making sixpence a day, often with no light but the winter fire, and often crowded away from this and reduced almost to starvation, if he spent but a penny for pens or paper.

Have you no money to buy books? Remember More, who borrowed Newton's *Principia* and copied it for himself.

Is it the multiplication table you wish to learn? Remember John Biddle, founder of English Unitarianism, the poorest of boys, afterward known throughout the world, who learned it up to a million by means of peas, marbles, and a bag of shot.

Is it music? Remember James Watt, developer of the steam engine, who, with no ear for music, mastered harmonies for himself because he had determined to build an organ.

Self-help has accomplished about all the great things of the world. How many, however, falter, faint, and dally with their purpose because they have no capital to start with, and wait for some good luck to give them a lift. But success is the child of drudgery and perseverance. It cannot be coaxed or bribed—pay the price and it is yours.

If you want knowledge, you must toil for it; if food, you must toil for it; accomplishment, you must toil for it; and if pleasure, you must toil for it. Toil is the law.

Even pleasure comes through toil. When one gets to the work one loves, one's life is a happy one.

Our greatest strength is developed, and our best work is done while we are struggling desperately for that which we do not possess.

Books and discourses can awaken and arouse you, and even hold up the sign of a wise finger-post to warn you from going astray at the start—but in the end, they cannot move you a single step on the road: it is your own legs only that can perform the journey.

"Why do so few of early promise, whose hopes, purposes, and resolves were as radiant as the colors of the rainbow, fail to distinguish themselves?" asks Daniel Wise.

"The answer," he goes on to say, "is obvious: they are not willing to devote themselves to that toilsome culture which is the price of great success. Whatever aptitude for particular pursuits nature may donate to her favorite children, she conducts none but the laborious and the studious to distinction.

"As the magnificent river, rolling in the pride of its mighty waters, owes its greatness to the hidden springs of mountain nooks, so does the wide-sweeping influence of distinguished individuals date its origin from hours of privacy, resolutely employed in efforts after self-development. The invisible spring of self-culture is the source of every great achievement.

"Away, then, you with all dreams of superiority, unless you are determined to dig after knowledge as those who have searched for concealed gold! Remember that we each have with ourselves the seminal principle of great excellence, and we may develop it by cultivation if we will TRY.

"Perhaps you are what the world calls *poor*. What of that? Most of those whose names are as household words were also the children of poverty. Captain Cook, the circumnavigator of the globe, was born in a mud hut, and started in life as a cabin-boy.

"Lord Eldon, who sat on the wool sack in the British Parliament for nearly half a century, was the son of a coal merchant. Franklin, the philosopher, diplomatist, and statesman, was but a poor printer's boy, whose highest luxury, at one time, was only a penny roll, eaten in the streets of Philadelphia. Each knew the pressure of limited circumstances, and demonstrated that poverty even is no insuperable obstacle to success.

"Up, then, and gird yourself for the work of self-cultivation! Set a high price on your leisure moments. They are sands of precious gold. Properly expended, they will procure for you a stock of great thoughts—thoughts that will fill, stir and invigorate, and expand the soul."

Do not trust what the lazy call the spur of the occasion. If you wish to wear spurs in the tournament of life, you must buckle them to your own heels before you enter the lists.

CHAPTER XVI
"I Will!"

Napoleon, while undergoing his examination at the military school in Paris, replied with such accuracy to all the questions proposed to him, that the professors and students were amazed. To terminate the examination, the following question was asked: "What would you do, if you were besieged in a place entirely destitute of provisions?" "As long as there was anything to eat in the enemy's camp," answered Napoleon, "I should not be at all concerned." A will finds a way.

Nothing ever seemed to daunt Napoleon. All through the Russian expedition, one of the most frightful experiences in history, he was calm, self-possessed, self-controlled, self-centered, ever believing in his destiny, and with no diminution of courage. Misfortune, disaster, obstacles, and sorrows which would crush and unbalance ordinary minds, never disturbed the depths of his serenity. When soldiers of all ranks by the score were blowing their brains out to escape misery, when the men were staining the snow with their blood, he never faltered, but cheered them and inspired them with hope and confidence in himself. And even in this extremity, when men were driven to desperation and reduced almost to starvation, they would have died for the Emperor if it had been necessary.

"Nature seems to have calculated," said he, "that I should endure great reverses. She has given me a mind of marble; thunder cannot ruffle it; the shafts merely glide along." Few men have ever had such remarkable self-control, such complete self-mastery as he, although in some directions he was weak.

Energy of will—self-originating force—is the soul of every great character. Where it is, there is life; where it is not, there is faintness, helplessness, and despondency.

We are not defeated until we give up. The point is, then, not to give up.

Those who allow their application of will to falter, or shirks their work on frivolous pretexts, is on the sure road to ultimate failure. Let any task be undertaken as a thing not possible to be evaded, and it will soon come to be performed with alacrity and cheerfulness.

In the world of action, *will is power*. Persistent will, with circumstances not altogether unfavorable, is victory; nay, in spite of circumstances altogether unfavorable, persistency will often carve out a way to unexpected success.

Fortune never will favor one who flings away the dice-box because the first throw brings a low number. There is only one thing that can give significance and dignity to human life—virtuous energy.

The business affairs of a gentleman named Rouss were once in a complicated condition, owing to his conflicting interests in various states, and he was thrown into prison. While confined he wrote on the walls of his cell: "I am forty years of age this day. When I am fifty, I shall be worth half a million; and by the time I am sixty, I shall be worth a million dollars."

He is now worth more than three million dollars.

Cornelius Vanderbilt, when but a youth, had gained such a reputation for overcoming obstacles, that his friends regarded anything which he undertook as virtually performed.

Louisa Alcott earned two hundred thousand dollars by her pen. Yet, when she was first dreaming of her power, her father handed her a manuscript one day that had been rejected by Mr. Fields, editor of the *Atlantic*, with the message: "Tell Louisa to stick to her teaching; she can never succeed as a writer."

"Tell him I *will* succeed as a writer, and some day I shall write for the *Atlantic*."

Not long after, she wrote for the *Atlantic*, a poem that Longfellow attributed to Emerson. And there came a time when she wrote in her diary:

"Twenty years ago, I resolved to make the family independent if I could. At forty, this is done. Debts all paid, even the outlawed ones, and we have enough to be comfortable. It has cost me my health, perhaps."

"Shall I go to the feast?" soliloquized an engineer in Holland one stormy day, "or shall I go and help my workmen take care of the dykes?"

He was soon to be married, and that evening a great feast was to be given in his honor. The ocean was beating furiously against the dykes, and the terror of the people was rising with the tide, for thousands of lives were protected by those massive stone walls.

"Take care of the dykes," he muttered to himself "the feast can get along without me or can be postponed, but take care of the dykes I must and will."

"Here comes the engineer! Thank God! Thank God!" shouted the men, as they saw him coming, for the wall was giving way, stone by stone, and they were nearly exhausted and discouraged.

The engineer had a rope fastened around his body, and other ropes around the bodies of several of his men, and they, were lowered amid the beating surf.

"More stones!" cried the men, "More mortar! everything is giving way."

"There are no more stones," was the answering shout.

"Take off your clothes," cried the engineer, "and with them stop the holes in the wall."

In the darkness and cold, amid the turbulent rush and roar of the waters, they crowded their clothes into the holes, praying as they worked. It seemed as if all their work would be in vain, however, when suddenly the wind changed and the sea subsided. What shouts went up when they knew that their villages were saved, and how they cheered their engineer, whose self-denial and stern determination had saved the dykes after all others had given up.

They can, who think they can.

"Well, I am a little late this morning; I guess I shall miss the train," says one man as he looks at his watch, and then mopes along as if he has decided to miss it. He hears the whistle and moves a little quicker. As the train nears the station he runs with all his might and arrives just in time to see the cars roll out. "Just my luck!" he exclaims, "I expected I would miss it when I started."

"Only three minutes to train time!" exclaims his neighbor as he looks at his watch; "I'll make it, though; good-by," he says to his wife, and tears down the street in a way to scare all the small boys. For fear of knocking some one down, or being hindered, he runs down the street, leaving the sidewalk, and enters the depot just as the train comes in. "That's a little the quickest time I ever made," he remarks to a friend; "but I told my wife I'd take this train, and here I am."

The second man had a determination to win, the first to miss. Each had the same time and distance. It was at the start that the race was really decided.

How mighty is resolution, when supported by an unconquerable will to carry it out; how feeble, when there is no real heart behind it!

Consider, for example, the story of William and Caroline Herschel, children of Isaac Herschel, a member of the band of the

Hanoverian Guards. The father's health had been seriously impaired by exposure in the army; but, although be was afflicted with asthma and rheumatism, he would often explain to William and Caroline what little he knew of the starry systems.

When Caroline was ten years old she could name the different constellations. She also learned to play the violin, while her brother was placed in the band, but was soon obliged to abandon it on account of ill health. He resolved to go to England, thinking it would afford him better opportunities for a start in life. He went to Leeds, where he secured a position as organist, being a fair musician, but subsequently removed to Bath. After his departure, the father died, and Caroline, who took a deep interest in her brother's welfare, was heart-broken. To her delight, however, she received an invitation from him to join him at Bath as a singer for his winter concerts.

She traveled six days and nights in a coach to a port in Holland, and sailed in a packet to Yarmouth. The vessel was wrecked, but Caroline with others was saved after a severe drenching in the sea. She hired a teamster to take herself and her trunk in a cart to meet the London stage-coach, but the horse ran away, throwing her and her trunk into a ditch. She finally reached her brother, and helped him greatly with his music, besides keeping house for him.

Her attachment for her brother was very strong. Both seemed to have the same thoughts and ambitions. Caroline took the deepest interest in his advancement, and cheerfully did everything possible for him.

Although William had attained a good position as a music-teacher in Bath, his mind was haunted by the lessons in astronomy which he had received from his father, and he bought all the books he could find on the subject, which only increased his determination to examine the heavens for himself. He was too poor to buy a telescope, so with indomitable will the two young astronomers decided to make one, although the work required an accurate knowledge of mathematics and optics.

With his sister's assistance, William succeeded in making a Newtonian telescope of five-foot focal length, the success of which so encouraged him that he began the construction of a twenty-foot reflector. They turned their little home into a telescope factory.

A foundry was established in the back garden, there were turning lathes in the bedrooms, the sound of hammers came from the garret, and the rasping of files could be heard all over the house. William was so enthusiastic that he hardly stopped work for his meals, while Caroline worked all the time when she was not singing at concerts, sometimes working all night. Of course everybody laughed at the amateurs, and wondered why they preferred to waste their time in such a visionary way instead of joining in youthful sports.

The twenty-foot telescope worked successfully. Imagine the delight of the young people when they first turned this great instrument to the sky and discovered Uranus. The news of the great discovery spread like wildfire, the Royal Society elected William to a fellowship, and his name became great in scientific circles.

Caroline was so elated over her brother's success that she refused to sing in the oratorios at Bristol or elsewhere, and could not be induced to leave him. The King appointed him Astronomer Royal, on a salary of 400 pounds a year, also allowing Caroline 50 pounds a year as his assistant; and with this fortune the brother and sister dedicated themselves anew to the study of astronomy.

Caroline would sweep the heavens every clear night with a small telescope, hunting intently for hours for comets or anything new and before unknown; while her brother, with the large one, penetrated deeper into space, resolving the nebulae into their component stars.

Caroline discovered eight comets, six of which had not been known before.

They had orders for telescopes from crowned heads and princes. These William manufactured by day, prosecuting his studies by night. The government granted him 4,000 pounds with which to manufacture a forty-foot telescope, which he succeeded in making after three years of almost incredible trials. When this instrument was first turned skyward there was great rejoicing, and the first night after it was completed William discovered the sixth satellite of Saturn.

Caroline had to undergo a great trial in her brother's marriage, but she gracefully yielded her post at the head of his household, and continued to assist him in every way.

She became so familiar with celestial phenomena that she felt quite at home among the stars, and could find her way among the planets and detect a comet rushing through space almost as easily as a stranger could walk in the streets of her native village.

Both were entertained by royalty. William was made Doctor of Laws, and he received the royal Hanoverian order of Knighthood. Caroline corresponded with the most learned men in Europe.

On the 22nd of August, 1822, came a great shock to Caroline in William's death. The object of her life, for whom she had lived, hoped, and toiled, had departed. She returned to her home in Hanover, where she spent the remainder of her life, keeping up her correspondence with the learned men, never relinquishing her interest in science until in 1848, at the age of ninety-eight, she died.

The strong determination of the brother and sister gave them a high rank among the greatest astronomers of all time. The Royal Society admitted Caroline to membership, and conferred upon her a gold medal.

"Though our character is formed by circumstances," says John Stuart Mill, "our own desires can do much to shape those circumstances; and what is really inspiriting and ennobling in the doctrine of free will, is the conviction that we have real power over the formation of our own character; our will, by influencing some of our circumstances, being able to modify our future habits or capacities of willing."

The timid and hesitating find everything impossible, chiefly because it seems so.

Those who can resolve vigorously upon a course of action, and who turn neither to the right nor to the left, though a paradise tempt them, who keep their eyes upon the goal, whatever distracts them, are almost sure of success.

Ben Franklin had this tenacity of purpose in a wonderful degree. When he started in the printing business in Philadelphia, he carried his material through the streets in a wheelbarrow. He hired one room fro his office, work room, and sleeping room. He found a formidable rival in the city and invited him to his room. Pointing to a piece of bread from which had just eaten his dinner, he said: "Unless you can live cheaper than I can, you cannot starve me out."

One talent with a will behind it will accomplish more than ten without it, as a thimbleful of powder in a rifle, the bore of whose barrel will give it direction, will do greater execution than a carload burned in the open air.

The greatest thing each of us can possibly do in this world is to make the most possible out of the stuff that has been given us. This is success, and there is no other. It is not a question of what some one else can do or become, but "What can I do?" How can I develop myself into the grandest possible self? How can I best improve my chance?

Were I called upon to express in a word the secret of so many failures among those who started out with high hopes, I should say they lacked will-power. They could not half will, and what hope is their for self-fulfillment without a will?

Without willpower, one is like an engine without steam—a mere sport of chance to be tossed about hither and thither, always at the mercy of those who *do* have wills.

One's strength of will is the test of one's possibilities.

As one has well said: "Those who are silent are forgotten; those who do not advance fall back; those who stop are overwhelmed, distanced, crushed; those who cease to become greater, become smaller; those who leave off give up; the stationary is the beginning of the end—it precedes death; to live is to achieve, to will without ceasing."

Can you will strongly enough and hold whatever you undertake with an iron grip, for it is the iron grip that takes the strong hold on life?

What chance is there in this crowding, pushing, greedy, selfish world, for the person with no will, no persistence?

The person without self-reliance and an iron will is the plaything of chance, the puppet of his or her environment, the slave of circumstances.

Are not doubts the greatest of your enemies? If you would succeed up to the limit of your possibilities, must you not constantly hold to the believe that you are success-organized, and that you will be successful, not matter what opposes you?

You are never to allow a shadow of doubt to enter your mind that the Creator intended you to win life's battle. Regard every suggestion that your life may be a failure, that you are not made like those who succeed, and that success is not for you, as a traitor, expel it from your mind as you would a thief from your house.

While there may be obstacles to be surmounted and difficulties to be vanquished, with "I will" as your watchword and relying upon your own noble purposes and indefatigable exertions, you will one day crown your brow with the knowledge of your attainment.

mane and uttered a terrific roar, which echoed through the hills. The sheep mother stood trembling, paralyzed with fear. But when this strange sound reached the lion cub's ears, he listened as though spellbound, and a strange feeling which he had never experienced surged through him.

The lion's roar had touched a chord in his nature that bad never before been touched. It aroused a new force within him which he had never before felt. New desires, a strange new consciousness of power possessed him. A new nature stirred in him, and instinctively, without a thought of what he was doing, he answered the lion's call with a corresponding roar.

Trembling with mingled fear, surprise, and bewilderment at the new powers aroused within him, the awakened animal went to his foster mother and nuzzled up against her, and then with a tremendous leap, started toward the lion on the hill.

The lost lion had found himself. Up to this time he had gamboled around his sheep mother just as though he were a lamb developing into a sheep, never dreaming he could do anything that his companions could not do, or that he had any more strength than the ordinary sheep. He never imagined that there was within him a power which would strike terror in the beasts of the jungle. He simply thought be was a sheep, and he would run at the sight of a dog and tremble at the howl of a wolf. Now he was amazed to see the dogs, the wolves, and other animals which formerly had so terrified him flee from him.

As long as this lion thought he was a sheep, he was as timid and retiring as a sheep; he had only a sheep's strength and a sheep's courage, and by no possibility could he have exerted the strength of a lion. If such a thing had been suggested to him he would have said, "How could I exert the strength of a lion? I am only a sheep, and just like other sheep. I cannot do what they cannot do." But when the lion was aroused in him, instantly he became a new creature, king of the

CHAPTER XVII
Something Touched Him

A cub lion was one day playing alone in the forest while his mother slept. As different objects attracted his attention, the cub thought be would explore a bit and see what the great world beyond his home was like. Before be realized it, though, he'd wandered so far that he couldn't find his way back.

He was lost.

Frightened, the cub ran frantically in every direction, calling for his mother. But he received no answer. Weary and not knowing what to do or where to turn, he continued calling out. A nearby sheep, hearing his pitiful cries, came to him and took him under her care—her own offspring having been taken from her.

The sheep became very fond of her foundling, though often she would become worried for him, as she would detect a strange, far-off look in his eyes which she could not understand.

The foster mother and her adopted lived very happily together, though he soon grew so much larger than herself that at times she was almost afraid of him.

Then one day a magnificent lion appeared, on the top of an opposite hill—sharply outlined against the sky. He shook his tawny forest, with no rivals save the tiger and the panther. This discovery doubled, trebled and quadrupled his conscious power, a power which it would not have been possible for him to exert a minute before he bad heard the lion's roar.

But for the roar of the lion on the distant hill, which had aroused the sleeping lion within him, he would have continued living the life of a sheep, perhaps never knowing that there was a lion in him. The roar of the lion had not added anything to his strength, had not put new power into him; it had merely aroused in him what was already there, simply revealed to him the power be already possessed. Never again, after such a startling discovery, could this young animal be satisfied to live a sheep's life. It would now be a lion's life, a lion's liberty, a lion's power—the jungle thereafter—for him.

There is in each of us, a sleeping lion. It is just a question of arousing it, just a question of something happening that will awaken us, stir the sleeping power within us.

When that occurs, we shall feel a new sense of power welling up within us, a power which we never before dreamed we possessed, and after which we will never be quite the same again: Every discovery of new powers, new assets in yourself, stimulates you tremendously to new efforts, to new endeavor.

Phillips Brooks—the 19th Century American Episcopal bishop and author of the famous carol "O Little Town of Bethlehem"—used to say that once we have discovered that we have been living but a half life, the other half will haunt us until we release it. And we will never again be content to live a half life.

There are men and women who have won distinction in every field who would not have believed that there was such a possibility for them until—because of answering some call—they had achieved it. The future successful executive may well be slumbering in the clerk, the errand boy, the waitress, the secretary, today.

It is the person you are capable of making, of becoming, not the person you have become, that is most important to you—and you ought not carry this enormous asset to your grave unused.

As a business person, you would not think of having a lot of idle capital in the bank, drawing no interest, uninvested, unused. Do you realize that this is exactly what you are doing with yourself? You have assets within you infinitely more valuable than money capital. Why do you not use these assets? This is exactly what you would ask a friend or business colleague who was letting his or wealth sit idle.

You know that you have a greater you within you. You instinctively feel it. Your intuition, your instinct, your ambition tell you that there is *a much bigger self in you than you have ever or used or developed*. Why don't you use it why don't you get at it, why don't you call it out, *why don't you stir it up*? Why don't you get the spark to this giant powder within you and explode it? It may be covered under all sorts of debris—doubt, lack of self-confidence, timidity, fear, worry, uncertainty, anxiety, hatred, jealousy, revenge, envy, selfishness—but these can all be neutralized by right thinking.

History is filled with stories of individuals who had long been "down-and-out," who had been considered "nobodies," "good-for-nothings," but who then changed suddenly, as though touched by a magic wand—something happened that quickened their spirit, and they became men and women of power—inspirers, helpers of others.

When you have once glimpsed or uncovered a bit of your potential pattern, when enough light is thrown upon it to enable you to see it—to *feel* it—you will never be content until you uncover the rest of the pattern. When you have felt beyond question that you have some latent power, some vast possibilities which you had never called out, it is impossible that you will ever again be satisfied with the half life you have been living. Your whole, newly discovered nature would revolt against it.

have been called to a higher, a finer purpose than you have previously been living.

Then you will know that you are not the tame, timid sheep that you had always thought you were.

Something happened which revealed the lion in you.

The most valuable thing which ever comes into our lives is that singular experience—that book, that sermon, that person, that incident, that emergency, that public lecture, that accident, that catastrophe . . . that *something*—which touches the springs of our inner natures and flings open the doors of our great within, revealing our hidden resources.

An honest dissatisfaction with our achievement, an instinctive feeling that there is something sublimely beautiful in life that we have never yet found, an intuition that this something will satisfy our inmost yearnings, is a lesson learned. It means we have more resources inside, and that until we find at least some measure of satisfaction from them, there is still more to do in order that we may quench our soul's thirst, satisfy our soul's hunger.

Most of us have glimpsed only a little bit of our great within. But this glimpse promises so much that we feel he must see the whole—and we will never be able to rest until we trace the whole.

The larger, grander, most superb thing we know and instinctively feel we ought to be beats so mightily so persistently beneath that which we presently are that we feel we must uncover it, we must develop it, we must use it. None of us can be satisfied while we're haunted by some sense that there is something within us that is greater, more capable, than we currently are.

And all of us have this feeling within us.

That unfilled part of ourselves is a prophecy of an infinitely larger and more magnificent whole, and we know we must find it.

This is the great object of our existence: We are here to find the complete pattern of what we can be.

The world has a right to expect those who have even partly discovered themselves, who have become even slightly conscious of their greater possibility, to hold up their heads, to do their work a little better, to be a little more dead-in-earnest, to live on a higher plane, to set a little better example in general than those who have not yet tasted their hidden power. The world needs great inspirers, great leaders, great examples. In a word or two, the world calls upon us to bring forth our own greatness to add to and complement its own.

When the consciousness of his heredity touched the lion cub, when his inheritance of strength, of terrific power, was revealed to him, he turned his back forever on the old life. Never again could be return to the sheepfold, never again could he be satisfied with his sheep nature, with the half life he had been living. From the moment he realized he was a lion, there was no more sheepfold for him. Freedom, the great open world, the jungle, the forest for him, for he felt his kingship, his power over all the things that had so terrified him in the past.

Perhaps you were reared under conditions which have kept you ignorant or only dimly aware of your own possibilities. You may have had an instinctive feeling that there was something in you which did not respond to the sheep call, that there was a something within you which did not fit your environment, which did not belong to the conditions in which you found yourself. You may have been conscious that there was something in you which never responded to the call which appealed to those about you. Then something happened to throw a light upon your real nature. You may have heard a voice that answered your yearning while you were reading an inspiring book, or while listening to a motivational speaker, and it open up a new compartment in your nature.

No matter where you hear this call, when you do hear it, something within you will answer the call and you will know that you

CHAPTER XVIII
How to Find Oneself

It's not what or who you are now, it's that bigger, grander person beating beneath the person you currently feel yourself to be that is important.

There is a legend that says "When God was equipping humans for their lifelong journey of exploration, the attendant good angel was about to add the gift of contentment and complete satisfaction. The Creator stayed the angel's hand. 'No,' He said. 'If you bestow that upon them, you will rob them forever of all joy of self-discovery.'"

The principal of a New York evening high school, telling an interviewer how she, the principal, had discovered herself, said: "When I felt that there was need of me in the world, I awoke to the fact that there must be a soul in me, a something bigger than I was, and therefore a something that I must give to others."

One of the greatest moment in our lives is the moment of self-discovery, that moment when we are given the first illuminating glimpse of the soul within, that moment which opens the door into the great within of ourselves and shows us our hitherto untapped possibilities.

One of the most difficult things in the world, though, is to get people to realize the extent of their latent powers, to believe in their own bigness, in their own possibilities. Most of us see only a part of ourselves, because we have only partially *discovered* ourselves.

"Each of us," said William James, "has resources of which he does not dream."

You have heard it before: All of the potencies and possibilities of a giant oak are wrapped up in the acorn, and under the right conditions they unfold to full in a perfect oak. When we see a scrub oak, which has come from a perfect acorn, we know that it has been dwarfed by wrong conditions, that only a very small part of the possibilities unfolded in the acorn were ever unfolded. The little scrub oak expresses only a fraction of the immense possibilities that lay buried in the parent acorn.

The same is true of each of us when we, too, are born into the world. We have latent forces, powers, and possibilities that are locked up in the human acorn, and which under the right conditions, can develop into the full and complete expression of the ideal man or woman we can be. And this is what Nature, in all her work, is ever after: the fully developed specimen that reaches up to the possibilities foreshadowed in the seed. She is not after the dwarf oak; she does not want the unripened wheat that has been starved and stunted by uncongenial soil, by droughts, or other unfavorable conditions. It is the perfect wheat that was foreshadowed in the parent kernel that she wants.

What you are capable of being and doing is your greatest life asset. What you are actually doing may be a dwarfed thing compared with the giant achievement you are capable of. It is not what you have done, but what you long to do, what you feel capable of doing that will—if you struggle to express it, give life to it—count the most.

Up to this time, all sorts of things may have happened to the possible man or the possible woman in you to limit your growth, to restrict you, to impoverish you. But it is that superb thing that is possible to you—that you *know* is there in you, that you *feel* in you—that you must strive to express. It is the man or the woman wrapped up in the human acorn that you should struggle to evolve.

Who can tell what unwritten books that would inspire or set the world thinking, may be in your lying in your undiscovered reserves? What possible harmonies and melodies may have been stifled, still silent in the octaves of your being? What masterfulness, what vast reserves of helpfulness, inspiration, encouragement may still lie uncovered within you?

You doubt that there is anything of the kind within you?

But you do not know. Many a man or women has carried for more than a century, locked up within himself or herself, the seeds of a mighty genius without even guessing at it. The problem is that very few of us ever make exploring voyages within ourselves, and so, sadly, we carry to our graves undiscovered continents of ability.

Most of us die with the great secret of our lives, the sealed message put into our hands at birth, still unread, because we have never learned how to open or how to read it.

Many of us say, say in excusing our lukewarm efforts, "If I only knew that I had the ability of a writer, a composer, a painter, a business executive, a self-employed person, there is not amount of hard work or drudgery I would not undertake. No matter how many years it might take, if I was sure of ultimate success, I would not mind the work or the time."

But how do you know, I ask? How can you be sure that you have not a lot of this ability locked up in yourself? If you have not tried your strength, how do you know what you may be able to do? You may have more ability slumbering within you than you dream of. Why waste your precious time thinking about other people's genius? Why not unlock your own, see what you have, bring it out into the light and develop it? You might have something within you much greater than anyone before you, waiting for your help to give it expression.

We know that even the great majority of men whom we call successful use only a comparatively small part of their ability because they never find all of themselves. So why should we put a narrow limit on *our* possibilities, remain paupers in achievement when we might be princes?

Thoreau said "The mass of men lead lives of quiet desperation." Stop being among them.

There are enough powers, enough resources in the minds of the people in the great failure army today—to which Thoreau referred—to revolutionize the world, if their sleeping potencies could be aroused; if they could only be made to believe in themselves. If they could only learn how to enter into the sleeping depths of their nature, to get hold of themselves, to arouse latent qualities and powers, they could do marvelous things.

The great problem is to know how to get at that force in the great within of ourselves and to put it to work to the best advantage. For whether life shall be a success or a failure depends upon the call we make on our resources, the extent to which we develop all our possibilities.

The other day I was trying to encourage a young man, who had the opportunity, to start out for himself, instead of settling down in a narrow groove to work for somebody else all his life. "I am afraid," he said, "I haven't the courage to take chances. I have always worked for somebody else. I have never made a program for myself; never started anything on my own responsibility. I don't dare to make the attempt lest I fail."

But we don't know what we can do until we try. Unused faculties never grow or strengthen.

The average person starting out in life has no means of knowing what his or her total assets are. Our systems of education do not help us discover our possibilities, and so most of us see only our assets that lie on the surface. If we are not instructed how to find those that are deep down below the surface, if we do not get into the right environment, we may never develop into the person it is possible for us to be.

We find ourselves in very different ways. Struggling with difficulties, disappointments, failures, great responsibilities, has been the means of recalling many human beings to themselves. In our efforts to overcome obstacles, we often find our larger selves.

For many of us, the greatness of our latent possibilities lies so deep in our natures that it takes the impact of a tremendous emergency, a great life, or national crisis to call it out. Any ordinary event, the easy way of prosperity, will not do it; it must be something which shakes us to the very center of our being and knocks out from under us every support. We must feel that finally we have nothing to lean upon but the creative power within, that our true selves must now rise out of the ashes of a burned fortune or apparently ruined hopes.

Like those plants which must be crushed before they will reveal their sweetest fragrances, or their beneficent properties, many of us never able to bring forth the sweetest thing in ourselves until we are crushed by some great sorrow. We go through half a life or more unconscious of the richness which lies buried within ourselves. Then suddenly, some great grief, some overwhelming misfortune reveals a wealth of personality, a power which neither we nor those who know us best dreamed we possessed.

Consider the story of Ulysses S. Grant: When he was forty years old, nobody outside of his own little community knew Grant. He had not shown the slightest sign of what was locked in him. No one ever dreamed there was anything remarkable in the man. Even he, no doubt, never dreamed what was inside of himself. Up to his thirty-ninth year or later, everybody who knew Grant would have laughed at the idea (as he would have done himself) that he had ability to take any prominent part in leading an army—*to say nothing of his becoming the 18th president of the United States!* He was graduated twenty-first in a class of thirty-nine at West Point. At thirty-two he was a nobody, forced to resign from the army because of his great weakness. He went into the custom house, the real estate business, worked in a store, in a tannery, and was a comparative failure in them all. It was the supreme emergency of a war which threatened to disrupt the nation that revealed the man to himself—and to the world.

The late Justice Miller, who was for years regarded as the ablest man in the United States Supreme Court, told me that he did not even begin to study law until he was thirty-seven years old. He had not found himself until then. But in a little more than ten years from that time he was on the Supreme Court Bench.

Many people pass their fiftieth, even their sixtieth milestone, before they find themselves, before something happens which unlocks a new door in the great within of themselves and reveals new powers, new resources, of which they had never before been conscious. Then in a few years after their discovery they have redeemed half a lifetime of ineffectiveness.

Boosting from the outside will never help us to discover ourselves. We do our greatest work, uncover most of our latent power, when we are struggling on our own to make good, when striving to make a place for ourselves in the world. Yet it is a strange fact that most people look for all their personal resources outside of themselves. They go through life complaining that they have nobody to help them, that they have no chance such as many others have, excusing themselves for their failure or mediocre success on the plea that they lack capital, or "pull," or opportunity, when they have locked up right within themselves vast assets of untold value which they have never developed and which they never can use until they have found and made them available.

For that reason, if all of the people who have done things worthwhile in the world would give an account of how they were awakened, tell of the things that had aroused their ambition—the incident, the circumstance, the book, the lecture, the sermon, the advice, or the catastrophe, the failures, the crisis, the emergency, the afflictions, the losses in their lives—that something or someone that gave them a glimpse of their own possibilities, uncovered powers which they never before dreamed they possessed, what a wonderful help it would be to the rest of us who are conscious that we have locked up within ourselves forces which have we have not aroused and which we cannot seem to get hold of, because we don't think we have "the luck" or "right circumstances" to do so.

A woman explaining to her husband why the bread she had baked had not turned out said, "There is as good a stuff in this loaf of bread as in any I have made, but nobody can eat this one because there is not enough yeast in it. It did not rise."

This is just what is the matter with many of us who have something greater within us that is lying dormant. We lack yeast. There is not enough of the rising quality to make us struggle to find and our develop their highest power.

There are a multitude of things which assist our self-discovery: keeping our minds in a positive, creative condition; keeping ourselves physically at the top of our condition, in our best health; maintaining a hopeful, determined attitude by keeping our minds free from fear and worry and anxiety. All these are great aids to self-discovery. And there is no secret about any of these things.

Self-depreciation closes the doors to the locked-up potencies and powers within. Faith and self-confidence opens the door and releases them.

Not long ago I wound my watch at night and in the morning I found that it had stopped.

The hands were just where they had been when I wound it. I took it up; but the hands did not move. Then I gave it a violent shaking and it started at once and ran until the mainspring was exhausted the following night.

The power which enabled the watch to do what it was made to do was there all the time.

All it needed was a little shaking up to start it going.

If you sense that greater something within that is not being fulfilled, put yourself in a position to hear the lion's roar that will stir the cub within you. Seek every possible experience which might shake open your nature and release new force.

Great lovers of music, after listening to a wonderful voice or going to an opera, feel something inside of them released, something which had been locked up before, something which they never really knew they possessed until then.

Sometimes a great play will produce a similar effect upon us. We leave the theater feeling conscious of possessing a decided enlargement within us, something that unlocks some latent forces within us. One of the great advantages of wide experience continually educating ourselves is that these help us to uncover more and more of our hidden powers. Human life is like a funnel: We enter into the small end at birth, and the farther we go the larger and larger grows the funnel. Our horizon keeps ever pushing out towards the infinite, and there seems no limit to our possible growth.

Men and women who are trying to make the most of their lives, never stop growing. They are always on the road towards self-discovery. They only pause along the way at rest stops in order to unpack a few things which they no longer need: impedimenta which they've learned are hampering them. Then they resume their journey.

You must do the same.

If you would get at your hidden resources, stimulate your growth and your power, you must be continually improving yourself, increasing your vision by closer and keener observation, constantly studying others, reading the life stories of great men and women, and associating with noble souls.

I know of no other means of self-discovery so potent as an inspiring book. It is a great thing to keep such books near you, because ideals become dim if we do not constantly stimulate them by the right mental food.

Listening to a great orator often stirs us to the very centers of our being, and awakens new impulses, new powers and determination in many a soul who up to that time had been asleep so far as knowing and utilizing his inner powers were concerned. Perhaps you have had this experience in listening to some great preacher or lecturer who seemed to open up a new world to you and give you a glimpse of realms in your nature which otherwise might have remained forever hidden.

The more highly we cultivate all our faculties, the more deeply we draw upon our resources, the more of our hidden selves we discover, and our lives become perpetual progress.

We are all in a continuous process of development, and yet we are also still strangers to the immense possibilities that sleep in the great within of ourselves. Uncovering these possibilities, finding our resources, should be the great object of every human being.

The wisest thought of the wise men of Greece was expressed in the two words carved over the entrance of the great Delphic Temple: *"Know Thyself!"*

"Know thyself!" This is really our chief business in this life: to learn to know ourselves; to realize the power that is ours.

PART III

LIFE STORIES OF SUCCESSFUL MEN AND WOMEN TOLD BY THEMSELVES

INTRODUCTORY NOTE

The great interest manifested in the life stories of successful men and women, which have been published from time to time in the magazine *Success* has actuated their production in book form. Many of these sketches have been revised and rewritten, and new ones have been added. They all contain the elements that make men and women successful; and they are intended to show that character, energy, and an indomitable ambition will succeed in the world, and that in this land, where all people are born equal and have an equal chance in life, there is no reason for despair. I believe that the ideal book for everyone aspiring toward a successful career should deal with concrete examples; for that which is taken from real life is far more effective than that which is culled from fancy. Character-building, therefore—its uplifting, energizing force—has been made the guiding principle behind these interviews.

CHAPTER XIX
Marshall Field

This world-renowned merchant is not easily accessible to interviews, and he seeks no fame for his business achievements. Yet, there is no story more significant, none more full of encouragement and inspiration.

In relating it, as he told it, I have removed my own interrogations, so far as possible, from the interview.

"I was born in Conway, Massachusetts," he said, "in 1835. My father's farm was among the rocks and hills of that section, and not very fertile. All the people were poor in those days. My father was a man who had good judgment, and he made a success out of the farming business. My mother was of a more intellectual bent. Both my parents were anxious that their boys should amount to something in life, and their interest and care helped me.

"I had but few books, scarcely any to speak of. There was not much time for literature. Such books as we had, I made use of.

"I had a leaning toward business, and took up with it as early as possible. I was naturally of a saving disposition: I had to be. Those were saving times. A dollar looked very big to us boys in those days;

and as we had difficult labor in earning it, we did not quickly spend it. I however,

DETERMINED NOT TO REMAIN POOR."

"Did you attend both school and college?"

"I attended the common and high schools at home, but not long. I had no college training. Indeed, I cannot say that I had much of any public school education. I left home when seventeen years of age, and of course had not time to study closely.

"My first venture in trade was made as clerk in a country store at Pittsfield, Massachusetts, where everything was sold, including dry goods. There I remained for four years, and picked up my first knowledge of business. I

SAVED MY EARNINGS AND ATTENDED STRICTLY TO BUSINESS,

and so made those four years valuable to me. Before I went West, my employer offered me a quarter interest in his business if I would remain with him. Even after I had been here several years, he wrote and offered me a third interest if I would go back.

"But I was already too well placed. I was always interested in the commercial side of life. To this I bent my energies; and

I ALWAYS THOUGHT I WOULD BE A MERCHANT.

"In Chicago, I entered as a clerk in the dry goods house of Cooley, Woodsworth & Co., in South Water street. There was no guarantee at that time that this place would ever become the western metropolis; the town had plenty of ambition and pluck, but the possibilities of greatness were hardly visible."

It is interesting to note in this connection how closely the story of Mr. Field's progress is connected with Chicago's marvelous growth. The city itself in its relations to the West, was

AN OPPORTUNITY.

A parallel, almost exact, may be drawn between the individual career and the growth of the town. Chicago was organized in 1837, two years after Mr. Field was born on the far-off farm in New England, and the place then had a population of a little more than four thousand. In 1856, when Mr. Field, fully equipped for a successful mercantile career, became a resident of the future metropolis of the West, the population had grown to little more than eighty-four thousand. Mr. Field's prosperity advanced with the growth of the city; with Chicago he was stricken but not crushed by the great fire of 1871; and with Chicago he advanced again to higher achievement and far greater prosperity than before the calamity.

"What were your equipments for success when you started as a clerk here in Chicago, in 1856?"

"Health and ambition, and what I believe to be sound principles;" answered Mr. Field. "And here I found that in a growing town, no one had to wait for promotion. Good business qualities were promptly discovered, and men were pushed forward rapidly.

"After four years, in 1860, I was made a partner, and in 1865, there was a partial reorganization, and the firm consisted after that of Mr. Leiter, Mr. Palmer and myself (Field, Palmer, and Leiter). Two years later Mr. Palmer withdrew, and until 1881, the style of the firm was Field, Leiter & Co. Mr. Leiter retired in that year, and since then it has been as at present (Marshall Field & Co.)."

"What contributed most to the great growth of your business?" I asked.

"To answer that question," said Mr. Field, "would be to review the condition of the West from the time Chicago began until the fire in 1871. Everything was coming this way; immigration, railways and water traffic, and Chicago was enjoying 'flush' times.

"There were things to learn about the country, and the man who learned the quickest fared the best. For instance, the comparative newness of rural communities and settlements made a knowledge of local solvency impossible. The old State banking system prevailed, and speculation of every kind was rampant.

A CASH BASIS

"The panic of 1857 swept almost everything away except the house I worked for, and *I learned that the reason they survived was because they understood the nature of the new country, and did a cash business.* That is, they bought for cash, and sold on thirty and sixty days; instead of giving the customers, whose financial condition you could hardly tell anything about, all the time they wanted. *When the panic came, they had no debts, and little owing to them,* and so they weathered it all right. *I learned what I consider my best lesson, and that was to do a cash business.*"

"What were some of the *principles* you applied to your business?" I questioned.

"*I made it a point that all goods should be exactly what they were represented to be. It was a rule of the house that an exact scrutiny of the quality of all goods purchased should be maintained, and that nothing was to induce the house to place upon the market any line of goods at a shade of variation from their real value. Every article sold must be regarded as warranted, and*

EVERY PURCHASER MUST BE ENABLED TO FEEL SECURE."

"Did you suffer any losses or reverses during your career?"

"No loss, except by the fire of 1871. It swept away everything—about three and a half millions. We were, of course, protected by insurance, which would have been sufficient against any ordinary calamity. But the disaster was so sweeping that some of the companies which had insured our property were blotted out, and a long time passed before our claims against others were settled. We managed, however, to start again. There were no buildings of brick or stone left standing, but there were some great shells of horse-car barns at State and Twentieth streets which were not burned, and I hired those. We put up signs announcing that we would continue business uninterruptedly, and then rushed the work of fitting things up and getting in the stock."

"Did the panic of 1873 affect your business?"

"Not at all. We did not have any debts."

"May I ask, Mr. Fields, what you consider to have been

THE TURNING POINT

in your career—the point after which there was no more danger?"

"Saving the first five thousand dollars I ever had, when I might just as well have spent the moderate salary I made. Possession of that sum, once I had it, gave me *the ability to meet opportunities*. That I consider the turning point."

"What trait of character do you look upon as having been the most essential in your career?"

"*Perseverance*," said Mr. Field. But Mr. Selfridge, his most trusted lieutenant, in whose private office we were, insisted upon the addition of *"good judgment"* to this.

"If I am compelled to lay claim to such traits," added Mr. Fields, "it is because I have tried to practice them, and the trying has availed me much. I have tried to make all my acts and commercial moves the result of definite consideration and sound judgment. *There were never any great ventures or risks*. I practiced honest, slow-growing business methods, and tried to back them with energy and good system."

At this point, in answer to further questions, Mr. Field disclaimed having overworked in his business, although after the fire of '71, he worked about eighteen hours a day for several weeks.

"My fortune, however, has not been made in that manner. I believe in reasonable hours, but close attention during those hours. I never worked very many hours a day. People do not work as many hours now as they once did. The day's labor has shortened in the last twenty years for everyone."

QUALITIES THAT MAKE FOR SUCCESS

"What, Mr. Field," I said, "do you consider to be the first requisite for success in life, so far as the young beginner is concerned?"

"The qualities of *honesty, energy, frugality, integrity,* are more necessary than ever today, and there is no success without them. They are so often urged that they have become commonplace, but they are really more prized than ever. And any good fortune that comes by such methods is deserved and admirable."

A COLLEGE EDUCATION AND BUSINESS

"Do you believe a college education for the young man to be a necessity in the future?"

"Not for business purposes. Better training will become more and more a necessity. The truth is, with most young men, a college education means that just at the time when they should be having business principles instilled into them, and be getting themselves energetically pulled together for their life's work, they are sent to college. Then intervenes what many a young man looks back on as the jolliest time of his life—four years of college. Often when he comes out of college the young man is unfitted by this good time to buckle down to hard work, and the result is a failure to grasp opportunities that would have opened the way for a successful career."

As to retiring from business, Mr. Field remarked:

"I do not believe that, when a man no longer attends to his private business in person every day, he has given up interest in affairs.

He may be, in fact should be, doing wider and greater work. There certainly is no pleasure in idleness. A man, upon giving up business, does not cease laboring, but really does or should do more in a larger sense. He should interest himself in public affairs. There is no happiness in mere dollars. After they are acquired, one can use but a moderate amount. It is given a man to eat so much, to wear so much, and to have so much shelter, and more he cannot use. When money has supplied these, its mission, so far as the individual is concerned, is fulfilled, and man must look further and higher. It is only in the wider public affairs, where money is a moving force toward the general welfare, that the possessor of it can possibly find pleasure, and that only in constantly doing more."

"What," I said, "in your estimation, is the greatest good a man can do?"

"The greatest good he can do is to cultivate himself, develop his powers, in order that he may be of greater use to humanity."

CHAPTER XX
Bell Telephone Talk
HINTS ON SUCCESS BY ALEXANDER G. BELL

Extremely polite, always anxious to render courtesy, no one carries great success more gracefully than Alexander G. Bell, the inventor of the telephone. His graciousness has won many a friend, the admiration of many more, and has smoothed many a rugged spot in life.

A NIGHT WORKER

When I first went to see him, it was about eleven o'clock in the morning, and he was in bed! The second time, I thought I would go somewhat later—at one o'clock in the afternoon. He was eating his breakfast, I was told; and I had to wait some time. He came in, apologizing profusely for keeping me waiting. When I told him I had come to interview him, in behalf of young people, about success—its underlying principles—he threw back his large head and laughingly said:

"'Nothing succeeds like success.' Success did you say? Why, that is a big subject—too big a one. You must give me time to think about it; and you having planted the seed in my brain, will have to wait for me."

When I asked what time I should call, he said: "Come any time, if it is only late. I begin my work at about nine or ten o'clock in the evening, and continue until four or five in the morning. Night is a more quiet time to work. It aids thought."

So, when I went to see him again, I made it a point to be late. He cordially invited me into his studio, where, as we both sat on a large and comfortable sofa, he talked long on

THE SUBJECT OF SUCCESS.

The value of this article would be greatly enhanced, if I could add his charming manner of emphasizing what he says, with hands, head, and eyes; and if I could add his beautiful distinctness of speech, due, a great deal, to his having given instruction to deaf mutes, who must read the lips.

"What do you think are the factors of success?" I asked. The reply was prompt and to the point.

PERSEVERANCE APPLIED TO A PRACTICAL END

"Perseverance is the chief; but perseverance must have some practical end, or it does not avail the man possessing it. A person without a practical end in view becomes a crank or an idiot. Such persons fill our insane asylums. The same perseverance that they show in some idiotic idea, if exercised in the accomplishment of something practicable, would no doubt bring success. Perseverance is first, but practicability is chief. The success of the Americans as a nation is due to their great practicability."

"But often what the world calls nonsensical, becomes practical, does it not? You were called crazy, too, once, were you not?"

"There are some things, though, that are always impracticable. Now, take, for instance, this idea of perpetual motion. Scientists have proved that it is impossible. Yet our patent office is continually beset by people applying for inventions on some perpetual motion machine. So the department has adopted a rule whereby a working model is always required of such applicants. They cannot furnish one. The impossible is incapable of success."

"I have heard of people dreaming inventions."

"That is not at all impossible. I am a believer in unconscious cerebration. The brain is working all the time, though we do not know it. At night, it follows up what we think in the daytime. When I have worked a long time on one thing, I make it a point to bring all the facts regarding it together before I retire; and I have often been surprised at the results. Have you not noticed that, often, what was dark and perplexing to you the night before, is found to be perfectly solved the next morning? We are thinking all the time; it is impossible not to think."

"Can everyone become an inventor?"

"Oh, no; not all minds are constituted alike. Some minds are only adapted to certain things. But as one's mind grows and one's knowledge of the world's industries widens, it adapts itself to such things as naturally fall to it."

Upon my asking the relation of health to success, the professor replied, "I believe it to be a primary principle of success: *'mens sana in corpore sano'*—a sound mind in a sound body. The mind in a weak body produces weak ideas; a strong body gives strength to the thought of the mind. Ill health is due to man's artificiality of living. He lives indoors. He becomes, as it were, a hothouse plant. Such a plant is never as successful as a hardy garden plant is. An outdoor life is necessary to health and success, especially in a youth."

"But is not hard study often necessary to success?"

"No; decidedly not. You cannot force ideas. Successful ideas are the result of slow growth. Ideas do not reach perfection in a day, no matter how much study is put upon them. It is *perseverance* in the pursuit of studies that is really wanted."

CONCENTRATION OF PURPOSE

"Next must come concentration of purpose and study. That is another thing I mean to emphasize. Concentrate all your thought upon the work in hand. The sun's rays do not burn until brought to a focus.

"I am now thinking about flying machines. Everything in regard to them, I pick out and read. When I see a bird flying in the air, I note its manner of flight, as I would not if I were not constantly thinking about artificial flight, and concentrating all my thought and observation upon it. It is like a man who has made the acquaintance of some new word that has been brought forcibly to his notice, although he may have come across it many times before, and not have noticed it particularly.

"*Man is the result of slow growth*; that is why he occupies the position he does in animal life. What does a pup amount to that has gained its growth in a few days or weeks, beside a man who only attains it in as many years. A horse is often a grandfather before a boy has attained his full maturity. The most successful men in the end are those whose success is the result of steady accretion. That intellectuality is more vigorous that has attained its strength gradually. It is the man who carefully advances step by step, with his mind becoming wider and wider—and progressively better able to grasp any theme or situation—persevering in what he knows to be practical, and concentrating his thought upon it, who is bound to succeed in the greatest degree."

YOUNG AMERICAN GEESE

"If a man is not hound down, he is sure to succeed. He may be bound down by environment, or by doting parental petting. In Paris, they fatten geese to create a diseased condition of the liver. A man stands with a box of very finely prepared and very rich food beside a revolving stand, and, as it revolves, one goose after another passes before him. Taking the first goose by the neck, he clamps down its throat a large lump of the food, whether the goose will or no, until its crop is well stuffed out, and then he proceeds with the rest in the same very mechanical manner. Now, I think, if those geese had to work hard for their own food, they would digest it better, and be far healthier geese. How many young American geese are stuffed in about the same manner at college and at home, by their rich and fond parents!"

UNHELPFUL READING

"Did everything you ever studied help you to attain success?"

"On the contrary, I did not begin real study until I was over sixteen. Until that time, my principal study was—reading novels." He laughed heartily at my evident astonishment. "They did not help me in the least, for they did not give me an insight into real life. It is only those things that give one a grasp of practical affairs that are helpful. To read novels continuously is like reading fairy stories or 'Arabian Nights' tales. It is a butterfly existence, so long as it lasts; but, some day, one is called to stern reality, unprepared."

INVENTIONS IN AMERICA

"You have had experience in life in Europe and in America. Do you think the chances for success are the same in Europe as in America?"

"It is harder to attain success in Europe. There is hardly the same appreciation of progress there is here. Appreciation is an element of success. Encouragement is needed. My thoughts run mostly toward inventions. In England, people are conservative. They are well contented with the old, and do not readily adopt new ideas. Americans more quickly appreciate new inventions.

Take an invention to an Englishman or a Scot, and he will ask you all about it, and then say your invention may be all right, but let somebody else try it first. Take the same invention to an American, and if it is intelligently explained, he is generally quick to see the feasibility of it. America is an inspiration to inventors. It is quicker to adopt advanced ideas than England or Europe. The most valuable inventions of this century have been made in America."

THE ORIENT

"Do you think there is a chance for Americans in the Orient?"

"There is only a chance for capital in trade. American labor cannot compete with Japanese and Chinese. A Japanese coolie, for the hardest kind of work, receives the equivalent of six cents a day; and the whole family, father, mother and children, work and contribute to the common good. A foreigner is only made use of until they have absorbed all his useful ideas; then he is avoided. The Japanese are ahead of us in many things."

ENVIRONMENT AND HEREDITY

"Do you think environment and heredity count in success?"

"Environment, certainly; heredity, not so distinctly. In heredity, a man may stamp out the faults he has inherited. There is no chance for the proper working of heredity. If selection could be carried out, a man might owe much to heredity. But as it is, only opposites marry. Blonde and light-complexioned people marry brunettes, and the tall marry the short. In our scientific societies, men only are admitted. If women who were interested especially in any science were allowed to affiliate with the men in these societies, we might hope to see some wonderful workings of the laws of heredity. A man, as a general rule, owes very little to what he is born with. A man is what he makes of himself.

"Environment counts for a great deal. A man's particular idea may have no chance for growth or encouragement in his community. Real success is denied that man, until he finds a proper environment.

"*America is a good environment for young men. It breathes the very spirit of success. I noticed at once, when I first came to this country, how the people were all striving for success, and helping others to attain success. It is an inspiration you cannot help feeling.* AMERICA IS THE LAND OF SUCCESS."

PROFESSOR BELL'S LIFE STORY

Alexander Graham Bell was born in Edinburgh, Scotland, March 3, 1847. His father, Alexander Melville Bell, now in Washington, D. C., was a distinguished Scottish educator, and the inventor of a system of "visible speech," which he has successfully taught to deaf mutes. His grandfather, Alexander Bell, became well known by the invention of a method of removing impediments of speech.

The younger Bell received his education at the Edinburgh High School and University; and, in 1867, he entered the University of London. Then, in his twenty-third year, his health failing from over-study, he came with his father to Canada, as he expressed it, "to die." Later, he settled in the United States, becoming first a teacher of deaf-mutes, and subsequently professor of vocal physiology in Boston University. In 1867, he first began to study the problem of conveying articulate sound by electric currents; which he pursued during his leisure time. After nine long years of research and experiment, he completed the first telephone, early in 1876, when it was exhibited at the Centennial Exposition, and pronounced the "wonder of wonders in electric telegraphy." This was the judgment of scientific men who were in a position to judge, and not of the world at large. People regarded it only as a novelty, as a curious scientific toy; and most business men doubted that it would ever prove a useful factor in the daily life of the world, and the untold blessing to mankind it has since become. All this skepticism he had to overcome. "A new art was to be taught to the world, a new industry created, business and social methods revolutionized."

"I WILL MAKE THE WORLD HEAR IT"

"It does speak," cried Sir William Thompson, with fervid enthusiasm; and Bell's father-in-law added: "I will make the world hear it." In less than a quarter of a century, it is conveying thought in every civilized tongue; Japan being the first country outside of the United States to adopt it. In the first eight years of its existence, the Bell Telephone Company declared dividends to the extent of $4,000,000; and the great sums of money the company earns for its stockholders is a subject of current comment and wonder. Some fierce contests have been waged over the priority of his invention, but Mr. Bell has been triumphant in every case.

He has become very wealthy from his invention. He has a beautiful winter residence in Washington; fitted up with a laboratory, and all sorts of electrical conveniences mostly of his own invention. His summer residence is at Cambridge, Massachusetts.

His wife, Mabel, the daughter of the late Gardiner G. Hubbard, is a deaf mute, of whose education he had charge when she was a child.

Mr. Bell, with one of his beautiful daughters, recently made a visit to Japan. The Order of the Rising Star, the highest order in the gift of the Japanese Emperor, was bestowed upon him.

He is greatly impressed by the character of the people; believing them capable of much greater advancement.

Mr. Bell is the inventor of the photophone, aiming to transmit speech by a vibratory beam of light. He has given much time and study to problems of multiplex telegraphy, and to efforts to record speech by photographing the vibrations of a jet of water.

Few inventors have derived as much satisfaction and happiness from their achievements as Mr. Bell. In this respect, his success has been ideal, and in impressive contrast with the experience of Charles Goodyear, the man who made india-rubber useful, and of some other well-known inventors, whose services to mankind brought no substantial reward to themselves.

Mr. Bell is in nowise spoiled by his good fortune; but is the same unpretending person today, that he was before the telephone made him wealthy and famous.

CHAPTER XXI
What Miss Mary E. Proctor Did to Popularize Astronomy

"You can never know what your possibilities are," said Miss Proctor, "till you have put yourself to the test. There are many, many women who long to do something, and could succeed, if they would only banish their doubts, and plunge in. For example, I was not at all sure that I could interest audiences with talks on astronomy, but, in 1893, I began, and since then have given between four and five hundred lectures."

Miss Proctor is so busy spreading knowledge of the beauties and marvels of the heavens, that she was at home in New York for only a two days' interval between tours, when she consented to talk to me about her work. This talk showed such enthusiasm and whole-souled devotion to the theme that it is easy to understand Miss Proctor's success as a lecturer, although she is physically diminutive, and is very domestic in her tastes.

AUDIENCES ARE APPRECIATIVE

"I am always nervous in going before an audience," she said, "but there is so much I want to tell them that I have no time at all to think of myself. I find that if the lecturer is really interested in the subject, those who come to listen usually are; and it is certainly true, as I have learned by going upon the platform, tired out from a long journey, that you cannot expect enthusiasm in your audience, unless you are enthusiastic yourself. But I think that audiences are very responsive and appreciative of intelligent efforts to interest them, and, therefore, I am sure, that if a woman possesses, or can acquire a thorough knowledge of some practical, popular subject, and has enthusiasm and a fair knowledge of human nature, she can attain success on the lecture platform.

"The field is broad, and far from overcrowded, and it yields bountifully to those who are willing to toil and wait. There is Miss Roberts, for instance, who commands large audiences for her lectures on music; and Mrs. Lemcke, who has been remarkably successful in her practical talks on cooking; and Mary E. Booth, who gives wonderfully instructive and entertaining lectures on the revelations of the microscope; and Miss Very, who takes audiences of children on most delightful and profitable imaginary trips to places of importance."

LECTURES TO CHILDREN

"Children, by the way, are my most satisfactory audiences. Grown-up people never become so absorbed. It is the greatest pleasure of my lecturing to talk to the little tots, and watch them drink it all in. Indeed, I prepared my very first lecture for children, but didn't deliver it. That episode marked the beginning of my career as a lecturer.

"Do you ask me to tell you about it? My father, Richard A. Proctor, wrote, as you know, many books on popular astronomy. When I was a girl I did not read them very carefully; my education at South Kensington, London, following a musical and artistic direction. In fact, I was ambitious to become a painter. But when my father died, in 1888, I found comfort in reading his books all over again; and as he had drilled me to write for his periodical, *Knowledge*, I began to write articles on astronomy for anyone who would accept them. One day, in the spring of 1893, I received a letter from Mrs. Potter Palmer, asking me if I would talk to an audience of children in the Children's Building at the World's Fair. The idea of lecturing was new to me, but I decided that I would try, at any rate, and so I took great pains to prepare a talk that I thought the children would understand, and be interested in. But when I reached the building, I found an audience, not of children, but of men and women. *There was hardly a child in all the assembled five hundred people.* It would never do to give them the childish talk I had prepared, and as it was my first attempt to talk from a platform, you can imagine my state of mind. I was determined, however, that my first effort should not be a fiasco, so I stepped out upon the platform and talked about the things that had most interested me in my father's books and conversations."

A LESSON IN LECTURING

"I have lectured a great many times since then, but my first lecture was the most trying. I am now glad that things happened as they did, for that experience taught me a valuable lesson. I learned not to commit my talks to memory, but merely to have the topics and facts and general arrangement of the lecture well in mind. By this method, I can change and adapt myself to my audience at any time; and I often have to do this. I am able to feel intuitively whether I have gained my listeners' sympathy and interest, and when I feel that I have not, I immediately take another tack. Another great advantage of not committing what you are going to say to memory, word for word, is the added color and animation and spontaneity which the conversational tone and manner gives the lecture."

THE STEREOPTICON

"My stereopticon pictures of the heavenly bodies are of great help to me. They naturally add much to the interest, and are really a revelation to most of my audiences, for the reason that they show things that can never be seen with the naked eye. How my father would have delighted in them, and how effectively he would have used them. But celestial photography had not been made practical at the time of his death; it is, indeed, quite a new art, although its general principles are very simple. A special lens and photographic plate are adjusted in the telescope, and the plate is exposed as in an ordinary camera, except that the exposure is much longer. It usually continues for about four hours, the greater the length of time the greater being the number of stars that will be seen in the photograph. After the developing, these stars appear as mere specks on the plate. That they are so small is not surprising, for most of them are stars that are never seen by the eye alone. When the photograph is enlarged by the stereopticon, the result is like looking at a considerable portion of the heavens through a powerful telescope.

"The children utter exclamations of delight when they see the pictures—the children, dear, imaginative little souls, it is my ambition to devote more and more of my time to them, and finally talk and write for them altogether. They are greatly impressed with the new world in the skies which is opened to them, and I like to think that these early impressions will give them an understanding and appreciation of the wonders of astronomy that will always be a pleasure to them."

"STORIES FROM STAR LAND"

"For the children, my first book, *Stories From Star-land*, was written. I tried to weave into it poetical and romantic ideas, that appeal to the imaginative mind of the child, and quicken the interest without any sacrifice of accuracy in the facts with which I deal. I wrote the book in a week. The publisher came to me one Saturday, and told me that he would like a children's book on astronomy. I devoted all my days to it till the following Saturday night, and on Monday morning took the completed manuscript to the publishing house. They seemed very much surprised that it should be finished so soon; but as a matter of fact it was not much more than the manual labor of writing out the manuscript that I did in that week. *The little book itself is the result of ten years' thought and study.*

"It is much the same with my lectures. I deliver them in a hasty, conversational tone, and they seem, as one of my listeners told me recently, to be 'just offhand chats.' But in reality I devote a great deal of labor to them, and am constantly adding new facts and new ideas."

CONCENTRATION OF ATTENTION

"I learned very soon after I began my work, that *I must give myself up to it absolutely* if I were to achieve success. There could be no side issues, nothing else to absorb any of my energy, or take any of my thought or time. One of the first things I did was to take a thorough course in singing, for the purpose of acquiring complete control of my voice. I put aside all social functions, of which I am rather fond and have since devoted my days and nights to astronomy—not that I work at night, except when I lecture; I rest and retire early, so that in the morning I may have the spirit and enthusiasm necessary to do good work.

"*Enthusiasm*, it seems to me, is an important factor in success. It combats discouragement, makes work a pleasure, and sacrifices easier.

"A great many women fail in special fields of endeavor, who might succeed if they were willing to sacrifice something, and would not let the distractions creep in. There is more in a woman's life to divert her attention from a single purpose than in a man's; but if the woman has chosen some line of effort that is worthy to be called life work, and if—refusing to be drawn aside—she keeps her eyes steadfastly upon the goal, I believe that she is almost certain to achieve success."

CHAPTER XXII
The Story of John Wannamaker

In a plain two-story dwelling, on the outskirts of Philadelphia, the future merchant prince was born, July 11, 1837. His parents were Americans in humble station; his mother being of that sturdy Pennsylvania Dutch stock which has no parallel except the Scotch for ruggedness. His father, a hardworking man, owned a brickyard in the close vicinity of the family residence. Little John earned his first money, seven big copper cents, by assisting his father. He was too small to do much, but turned the bricks every morning as they lay drying in the summer sun. As he grew older and stronger, the boy was given harder tasks around the brickyard.

He went to school a little, not much, and he assisted his mother in the house a great deal. His father died when John was fourteen, and this changed the whole course of his life. He abandoned the brickyard and secured a place in a bookstore owned by Barclay Lippincott, on Market Street, Philadelphia, at a salary of one dollar and twenty-five cents a week.

It was a four-mile walk from his home to his place of business. Cheerfully he trudged this distance morning and night; purchasing an apple or a roll each noon for luncheon, and giving his mother all the money that he saved. He used to deny himself every comfort, and the only other money that he ever spent was on books for his mother. This seems to have been the boy's chief source of pleasure at that period. Even to-day, he says of his mother: "Her smile was a bit of heaven, and it never faded out of her face till her dying day." Mrs. Wanamaker lived to see her son famous and wealthy.

HIS CAPITAL AT FOURTEEN

John Wanamaker, the boy, had no single thing in all his surroundings to give him an advantage over any one of hundreds of other boys in the city of Philadelphia. Indeed, there were hundreds and hundreds of other boys of his own age for whom anyone would have felt safe in prophesying a more notable career. His capital was not in money. Very few boys in all that great city had less money than John Wanamaker, and comparatively few families of average position but were better off in the way of worldly goods. John Wanamaker's capital, that stood him in such good stead in after life, comprised good health, good habits, a clean mind, thrift in money matters, and tireless devotion to whatever he thought to be duty.

People who were well acquainted with John Wanamaker when he was a book publisher's boy, say that he was exceptionally promising as a boy; that he was studious as well as attentive to business. He did not take kindly to rough play, or do much playing of any kind. He was earnest in his work, unusually earnest for a boy. And he was saving of his money.

When, a little later, he went to a Market street clothing house and asked for a place, he had no difficulty in getting it, nor had he any trouble in holding it, and here he could earn twenty-five cents a week more wages.

TOWER HALL CLOTHING STORE

Men who worked with him in the Tower Hall Clothing Store say that he was always bright, willing, accommodating, and very seldom out of temper. His effort was to be first at the store in the morning, and he was very likely to be one of the last, if not the last, at the store in the evening. If there was an errand, he was always prompt and glad to do it. And so the store people liked him, and the proprietor liked him, and, when he began to sell clothing, the customers liked him. He was considerate of their interests. He did not try to force undesirable goods upon them. He treated them so that when they came again they would be apt to ask, "Where is John?"

HIS AMBITION AND POWER AS AN ORGANIZER AT SIXTEEN

Colonel Bennett, the proprietor of Tower Hall, said of him at this time:

"John was certainly the most ambitious boy I ever saw. I used to take him to lunch with me, and he used to tell me how he was going to be a great merchant.

"He was very much interested in the temperance cause; and had not been with me long before he persuaded most of the employees in the store to join the temperance society to which he belonged. He was always organizing something. He seemed to be a natural-born organizer. This faculty is largely accountable for his great success in afterlife."

THE Y. M. C. A.

Young Wanamaker's religious principles were always at the forefront in whatever he did. His interest in Sunday School work, and his skill as an organizer became well known. And so earnestly did he engage in the work of the Young Men's Christian Association, that he was appointed the first salaried secretary of the Philadelphia branch, at one thousand dollars a year. Never since has a secretary enrolled so many members in the same space of time. He passed seven years in this arduous work.

OAK HALL

He saved his money; and, at twenty-four, formed a partnership with his brother-in-law Nathan Brown, and opened Oak Hall Clothing store, in April, 1861. Their united capital was only $3,500; yet Wanamaker's capital of popular good-will was very great. He was already a great power in the city. I can never forget the impression made upon my mind, after he had been in business but a few months, when I visited his Bethany Sunday School, established in one of the most unpromising sections of the city, which had become already a factor for good, with one of the largest enrollments in the world. And he was foremost in every form of philanthropic work.

It was because of his great capacity to do business that Wanamaker had been able to "boom" the Young Men's Christian Association work. He knew how to do it. And he could "boom" a Sunday School, or anything else that he took hold of. He had

A HEAD BUILT FOR BUSINESS,

whatever the business might be. And as for Oak Hall, he knew just what to do with it.

The first thing he did was to multiply his working capital by getting the best help obtainable for running the store.

At the very outset, John Wanamaker did what almost any other business man would have stood aghast at. He chose the best man he knew as a salesman in the clothing business in Philadelphia—the man of the most winning personality who could attract trade—and agreed to pay him $1,350 for a year—one-third of the entire capital of the new concern.

It has been a prime principle with this merchant prince not only to deal fairly with his employees, but to make it an object for them to earn money for him and to stand by him.

Capacity has been the first demand. *He engaged the very best men to be had.* There are today dozens of men in his employ who receive larger salaries than are paid to cabinet ministers. All the employees of the Thirteenth Street store, which he occupied in 1877, participate in *a yearly division of profits. Their share at the end of the first year amounted to* $109,439.68.

HIS RELATION TO CUSTOMERS

A considerable portion of the trade of the new store came from people in the country districts. Mr. Wanamaker had a way of getting close to them and gaining their good will. He understood human nature. He put his customer at ease. He showed interest in the things that interested the farmer. An old employee of the firm says: "John used to put a lot of chestnuts in his pocket along in the fall and winter, and, when he had one of these countrymen in tow, he'd slip a few of the nuts into the visitor's hand and both would go munching about the store."

Wanamaker was the first to introduce the "one-price system" into the clothing trade. It was the universal rule in those days, in the clothing trade, not to mark the prices plainly on the goods that were for sale. Within rather liberal bounds, the salesman got what he could from the customer. Mr. Wanamaker, after a time, instituted at Oak Hall the plan of "but one price and that plainly marked." In doing this he followed the cue of Stewart, who was the first merchant in the country to introduce it into the dry-goods business.

The great Wanamaker store of 1877 went much further:

He announced that *those who bought goods of him were to be satisfied with what they bought, or have their money back.*

To the old mercantile houses of the city, this seemed like committing business suicide.

It was, also, unheard-of that special effort should be made to add to the comfort of visitors; to make them welcome whether they cared to buy or not; to induce them to look upon the store as a meeting-place, a rendezvous, a resting place—a sort of city home, almost.

THE MERCHANT'S ORGANIZING FACULTY

was so great that General Grant once remarked to George W. Childs that Wanamaker would have been a great general if his lot had been that of army service.

Wanamaker used to buy goods of Stewart, and the New York merchant remarked to a friend: "If young Wanamaker lives, he will be a greater merchant than I ever was."

Sometime in recent years, since Wanamaker bought the Stewart store, he said to Frank G. Carpenter:

"A. T. Stewart was a genius. I have been surprised again and again as I have gone through the Broadway and Tenth Street building, to find what a knowledge he had of the needs of a mercantile establishment. Mr. Stewart put up a building which is today, I believe, better arranged than any of the modern structures. He seemed to know just what was needed.

"I met him often when I was a young man. I have reason to think that he took a liking to me. One day, I remember, I was in his woolen department buying some stuffs for my store here, when he came up to me and asked if I would be in the store for fifteen minutes longer. I replied that I would. At the end of fifteen minutes he returned and handed me a slip of paper, saying:

"'Young man, I understand that you have a mission school in Philadelphia; use that for it.'

"Before I could reply he had left. I looked down at the slip of paper. It was a check for one thousand dollars."

Wanamaker early showed himself the peer of the greatest merchants. He created the combination or department store. He lifted the retail clothing business to a higher plane than it had ever before reached. In ten years from the time he began to do business for himself, he had absorbed the space of forty-five other tenants and become the leading merchant of his native city. Four years later, he had purchased, for $450,000, the freight depot of the Pennsylvania Railroad, covering the entire square where his present great store is located. The firm name became simply John Wanamaker. His lieutenants and business partners therein are his son Thomas B. Wanamaker, and Robert C. Ogden. Their two Philadelphia establishments alone do a business of between $30,000,000 and $40,000,000 annually. Mr. Wanamaker's private fortune is one of the most substantial in America.

ATTENTION TO DETAILS

Yet in all these years he has been early and late at the store, as he was when a boy. He has always seen to it that customers have prompt and careful attention. He early made the rule that if a sale was missed, a written reason must be rendered by the salesman. There was no haphazard business in that store—nothing of the happy-go-lucky style. Each man must be alert, wide-awake, attentive, or there was no place for him at Oak Hall.

THE MOST RIGID ECONOMY

has been always a part of the system. It is told of him that, in the earlier days of Oak Hall, he used to gather up the short pieces of string that came in on parcels, make them into a bunch, and see that they were used when bundles were to be tied. He also had a habit of smoothing out old newspapers, and seeing that they were used as wrappers for such things as did not require a better grade of paper.

The story has been often related of the first day's business at the original store in '61, when Wanamaker delivered the sales by wheeling a push-cart.

ADVERTISING

The first day's business made a cash profit of thirty-eight dollars; and the whole sum was invested in one advertisement in the next day's *Inquirer*.

His advertising methods were unique; he paid for the best talent he could get in this line.

Philadelphia woke one morning to find "W. & B." in the form of six-inch square posters stuck up all over the town. There was not another letter, no hint, just "W. & B." Such things are common enough now, but then the whole city was soon talking and wondering what this sign meant. After a few days, a second poster modestly stated that Wanamaker & Brown had begun to sell clothing at Oak Hall. Before long there were great signs, each 100 feet in length, painted on special fences built in a dozen places about the city, particularly near the railroad stations.

These told of the new firm and were the first of a class that is now seen all over the country. Afterwards

BALLOONS

more than twenty feet high were sent up, and a suit of clothes was given to each person who brought one of them back. Whole counties were stirred up by the balloons. It was grand advertising, imitated since by all sorts of people. When the balloon idea struck the Oak Hall management it was quickly found that the only way to get these air-ships was to make them, and so, on the roof of the store, the cotton cloth was cut and oiled and put together. Being well built, and tied very tightly at the neck, they made long flights and some of them were used over and over again. In one instance, a balloon remained for more than six months in a cranberry swamp, and when the great bag was discovered, slowly swaying in the breeze, among the bushes, the frightened Jerseymen thought they had come upon an elephant, or, maybe, a survivor of the mastodons. This made more advertising of the very best kind for the clothing store—the kind that excites interested, complimentary talk.

SEIZING OPPORTUNITIES

Genius consists in taking advantage of opportunities quite as much as in making them.

Here was a young man doing things in an advertising way regardless of the custom of the business world, and with a wonderful knowledge of human nature. He took common-sense advantage of opportunities that were open to everybody.

Soon after the balloon experience, tally-ho coaching began to be a Philadelphia fad of the very exclusives. Immediately afterwards a crack coach was secured, and six large and spirited horses were used instead of four, and Oak Hall employees, dressed in the style of the most ultra coaching set, traversed the country in every direction, scattering advertising matter to the music of the horn. Sometimes they would be a week on a trip. No wonder Oak Hall Nourished. It was kept in the very front of the procession all the time.

A little later, in the yachting season, the whole town was attracted and amused by processions and scatterings of men, each wearing a wire body frame that supported a thin staff from which waved a wooden burgee, or pointed flag reminding them of Oak Hall. Nearly two hundred of these prototypes of the "Sandwich man" were often out at one time.

But it was not only in the quick catching of a novel advertising thought that the new house was making history; in newspaper advertising, it was even further in advance. The statements of store news were crisp and unhackneyed, and the first artistic illustrations ever put into advertisements were used there. So high was the grade of this picture work that art schools regularly clipped the illustrations as models; and the world-famous Shakespearian scholar, Dr. Horace Howard Furness, treasured the original sketches of "The Seven Ages" as among the most interesting in his unique collection.

PUSH AND PERSISTENCE

"The chief reason," said Mr. Wanamaker upon one occasion, "that everybody is not successful is the fact that they have not enough persistency. I always advise young men who write me on the subject to do one thing well, throwing all their energies into it."

To his employees he once said: "We are very foolish people if we shut our ears and eyes to what other people are doing. I often pick up things from strangers. As you go along, pick up suggestions here and there, jot them down and send them along. Even writing them down helps to concentrate your mind on that part of the work. You need not be afraid of overstepping the mark. The more we push each other, the better."

"TO WHAT, MR. WANAMAKER, DO YOU ATTRIBUTE YOUR GREAT SUCCESS?"

In reply to this question when asked, he replied: "To thinking, toiling, trying, and trusting in God."

A serene confidence in a guiding power has always been one of the Wanamaker characteristics. He is always calm. Under the greatest stress he never loses his head.

In one physical particular, Mr. Wanamaker is very remarkable. He can work continually for a long time without sleep and without evidence of strain, and make up for it by a good rest afterwards.

When upon one occasion he was asked to name the essentials of success, he replied, curtly: "I might write a volume trying to tell you how to succeed. *One way is to not be above taking a hint from a master.* I don't care to tell why I succeeded; because I object to talking about myself—it isn't modest."

A feature of his make-up that has contributed largely to his success is his ability to concentrate his thoughts. No matter how trivial the subject brought before him, he takes it up with the appearance of one who has nothing else on his mind.

HIS VIEWS ON BUSINESS

When asked whether the small tradesmen has any "show" today against the great department stores, he said:

"All of the great stores were small at one time. Small stores will keep on developing into big ones. You wouldn't expect a man to put an iron band about his business in order to prevent expansion, would you? There are, according to statistics, a greater number of prosperous small stores in the city than ever before. What better proof do you want?

"The department store is a natural product, evolved from conditions that exist as a result of fixed trade laws. Executive capacity, combined with command of capital, finds opportunity in these conditions, which are harmonious with the irresistible determination of the producer to meet the consumer directly, and of merchandise to find distribution along the lines of least resistance. Reduced prices stimulate consumption, and increase employment; and it is sound opinion that the increased employment created by the department stores goes to women without curtailing that of men. In general it may be stated that large retail stores have shortened the hours of labor; and by systematic discipline have made it lighter. The small store is harder upon the sales-person and clerk. The effects upon the character and capacity of the employees are good. A well ordered, modern retail store is the means of education in spelling, writing, English language, system and method. Thus it becomes to the ambitious and serious employees, in a small way, a university, in which character is broadened by intelligent instruction practically applied."

When asked if a man with means but no experience would be safe in embarking in a mercantile business, he replied quickly:

"A man can't drive a horse who has never seen one. No; a man must have training, must know how to buy and sell; only experience teaches that."

I have heard people marvel at the unbroken upward course of Mr. Wanamaker's career, and lament that they so often make mistakes. But hear him:

"Who does not make mistakes? Why, if I were to think only of the mistakes I have made, I should be miserable indeed."

I have heard it said a hundred times that Mr. Wanamaker started when success was easy.

Here is what he says himself about it:

"I think I could succeed as well now as in the past. It seems to me that the conditions of today are even more favorable to success than when I was a boy. There are better facilities for doing business, and more business to be done. Information in the shape of books and newspapers is now in the reach of all, and the young man has two opportunities where he formerly had one.

"We are much more afraid of combinations of capital than we have any reason for being.

"Competition regulates everything of that kind. No organization can make immense profits for any length of time without its field soon swarming with competitors. It requires brain and muscle to manage any kind of business, and the same elements which have produced business success in the past will produce it now, and will always produce it."

PUBLIC SERVICE

With the exception of his term of service as postmaster-general of the United States in President Harrison's cabinet—a service which was marked by great executive ability and the institution of many reforms—Mr. Wanamaker has devoted his attention almost entirely to his business and his church work.

Yet as a citizen he has always taken a most positive course in opposition to the evils that threaten society. He has been forever prompted by his religious convictions to pursue vice either in the "dive," or in municipal, state or national life. He hates a barroom, but he hates a treasury looter far more fiercely. His idea of Christian duty was evidently derived from the scene wherein the Master took a scourge and drove the corrupt traders and officeholders out of the temple. It is vigorous, it is militant; but it makes enemies. Consequently, Mr. Wanamaker is not without persistent maligners; getting himself well hated by the worst men in the community.

INVEST IN YOURSELF

Mr. Wanamaker's views of what life is for are well expressed in the following excerpt from one of his addresses to young men.

In the course of his address, he related that he was once called upon to invest in an expedition to recover Spanish mahogany and doubloons from the Spanish Main, which, for half a century, had lain under the rolling waves in sunken frigates. "But, young men," he continued, "I know of better expeditions than this right at home, deep down under the sea of neglect and ignorance and discouragement. Near your own feet lie treasures untold, and you can have them all for your own by earnest watch and faithful study and proper care.

"Let us not be content to mine the most coal, make the largest locomotives and weave the largest quantities of carpets; but, amid the sounds of the pick, the blows of the hammer, the rattle of the looms, and the roar of the machinery, take care that the immortal mechanism of God's own hand—the mind—is still full-trained for the highest and noblest service.

"This is the most enduring kind of property to acquire, a property of soul which no disaster can wreck or ruin. Whatever may be the changes that shall sweep over our fair land, no power can ever take away from you your investments in knowledge."

AT HOME

Like all other magnetic and forceful men, Mr. Wanamaker is striking in appearance, strong rather than handsome. He has a full, round head, a broad forehead, a strong nose, heavy-lidded eyes that flash with energy, heavy jaws that denote strength of will, and tightly closed lips that just droop at the corners, giving an ever-present touch of sedateness. His face is as smooth as a boy's and as mobile as an actor's; and, when lighted up in discussion, it beams with expression. He wears a hat that is only six and seven-eighths in size, but is almost completely circular in form. He is almost six feet tall and finely built, and all his motions have in them the springiness of health. Nobody ever saw him dressed in any other color than black, with a black necktie under a "turn-down" collar. But he always looks as trim as if he were just out of the hands of both tailor and barber.

It is his delight to pass much time at his country seat in Jenkintown. He is fond of the field and the river, the trees and flowers, and all the growths with which God has beautified the earth. His house is a home-like structure, with wide piazzas, standing upon the crest of a hill in the midst of a noble lawn. A big rosery and orchid house stand near by. The before-breakfast ramble of the proprietor is finished in the flower garden, and every guest is laden with floral trophies.

Mr. Wanamaker was married, while he was the Secretary of the Y. M. C. A., to one whom he met at a church service, and who has been in full sympathy with his religious activities. He has been for forty years superintendent of the Bethany Sunday School in Philadelphia. He began with two teachers and twenty-seven pupils; and at the recent anniversary reported a school of 4,500, a church with 3,700 members, 500 having been added during the past year, several branches, and scores of department organizations.

John Wanamaker says today that his business success is due to his religious training. He is first of all a Christian.

The lesson of such a life should be precious to every young man. It teaches the value of untiring effort, of economy, of common sense applied to common business. I know of no career in this country that offers more encouragement to young people. It shows what persistency can do; it shows what intelligent, well directed, tireless effort can do; and it proves that a man may devote himself to helping others, to the Sunday School, to the Church, to broad philanthropy, and still be wonderfully successful in a business way.

CHAPTER XXIII

Giving Up Five Thousand Dollars a Year to Become a Sculptor

"My life?" queried F. Wellington Ruckstuhl, one of the foremost sculptors of America, as we sat in his studio looking up at his huge figure of 'Force.' "When did I begin to sculpture? As a child I was forever whittling, but I did not have dreams then of becoming a sculptor. It was not till I was thirty-two years of age. And love, disappointment in my first love played a prominent part."

"But as a boy, Mr. Ruckstuhl?"

"I was a poet. Every sculptor or artist is necessarily a poet. I was always reaching out and seeking the beautiful. My father was a foreman in a St. Louis machine shop. He came to this country in a sailing ship from Alsace, by way of the Gulf to St. Louis, when I was but six years old. He was a very pious man and a deacon in a church. One time, Moody and Sankey came to town, and my father made me attend the meetings; I think he hoped that I would become a minister. Between the ages of fourteen and nineteen, I worked in a photographic supply store; wrote one hundred poems, and read incessantly. I enlarged a view of the statue of Nelson in Trafalgar Square, London, into a 'plaster sketch,' ten times as large as the picture, but still I did not know my path. I began the study of philosophy, and kept up my reading for ten years. My friends thought I would become a literary man. I wrote for the papers, and belonged to a prominent literary club. I tried to analyze myself. 'I am a man,' I said, 'but what am I good for? What am I to make of this life?' I drifted from one position to another. Every one was sorry to part with my services, for I always did my duties as well as they could be done. When I was twenty-five years of age, the girl to whom I was attached was forced by her mother to marry a wealthy man. She died a year afterwards; and I 'pulled up stakes,' and started on a haphazard, reckless career. I went to Colorado, drifted into Arizona, prospected, mined, and worked on a ranch. I went to California, and at one time thought of shipping for China. My experiences would fill a book. Again I reached St. Louis. For a year, I could not find a thing to do, and became desperate."

"And you had done nothing at art so far?" I asked.

"At that time, I saw a clay sketch. I said to myself, 'I can do as well as that,' and I copied it. My second sketch admitted me to the St. Louis Sketch Club. I told my friends that I would be a sculptor. They laughed and ridiculed me. I had secured a position in a store, and at odd times worked at what I had always loved, but had only half realized it. Notices appeared in the papers about me, for I was popular in the community. I entered the competition for a statue of General Frank R. Blair. I received the first prize, but when the committee discovered that I was only a bill clerk in a store, they argued that I was not competent to carry out the work; although I was given the first prize model and the one hundred and fifty dollars accompanying it."

"But that inspired you?"

"Yes, but my father and mother put every obstacle in the way possible. I was driven from room to room. I was not even allowed to work in the attic." Here Mr. Ruckstuhl laughed. "You see what genius has to contend with. I was advanced in position in the store, till I became assistant manager, at two thousand dollars a year. When I told the proprietor that I had decided to be a sculptor, he gazed at me in blank astonishment. 'A sculptor?' he queried incredulously, and made a few very discouraging remarks, emphasized with dashes. 'Why, young man, are you going to throw up the chance of a lifetime? I will give you five thousand dollars a year, and promote you to be manager if you will remain with me.'

"But I had found my life's work," said Mr. Ruckstuhl, turning to me. "I knew it would be a struggle through poverty, till I attained fame. But I was confident in myself, which is half of the battle."

"And you went abroad?"

"Yes, with but two hundred and fifty dollars," he replied. "I traveled through Europe for five months and visited the French Salon. I said to myself, 'I can do that, and that,' and my confidence grew. But there was some work that completely 'beat' me. I returned to America penniless, but with a greater insight into art. I determined that I would retrace my steps to Paris, and study there for three years, and thought that would be sufficient to fully develop me. My family and friends laughed me to scorn, and I was discouraged by everyone. In four months, in St. Louis, I secured seven orders for busts, at two hundred dollars each, to be done after my return from France. That shows that some persons had confidence in me and in my talent.

"O, the student life in Paris! How I look back with pleasure upon those struggling, yet happy days! In two months, I started on my female figure of 'Evening,' in the nude, that is now in the Metropolitan Museum of Art. I finished it in nine months, and positively sweat blood in my work. I sent it to the Salon, and went to Italy. When I returned to Paris, I saw my name in the paper with honorable mention. I suppose you can realize my feelings; I experienced the first flush of victory. I brought it to America, and exposed it in St. Louis.

Strange to say, I rose in the estimation of even my family. My father actually congratulated me. A wealthy man in St. Louis gave me three thousand dollars to have my 'Evening' put into marble. I returned with it to Paris, and in a month and a quarter it was exhibited in the Salon. At the World's Fair, at Chicago, it had the place of honor, and received one of the eleven grand medals given to American sculptors. In 1892, I came to New York. This statue of 'Force' will be erected, with my statue of 'Wisdom,' on the new Court of Appeals in New York."

We gazed at it, seated, and clothed in partial armor, of the old Roman type, and holding a sword across its knees. The great muscles spoke of strength and force, and yet, with it all, there was an almost benign look upon the military visage.

"There is force and real action there withal, although there is repose." I said in admiration.

"Oh," said Mr. Ruckstuhl, "that's it, and that is what it is so hard to get! That is what every sculptor strives for; and, unless he attains it, his work, from my point of view, is worthless. There must be life in a statue; it must almost breathe. In repose there must be dormant action that speaks for itself."

"Is most of your work done under inspiration?" I asked.

"There is nothing—and a great deal—in so-called inspiration. I firmly believe that we mortals are merely tools, mediums, at work here on earth. I peg away, and bend all my energies to my task. I simply accomplish nothing. Suddenly, after considerable preparatory toil, the mist clears away; I see things clearly; everything is outlined for me. I believe there is a conscious and a subconscious mind. The subconscious mind is the one that does original work; it cannot be affected by the mind that is conscious to all our petty environments. When the conscious mind is lulled and silenced, the subconscious one begins to work. That I call inspiration."

"Are you ever discouraged?" I asked out of curiosity.

"Continually," replied Mr. Ruckstuhl, looking down at his hands, soiled with the working clay. "Some days I will be satisfied with what I have done. It will strike me as simply fine. I will be as happy as a bird, and leave simply joyous. The following morning, when the cloths are removed, I look at my previous toil, and consider it vile. I ask myself: 'Are you a sculptor or not? Do you think that you ever will be one? Do you consider that art?' So it is, till your task is accomplished. You are your own critic, and are continually distressed at your inability to create your ideals."

Mr. F. Wellington Ruckstuhl is forty-six years of age; neither short nor tall; a brilliant man, with wonderful powers of endurance, for his work is more exacting and tedious than is generally supposed.

"I have simply worked a month and a quarter on that statue," he said. "Certain work dissatisfied me, and I obliterated it. I have raised that head three times. My eyes get weary, and I become physically tired. On such occasions I sit down and smoke a little to distract my thoughts, and to clear my mind. Then my subconscious mind comes into play again," he concluded with a smile.

Mr. Ruckstuhl's best known works are "Mercury Teasing the Eagle of Jupiter," which is of bronze, nine feet high, which he made in Paris; a seven-foot statue of Solon, erected in the Congressional Library, at Washington; busts of Franklin, Goethe and Macaulay, on the front of the same library; and the eleven-foot statue of bronze of "Victory," for the Jamaica soldiers' and sailors' monument. In competition, he won the contract for an equestrian statue of General John F. Hartrauft, ex-Governor of Pennsylvania, which he also made in Paris. It is considered the finest piece of work of its kind in America. Besides this labor, he has made a number of medallions and busts; and with the completion of his statue of "Force," he will have made a wonderful record.

"Art was in me as a child," he said: "I was discouraged whenever it beckoned me, but finally claimed me. I surrendered a good position to follow it, whether it led through a thorny road or not. A sculptor is an artist, a musician, a poet, a writer, a dramatist—to throw action, breath and life, music and a soul into his creation. I can pick up an instrument and learn it instantly; I can sing, and act, so I am in touch with the sympathies of the beings that I endeavor to create. You will find most sculptors and artists of my composite nature.

"There," said Mr. Ruckstuhl, and he stretched out his arm, with his palm downward, and moved it through the air, as he gazed into distance, "you strive to create the imagination of your mind, and it comes to you as if sent from another world."

"You strive." That is the way to success.

CHAPTER XXIV
John D. Rockefeller

The richest man in the United States, John Davidson Rockefeller, has consented to break his rule never to talk for publication; and he has told me the story of his early struggles and triumphs, and given utterance to some strikingly interesting observations anent the same. In doing so, he was influenced by the argument that there is something of helpfulness, of inspiration, in the career of every self-made man.

While many such careers have been prolific of vivid contrasts, this one is simply marvelous. Whatever may be said by political economists of the dangers of vast aggregations of wealth in the hands of the few, there can be no question of the extraordinary interest attaching to the life story of a man who was a farm laborer at the age of fifteen, who left school at eighteen, because he felt it to be his duty to care for his mother and brother, and who, at the zenith of his business career, has endowed Chicago University with $7,500,000 out of a fortune estimated at over $300,000,000—probably the largest single fortune on earth.

The story opens in a fertile valley in Tioga County, New York, near the village of Richford, where John D. Rockefeller was born on his father's farm in July, 1838. The parents of the boy were church-going, conscientious, debt-abhorring folk, who preferred the independence of a few acres to a mortgaged domain. They were Americans to the backbone, intelligent, industrious people, not very poor and certainly not very rich, for at fourteen John hired out to neighboring farmers during the summer months in order to earn his way and not be dependent upon those he loved. His father was able to attend to the little farm himself: and thus it happened that the youth spent several summers away from home, toiling from sunrise to sunset, and sharing the humble life of the people he served.

HIS EARLY DREAM AND PURPOSE

Did the tired boy, peering from his attic window, ever dream of his future?

He said to a youthful companion of Richford, a farmer's boy like himself: "I would like to own all the land in this valley, as far as I can see. I sometimes dream of wealth and power. Do you think we shall ever be worth one hundred thousand dollars, you and I? I hope to—some day."

Who can estimate the influence such a life as this must have had upon the future multimillionaire? I asked Mr. Rockefeller about this, and found him enthusiastic over the advantages which he had received from his rural surroundings, and full of faith in the ability of the country boy to surpass his city cousin.

"To my mind," he said, "there is something unfortunate in being born in a city. Most young men raised in New York and other large centers have not had the struggles which come to us who were reared in the country. It is a noticeable fact that the country men are crowding out the city fellows who have wealthy fathers. They are willing to do more work and go through more for the sake of winning success in the end. Sons of wealthy parents haven't a ghost of a show in competition with the fellows who come from the country with a determination to do something in the world."

The next step in the young man's life was his going to Cleveland, Ohio, in his sixteenth year.

"That was a great change in my life," said he. "Going to Cleveland was my first experience in a great city, and I shall never forget those years. I began work there as an office boy, and learned a great deal about business methods while filling that position. But what benefitted me most in going to Cleveland was the new insight I gained as to what a great place the world really is. I had plenty of ambition then, and saw that, if I was to accomplish much, I would have to work very, very hard, indeed."

SCHOOL DAYS

He found time, during the year 1854, to attend the sessions of the school which is now known as the Central High School. It was a brick edifice, surrounded by grounds which contained a number of hickory trees. It has long since been superseded by a larger and handsomer building, but Andrew J. Freese, the teacher, is still living. It is one of the proudest recollections of this delightful old gentleman's life that John D. Rockefeller went to school with him. I visited him at his residence in Cleveland the other day, and he said:

"John was one of the best boys I had. He was always polite, but when the other boys threw hickory clubs at him, or attempted any undue familiarities with him, he would stop smiling and sail into them. Young Hanna—Marcus A. Hanna—who was also a pupil, learned this, to his cost, more than once, and so did young Jones, the present Nevada senator. I have had several very distinguished pupils, you see, and one of my girls is now Mrs. John D. Rockefeller. I had Edward Wolcott, the Colorado senator, later on. Yes, John was about as intelligent and well-behaved a chap as I ever had. Here is one of his essays which you may copy, if you wish."

Mr. Rockefeller, I am quite sure, will pardon me for copying his composition at this late day, for its tone and subject matter reflect credit upon him:

"Freedom is one of the most desirable of all blessings. Even the smallest bird or insect loves to be free. Take, for instance, a robin that has always been free to fly from tree to tree, and sing its cheerful song from day to day—catch it, and put it into a cage which is to it nothing less than a prison, and, although it may be there tended with the choicest care, yet it is not content.

How eloquently does it plead, though in silence, for liberty. From day to day it sits mournfully upon its perch, meditating, as it were, some way for its escape, and when at last this is effected, how cheerfully does it wing its way out from its gloomy prison-House to sing undisturbed in the branches of the first trees.

"If even the birds of the air love freedom, is it not natural that man, the lord of creation, should? I reply that it is, and that it is a violation of the laws of our country, and the laws of our God, that man should hold his fellow man in bondage. Yet how many thousands there are at the present time, even in our own country, who are bound down by cruel masters to toil beneath the scorching sun of the South. How can America, under such circumstances, call herself free? Is it extending freedom by granting to the South one of the largest divisions of land that she possesses for the purpose of holding slaves? It is a freedom that, if not speedily checked, will end in the ruin of our country."

It was greatly to the regret of the teacher that John came to him one day to announce his purpose to leave school. Mr. Freese urged him to remain two years longer, in order that he might complete the course, but the young man told him he felt obliged to earn more money than he was getting, because of his desire to provide for his mother and brother. He had received an offer, he said, of a place on the freight docks as a bill clerk, and this job would take him away from his studies.

A RAFT OF HOOP POLES

A short time afterwards, when Mr. Freese visited his former pupil at the freight dock, he found the young man seated on a bale of goods, bill book and pencil in hand. Pointing to a raft of hoop poles in the water, John told his caller that he had purchased them from a Canadian who had brought them across Lake Erie, expecting to sell them. Failing in this, the owner gladly accepted a cash offer from young Rockefeller, who named a price below the usual market rates. The young man explained that he *had saved a little money out of his wages*, and that this was his first speculation. He afterwards told Mr. Freese that he rafted the purchase himself to a flourmill, and disposed of his bargain at a profit of fifty dollars.*

THE ODOR OF OIL

It was Mr. Freese, too, who first got the young man interested in oil. They were using sperm oil in those days, at a dollar and a half a gallon. Somebody had found natural petroleum, thick, slimy, and foul-smelling, in the Pennsylvania creeks, and a quantity of it had been received in Cleveland by a next-door neighbor of the schoolmaster. The neighbor thought it could be utilized in some way, but his experiments were as crude as the ill-favored stuff itself. These consisted of

---

* This hoop pole story is matched by another, related by a friend, of Rockefeller's later warehouse days in Cleveland. He one day bought a lot of beans. He bought them cheap, because they were damaged. Instead of selling them at a slight advance, as most dealers would have done, he spent all his spare time, for weeks, in the attic of his warehouse, sorting over those beans He took out all the blackened and injured ones, and in the end he got a fancy price for the remainder, because they were of extra quality.

boiling, burning, and otherwise testing the oil, and the only result was the incurring of the disfavor of the near-by residents. The young man became interested at once. He, too, experimented with the black slime, draining off the clearer portions and touching matches to it.

The flames were sickly, yellow, and malodorous.

"*There must be some way of deodorizing this oil,*" said John, "*and I will find it.* There ought to be a good sale for it for illuminating purposes, if the good oil can be separated from the sediment, and that awful smell gotten rid of."

How well the young man profited by the accidental meeting is a matter of history. But I am digressing.

HIS FIRST LEDGER, AND THE ITEMS IN IT

While in Cleveland, slaving away at his tasks, Mr. Rockefeller was training himself for the more busy days to come. He kept a small ledger in which he entered all his receipts and expenditures, and I had the privilege of examining this interesting little book, and having its contents explained to me. It was nothing more than a small, paper-backed memorandum book.

"When I looked this book up the other day, I thought I had but the cover," said Mr. Rockefeller, "but, on examination, I perceived that I had utilized the cover to write on. In those days I was very economical, just as I am economical now. Economy is a virtue. I hadn't seen my little ledger for a long time, when I found it among some old things. It is more than forty-two years ago since I wrote what it contains. I called it 'Ledger A,' and I wouldn't exchange it now for all the ledgers in New York city and their contents. A glance through it shows me how carefully I kept account of my receipts and disbursements. I only wish more young men could be induced to keep accounts like this nowadays. It would go far toward teaching them the value of money.

"Every young man should take care of his money. I think it is a man's duty to make all the money he can, keep all he can, and give away all he can. I have followed this principle religiously all my life, as is evidenced in this book. It tells me just what I did with my money during my first few years in business. Between September, 1855, and January, 1856, I received just fifty dollars. Out of this sum I paid for my washing and my board, and managed to save a little besides. I find, in looking through the book, that I gave a cent to Sunday school every Sunday. It wasn't much, but it was all that I could afford to give to that particular object. *What I could afford to give to the various religious and charitable works, I gave regularly. It is a good habit for a young man to get into.*

"During my second year in Cleveland, I earned twenty-five dollars a month. I was beginning to be a capitalist," said Mr. Rockefeller, "and I suppose I ought to have considered myself a criminal for having so much money. I paid all my own bills at this time, and had some money to give away. I also had the happiness of saving some. I am not sure, but I was more independent then than now. I couldn't buy the most fashionable cut of clothing, but I dressed well enough. I certainly did not buy any clothes I couldn't pay for, as some young men do that I know of. I didn't make any obligations I could not meet, and *my earnest advice is for every young man to live within his means. One of the swiftest 'toboggan slides' I know of, is for a young fellow just starting out into the world to go into debt.*

"During the time between November, 1855, and April, 1856, I paid out just nine dollars and nine cents for clothing. And there is one item that was certainly extravagant as I usually wore mittens in the winter. This item is for fur gloves, two dollars and a half. In this same period I gave away five dollars and fifty-eight cents. In one month I gave to foreign missions, ten cents, to the mite society, fifty cents, and twelve cents to the Five Points Mission, in New York. I wasn't living here then, of course, but I suppose I thought the Mission needed money. These little contributions of mine were not large, but they brought me into direct contact with church work, and that has been a benefit to me all my life. It is a mistake for a man to think that he must be rich to help others."

TEN THOUSAND DOLLARS

He earned and saved ten thousand dollars before he was twenty-five years old.

Before he attained his majority, Rockefeller formed a partnership with another young man named Hewett, and began a warehouse and produce business. This was the natural outgrowth of his freight clerkship on the docks. *In five years, he had amassed about ten thousand dollars* besides earning a reputation for business capacity and probity.

HE REMEMBERED THE OIL

He never forgot those experiments with the crude oil. Discoveries became more and more frequent in the Pennsylvania oil territory. There was a rush of speculators to the new land of fortune. Men owning impoverished farms suddenly found themselves rich. Thousands of excited men bid wildly against each other for newly-shot wells, paying fabulous sums occasionally for dry holes.

KEEPING HIS HEAD

John D. Rockefeller looked the entire field over carefully and calmly. Never for a moment did he lose his head. His Cleveland bankers and business friends had asked him to purchase some wells, if he saw fit, offering to back him up with $75,000 for his own investment (he was worth about $10,000 at the time), and to put in $400,000 more on his report.

The business judgment of this young man at twenty-five was so good, that his neighbors were willing to invest half a million dollars at his bidding.

He returned to Cleveland without investing a dollar. Instead of joining the mad crowd of producers, he sagaciously determined to begin at the other end of the business—the refining of the product.

THERE WAS MORE MONEY IN A REFINERY

The use of petroleum was dangerous at that time, on account of the highly inflammable gases it contained. Many persons stuck to candles and sperm oil through fear of an explosion if they used the new illuminant. The process of removing these superfluous gases by refining, or distilling, as it was then called, was in its infancy. There were few men who knew anything about it.

Among Rockefeller's acquaintances in Cleveland was one of these men. His name was Samuel Andrews. He had worked in a distillery, and was familiar with the process. He believed that there was a great business to be built up by removing the gases from the crude oil and making it safe for household use. Rockefeller listened to him, and became convinced that he was right. Here was a field as wide as the world, limited only by the production of crude oil. It was a proposition on which he could figure and make sure of the result. It was just the thing Rockefeller had been looking for. He decided to leave the production of oil to others, and to devote his attention to preparing it for market.

Andrews was a brother commission merchant. The two started a refinery, each closing out his former business connection. In two weeks it was running night and day to fill orders. So great was the demand, and so great was the judgment of young Rockefeller—seeing what no one else had seen.

A second refinery had to be built at once, and in two years their plants were turning out two thousand barrels of refined petroleum per day. Henry M. Flagler, already wealthy, came into the firm, the name of which then became Rockefeller, Flagler and Andrews.

More refineries were built, not only at Cleveland, but also at other advantageous points. Competing refineries were bought or rendered ineffective by the cutting of prices.

It is related that Mr. Andrews became one day dissatisfied, and he was asked, "What will you take for your interest?" Andrews wrote carelessly on a piece of paper, "One million dollars." Within twenty-four hours he was handed that amount; Mr. Rockefeller saying, "Cheaper at one million than ten." In building up the refinery business Rockefeller was the head; the others were the hands. He was always the general commanding, the tactician. He made the plans and his associates carried them out. Here was the post for which he had fitted himself, and in which his genius for planning had full sway. In the conduct of the refinery affairs, as in every enterprise in which he has taken part, he exemplified another rule to which he had adhered from his boyhood days. He was the leader in whatever he undertook. In going into any undertaking, John D. Rockefeller has made it his rule to have the chief authority in his own hands or to have nothing to do with the matter.

STANDARD OIL

In 1870, when Mr. Rockefeller was thirty-two years old, the business was merged into the Standard Oil Company, starting with a capital of one million dollars. Other pens have written the later story of that great corporation; how it started pipe lines to carry the oil to the seaboard; how it earned millions in by-products which had formerly run to waste; how it covered the markets of the world in its keen search for trade, distancing all competition, and cheapening its own processes so that its dividends in one year, 1899, amounted to $23,000,000 in excess of the fixed dividend upon the whole capital stock. This is the outcome of thirty years' development. The corporation is now the greatest business combination of modern times, or of any age of the world. Mr. Rockefeller's annual income from his holdings of Standard Oil stock is estimated at about sixteen millions of dollars.

MR. ROCKEFELLER'S PERSONALITY

The brains of all this, the owner of the largest percentage of the stock in the parent corporation, and in most of the lesser ones, is now sixty-two years old. His personality is simple and unaffected, his tastes domestic, and the trend of his thoughts decidedly religious. His Cleveland residential estate is superb, covering a large tract of park-like land, but even there he has shown his unselfishness by donating a large portion of his land to the city for park purposes. His New York home is not a pretentious place, solid, but by no means elegant in outward appearance. Between the two homes he divides his time with his wife and children. He is an earnest and hard-working member of the Fifth Avenue Baptist Church, in New York, and does much to promote the good work carried on by that organization. He is particularly interested in the Sunday-school work.

AT THE OFFICE

He arises early in the morning, at his home, and, after a light breakfast, attends to some of his personal affairs there. He is always early on hand at the great Standard Oil building on lower Broadway, New York, and, during the day, he transacts business connected with the management of that vast corporation. There is hardly one of our business men of whom the public at large knows so little. He avoids publicity as most men would the plague. The result is that he is the only one of our very wealthy men who maintains the reputation of being different from the ordinary run of mortals. To most newspaper readers, he is a man of mystery, a sort of financial wizard who sits in his office and heaps up wealth after the fashion of Aladdin and other fairy-tale heroes.

All this is wide of the mark. It would be hard to find a more commonplace, matter-of fact man than John D. Rockefeller. His tall form, with the suggestion of a stoop in it, his pale, thoughtful face and reserved manner, suggest the scholar or professional man rather than an industrial Hercules or a Napoleon of finance. He speaks in a slow, deliberate manner, weighing each word. There is nothing impulsive or bombastic about him. But his conversation impresses one as consisting of about one hundred per cent of cold, compact, boiled-down common sense.

Here is to be noted one characteristic of the great oil magnate which has helped to make him what he is. The popular idea of a multimillionaire is a man who has taken big risks, and has come out luckily. He is a living refutation of this conception. He is careful and cautious by nature, and he has made these traits habitual for a lifetime; he conducts all his affairs on the strictest business principles.

FORESIGHT

The qualities which have made him so successful are largely those which go to the making of any successful business man, industry, thrift, perseverance, and foresight. Three of these qualities would have made him a rich man; the last has distinguished him as the richest man. One of his business associates said of him, the other day:

"I believe the secret of his success, so far as there is any secret, lies in power of foresight, which often seems to his associates to be wonderful. It comes simply from his habit of looking at every side of a question, of weighing the favorable and unfavorable features of a situation, and of sifting out the inevitable result through his unfailing good judgment."

This is his own personal statement, put into other words, so it may be accepted as true. The encouraging part of it is that, while such foresight as Rockefeller displays may be ascribed partly to natural endowment, both he and his friend say that it is more largely a matter of habit, made effective by continual practice.

HYGIENE

At noon he takes a very simple lunch at his club, or at some downtown restaurant. The lunch usually consists of a bowl of bread and milk. He remains at the office until late in the afternoon, and before dinner he takes some exercise. *In winter, he skates when possible.* And at other seasons of the year he nearly always drives in the park or on the avenues. Mr. Rockefeller has great faith in fresh air as a tonic.

AT HOME

The evenings are nearly always spent at home, for neither Mr. Rockefeller nor any of the children are fond of "society," as the word is understood in New York. The children seem to have inherited many of their father's sensible ideas, and John D. Rockefeller, Jr., has apparently escaped the fate of most rich men's sons. He has a deep sense of responsibility as the heir-apparent to so much wealth; and, since his graduation from college, he has devoted himself to a business career, starting at the bottom and working upward, step by step. It is now generally known that he has been very successful in his business ventures, and he bids fair to become a worthy successor to his father. He is now actively engaged in important philanthropic enterprises in New York. Miss Bessie became the wife of a poor clergyman of the Baptist Church in Cleveland; while Miss Alta is married to a prominent young business man in Chicago.

PHILANTHROPY

Mr. Rockefeller has during many years turned over to his children a great many letters from needy people, asking them to exercise their own judgment in distributing charities.

While he has himself given away millions for education and charity, he would have given more were it not for his dread of seeming ostentatious. But he never gives indiscriminately, nor out of hand. When a charity appeals to him, he investigates it thoroughly, just as he would a business scheme. If he decides that its object is worthy, he gives liberally; otherwise, not a cent can be got out of him.

It may be imagined that such a man is busy to the full limit of his working capacity. This is true. He is too busy for any of the pastimes and pleasures in which most wealthy men seek diversion. He is thoroughly devoted to his home and family, and spends as much as possible of his time with them. He is a man who views life seriously, but in his quiet way he can get as much enjoyment out of a good story or a meeting with an old friend as can any other man.

PERSEVERANCE

When I asked Mr. Rockefeller what he considers has most helped him in obtaining success in business, he answered: "It was early training, and the fact that I was willing to persevere. I do not think there is any other quality so essential to success of any kind as the quality of perseverance. It overcomes almost everything, even nature."

It is to be said of his business enterprises, looking at them in a large way, that he has given to the world good honest oil, of standard quality; that his employees are always well paid; that he has given away more money in benevolence than any other business man in America.

And everything about the man indicates that he is likely to "persevere" in the course he has so long pursued turning his vast wealth into institutes for public service.

A GENIUS FOR MONEY MAKING

"There are men born with a genius for money-making," says Mathews. "They have the instinct of accumulation. The talent and the inclination to convert dollars into doubloons by bargains or shrewd investments are in them just as strongly marked and as uncontrollable as were the ability and the inclination of Shakespeare to produce *Hamlet* and *Othello*, of Raphael to paint his cartoons, of Beethoven to compose his symphonies, or Morse to invent an electric telegraph. As it would have been a gross dereliction of duty, a shameful perversion of gifts, had these latter disregarded the instincts of their genius and engaged in the scramble for wealth, so would a Rothschild, an Astor, and a Peabody have sinned had they done violence to their natures, and thrown their energies into channels where they would have proved dwarfs and not giants."

The opportunity which came to young Rockefeller does not occur many times in many ages: and in a generous interpretation of his opportunity he has already invested a great deal of his earnings in permanently useful philanthropies.

CHAPTER XXV

A Talk With Edison

Dramatic Incidents In His Early Life

To discover the opinion of Thomas A. Edison concerning what makes and constitutes success in life is an easy matter—if one can first discover Mr. Edison. I camped three weeks in the vicinity of Orange, N. J., awaiting the opportunity to come upon the great inventor and voice my questions. It seemed a rather hopeless and discouraging affair until he was really before me; but, truth to say, he is one of the most accessible of men, and only reluctantly allows himself to be hedged in by pressure of endless affairs.

"Mr. Edison is always glad to see any visitor," said a gentleman who is continually with him, "except when he is hot on the trail of something he has been working for, and then it is as much as a man's head is worth to come in on him."

He certainly was not hot on the trail of anything on the morning when, for the tenth time, I rang at the gate in the fence which surrounds the laboratory on Valley Road, Orange. A young man appeared, who conducted me up the walk to the Edison laboratory office.

THE LIBRARY

is a place not to be passed through without thought, for, with a further store of volumes in his home, it contains one of the most costly and well-equipped scientific libraries in the world; the collection of writings on patent laws and patents, for instance, is absolutely exhaustive. It gives, at a glance, an idea of the breadth of thought and sympathy of this man who grew up with scarcely a common school education.

On the second floor, in one of the offices of the machine shop, I was asked to wait, while a grimy youth disappeared with my card, which he said he would "slip under the door of Mr. Edison's office."

"Curious," I thought; "what a lord this man must be if they dare not even knock at his door!"

Thinking of this and gazing out the window, I waited until a working man, who had entered softly, came up beside me. He looked with a sort of "Well, what is it?" in his eyes, and quickly it began to come to me that the man in the sooty, oil-stained clothes was Edison himself. The working garb seemed rather incongruous, but there was no mistaking the broad forehead, with its shock of blackish hair streaked with gray. The gray eyes, too, were revelations in the way of alert comprehensiveness.

"Oh!" was all I could get out at the time.

"Want to see me?" he said, smiling in the most youthful and genial way.

"Why—yes, certainly, to be sure," I stammered.

He looked at me blankly.

"You'll have to talk louder," said an assistant who worked in another portion of th room; "he don't hear well."

This fact was new to me, but I raised my voice with celerity, and piped thereafter in an exceedingly shrill key. After the usual humdrum opening remarks, in which he acknowledged his age as fifty-two years, and that he was born in Erie county, O., of Dutch parentage, the family having emigrated to America in 1730, the particulars began to grow more interesting.

His great-grandfather, I learned, was a banker of high standing in New York; and, when Thomas was but a child of seven years, the family fortune suffered reverses so serious as to make it necessary that he should become a wage-earner at an unusually early age, and that the family should move from his birthplace to Michigan.

"Did you enjoy mathematics as a boy?" I asked.

"Not much," he replied. "I tried to read Newton's *Principia* at the age of eleven. That disgusted me with pure mathematics, and I don't wonder now. I should not have been allowed to take up such serious work."

"You were anxious to learn?"

"Yes, indeed, *I attempted to read through the entire Free Library at Detroit,* but other things interfered before I had done."

A CHEMICAL NEWSBOY

"Were you a book-worm and dreamer?" I questioned.

"Not at all," using a short, jerky method, as though he were unconsciously checking himself up. "I became a newsboy, and liked the work. Made my first *coup* as a newsboy in 1869."

"What was it?" I ventured.

"I bought up on 'futures' a thousand copies of the *Detroit Free Press* containing important war news—gained a little time on my rivals, and sold the entire batch like hot cakes. The price reached twenty-five cents a paper before the end of the route," and he laughed. "I ran the *Grand Trunk Herald*, too, at that time—a little paper I issued from the train."

"When did you begin to be interested in invention?" I questioned.

"Well," he said, "I began to dabble in chemistry at that time. I fitted up a small laboratory on the train."

In reference to this, Mr. Edison subsequently admitted that, during the progress of some occult experiments in this workshop, certain complications ensued in which a jolted and broken bottle of sulphuric acid attracted the attention of the conductor. He, who had been long suffering in the matter of unearthly odors, promptly ejected the young devotee and all his works. This incident would have been only amusing but for its relation to, and explanation of, his deafness. A box on the ear, administered by the irate conductor, caused the lasting deafness.

TELEGRAPHY

"What was your first work in a practical line?" I went on.

"A telegraph line between my home and another boy's, I made with the help of an old river cable, some stove-pipe wire, and glass-bottle insulators. I had my laboratory in the cellar and studied telegraphy outside."

"What was the first really important thing you did?"

"I saved a boy's life."

"How?"

"The boy was playing on the track near the depot. I saw he was in danger and caught him, getting out of the way just in time. His father was station-master, and taught me telegraphy in return."

Dramatic situations appear at every turn of this man's life. He seems to have been continually arriving on the scene at critical moments, and always with the good sense to take things in his own hands. The chance of learning telegraphy only gave him a chance to show how apt a pupil he was, and the railroad company soon gave him regular employment. A seventeen, he had become one of the most expert operators on the road.

"Did you make much use of your inventive talent at this time?" I questioned.

"Yes," he answered. "I invented an automatic attachment for my telegraph instrument which would send in the signal to show I was awake at my post, when I was comfortably snoring in a corner. I didn't do much of that, though," he went on; "for some such boyish trick sent me in disgrace over the line into Canada."

"Were you there long?"

"Only a winter. If it's incident you want, I can tell you one of that time. The place where I was and Sarnier, the American town, were cut off from telegraphic and other means of communication by the storms, until I got at a locomotive whistle and tooted a telegraphic message. I had to do it again and again, but eventually they understood over the water and answered in the same way."

According to his own and various recorded accounts, Edison was successively in charge of important wires in Memphis, Cincinnati, New Orleans, and Louisville. He lived in the free-and-easy atmosphere of the tramp operators—a boon companion with them, yet absolutely refusing to join in the dissipations to which they were addicted. So highly esteemed was he for his honesty, that it was the custom of his colleagues, when a spree was on hand, to make him the custodian of those funds which they felt obliged to save. On a more than usually hilarious occasion, one of them returned rather the worse for wear, and knocked the treasurer down on his refusal to deliver the trust money; the other depositors, we may be glad to note, gave the ungentlemanly tippler a sound thrashing.

HIS USE OF MONEY

"Were you good at saving your own money?" I asked.

"No," he said, smiling. "I never was much for saving money, as money. I devoted every cent, regardless of future needs, to scientific books and materials for experiments."

"You believe that an excellent way to succeed?"

"Well, it helped me greatly to future success."

INVENTIONS

"What was your next invention?" I inquired.

"An automatic telegraph recorder-a machine which enabled me to record dispatches at leisure, and send them off as fast as needed."

"How did you come to hit upon that?"

"Well, at the time, I was in such straits that I had to walk from Memphis to Louisville. At the Louisville station they offered me a place. I had perfected a style of handwriting which would allow me to take legibly from the wire, long hand, forty-seven and even fifty-four words a minute, but I was only a moderately rapid sender. I had to do something to help me on that side, and so I thought out that little device."

Later I discovered an article by one of his biographers, in which a paragraph referring to this Louisville period, says:

"True to his dominant instincts, he was not long in gathering around him a laboratory, printing office, and machine shop. He took press reports during his whole stay, including on one occasion, the Presidential message, by Andrew Johnson, and this at one sitting, from 3.30 P.M. to 4.30 A.M.

"He then paragraphed the matter he had received over the wires, so that printers had exactly three lines each, thus enabling them to set up a column in two or three minutes' time. For this, he was allowed all the exchanges he desired, and the Louisville press gave him a dinner."

"How did you manage to attract public attention to your ability?" I questioned.

"I didn't manage," said the Wizard. "Some things I did created comment. A device that I invented in 1868, which utilized one submarine cable for two circuits, caused considerable talk, and the Franklin telegraph office of Boston gave me a position."

It is related of this, Mr. Edison's first trip East, that he came with no ready money and in a rat her dilapidated condition. His colleagues were tempted by his "hayseed" appearance to "salt" him, as professional slang terms the process of giving a receiver matter faster than he can record it. For this purpose, the new man was assigned to a wire manipulated by a New York operator famous for his speed. But there was no fun at all. Notwithstanding the fact that the New Yorker was in the game and was doing his most speedy clip, Edison wrote out the long message accurately, and, when he realized the situation, was soon firing taunts over the wire at the sender's slowness.

"Had you patented many things up to the time of your coming East?" I queried.

"Nothing," said the inventor, ruminatively. "I received my first patent in 1869."

"For what?"

"A machine for recording votes, and designed to be used in the State Legislature."

"I didn't know such machines were in use," I ventured.

"They aren't," he answered, with a merry twinkle. "The better it worked, the more impossible it was; the sacred right of the minority, you know—couldn't filibuster if they used it—didn't use it."

"Oh!"

"Yes, it was an ingenious thing. Votes were clearly pointed and shown on a roll of paper, by a small machine attached to the desk of each member. I was made to learn that such an innovation was out of the question, but it taught me something."

"And that was?"

"To be sure of the practical need of and demand for a machine, before expending time and energy on it."

"Is that one of your maxims of success?"

"It is. It is a good rule to give people something they want, and they will pay money to get it."

HIS ARRIVAL AT THE METROPOLIS

In this same year, Edison removed from Boston to New York, friendless, and in debt on account of the expenses of his experiment. For several weeks he wandered about the town with actual hunger staring him in the face. It was a time of great financial excitement, and with that strange quality of Fortunism, which seems to be his chief characteristic, he entered the establishment of the Law Gold Reporting Company just as their entire plant had shut down on account of an accident in the machinery that could not be located. The heads of the firm were anxious and excited to the last degree, and a crowd of the Wall street fraternity waited about for the news which came not. The shabby stranger put his finger on the difficulty at once, and was given lucrative employment. In the rush of the metropolis, a man finds his true level without delay especially when his talents are of so practical, and brilliant a nature as were this young telegrapher's. It would be an absurdity to imagine an Edison hidden in New York. Within a short time, he was presented with a check for $40,000, as his share of a single invention—an improved stock printer. From this time, a national reputation was assured him. He was, too, now engaged upon the duplex and, quadruplex systems—systems for sending two and four messages at the same time over, a single wire—which were to inaugurate almost a new era in telegraphy.

MENTAL CONCENTRATION

Recalling the incident of the Law Gold Reporting Company, I inquired: "Do you believe want urges a man to greater efforts, and so to greater success?"

"It certainly makes him keep a sharp look out. I think it does push a man along."

"Do you believe that invention is a gift, an acquired ability?"

"I think it's born in a man."

"And don't you believe that familiarity with certain mechanical conditions and defects naturally suggests improvements to any one?"

"No. Some people may be perfectly familiar with a machine all their days, knowing it inefficient, and never see a way to improve it."

"What do you think is the first requisite for success in your field, or any other?"

"*The ability to apply your physical and mental energies to one problem incessantly without growing weary.*"

TWENTY HOURS A DAY

"Do you have regular hours, Mr. Edison?" I asked.

"Oh," he said, "I do not work hard now. I come to the laboratory about eight o'clock every day and go home to tea at six, and then I study or work on some problem until eleven, which is my hour for bed."

"Fourteen of fifteen hours a day can scarcely be called loafing," I suggested.

"Well," he replied, "for fifteen years I have worked on an average of twenty hours a day."

When he was forty-seven years old, he estimated his true age at eighty-two, since working only eight hours a day would have taken till that time.

Mr. Edison has sometimes worked sixty consecutive hours upon one problem. Then after a long sleep, he was perfectly refreshed and ready for another.

A RUN FOR BREAKFAST

Mr. Dicks on, a neighbor and familiar, gives an anecdote told by Edison which well illustrates his untiring energy and phenomenal endurance. In describing his Boston experience, Edison said he bought Faraday's works on electricity, commenced to read them at three o'clock in the morning and continued until his roommate arose, when they started on their long walk to get breakfast. That object was entirely subordinated in Edison's mind to Faraday, and he suddenly remarked to his friend: "'Adams, I have got so much to do and life is so short, that I have got to hustle,' and with that I started off on a dead run for my breakfast."

"I've known Edison since he was a boy of fourteen," said another friend; "and of my; own knowledge I can say he never spent an idle day in his life. Often, when he should have been asleep, I have known him to sit up half the night reading. He did not take to novels or wild Western adventures, but read works on mechanics, chemistry, and electricity; and he mastered them too. But in addition to his reading, which he could only indulge in at odd hours, he carefully cultivated his wonderful powers of observation, till at length, when he was not actually asleep, it may be said he was learning all the time."

NOT BY ACCIDENT AND NOT FOR FUN

"Are your discoveries often brilliant intuitions? Do they come to you while you are lying awake nights?" I asked him.

"I never did anything worth doing by accident," he replied, "nor did any of my inventions come indirectly through accident, except the phonograph.* No, when I have fully decided that a result is worth getting, I go about it, and make trial after trial, until it comes.

"I have always kept," continued Mr. Edison, "strictly within the lines of commercially useful inventions. I have never had any time to put on electrical wonders, valuable only as novelties to catch the popular fancy."

"I LIKE IT—I HATE IT"

"What makes you work?" I asked with real curiosity. "What impels you to this constant, tireless struggle? You have shown that you care comparatively nothing for the money it makes you, and you have no particular enthusiasm for the attending fame. What is it?"

"I like it," he answered, after a moment of puzzled expression. "I don't know any other reason. Anything I have begun is always on my mind, and I am not easy while away from it, until it is finished; and then I hate it."

"Hate it?" I said.

"Yes," he affirmed, "when it is all done and is a success, I can't bear the sight of it. I haven't used a telephone in ten years, and I would go out of my way any day to miss an incandescent light."**

---

* I was singing to the mouthpiece of a telephone," said Edison, "when the vibrations of my voice caused a fine steel point to pierce one of my fingers held just behind it. That set me to thinking. If I could record the motions of the point and send it over the same surface afterward, I saw no reason why the thing would not talk. I determined to make a machine that would work accurately, and gave my assistants the necessary instructions, telling them what I had discovered. That's the whole story. The phonograph is the result of the pricking of a finger."

** After I have completed an invention," remarked Edison, upon another occasion, "I seem to lose interest in it. One might think that the money value of an invention constitutes its reward to the man who loves his work. But, speaking for myself, I can honestly say this is not so. Life was never more full of joy to me, than when, a poor boy, I began to think out improvements in telegraphy, and to experiment with the cheapest and crudest appliances. But now that I have all the appliances I need, and am my own master, I continue to find my greatest pleasure, and so my reward, in the work that precedes what the world calls success."

DOING ONE THING EIGHTEEN HOURS IS THE SECRET

"You lay down rather severe rules for one who wishes to succeed in life," I ventured, "working eighteen hours a day."

"Not at all," he said. "You do something all day long, don't you? Every one does. If you get up at seven o'clock and go to bed at eleven, you have put in sixteen good hours, and it is certain with most men, that they have been doing something all the time. They have been either walking, or reading, or writing, or thinking. The only trouble is that they do it about a great many things and I do it about one. If they took the time in question and applied it in one direction, to one object, they would succeed. Success is sure to follow such application. The trouble lies in the fact that people do not have an object—one thing to which they stick, letting all else go. Success is the product of the severest kind of mental and physical application."

POSSIBILITIES IN THE ELECTRICAL FIELD

"You believe, of course," I suggested, "that much remains to be discovered in the realm of electricity?"

"It is the field of fields," he answered. "We can't talk of that, but it holds the secrets which will reorganize the life of the world."

"You have discovered much about it," I said, smiling.

"Yes," he said, "and yet very little in comparison with the possibilities that appear."

ONLY SIX HUNDRED INVENTIONS

"How many inventions have you patented?"

"Only six hundred," he answered, "but I have made application for some three hundred more."

"And do you expect to retire soon, after all this?"

"I hope not," he said, almost pathetically. "I hope I will be able to work right on to the close. I shouldn't care to loaf."

HIS COURTSHIP AND HIS HOME

The idea of the great electrician's marrying was first suggested by an intimate friend, who told him that his large house and numerous servants ought to have a mistress. Although a very shy man, he seemed pleased with the proposition, and timidly inquired whom he should marry. The friend, annoyed at his apparent want of sentiment, somewhat testily replied, "Anyone." But Edison was not without sentiment when the time came. One day, as he stood behind the chair of a Miss Stillwell, a telegraph operator in his employ, he was not a little surprised when she suddenly turned round and said:

"Mr. Edison, I can always tell when you are behind me or near me."

It was now Miss Stillwell's turn to be surprised, for, with characteristic bluntness and ardor, Edison fronted the young lady, and, looking her full in the face, said:

"I've been thinking considerably about you of late, and, if you are willing to marry me, I would like to marry you."

The young lady said she would consider th matter, and talk it over with her mother. The result was that they were married a month later, and the union proved a very happy one.

It was in fact no more an accident than other experiments in the Edison laboratory—his bride having been long the subject of the Wizard's observation—her mental capacity, her temper and temperament, her aptitude for home-making being duly tested and noted.

CHAPTER XXVI
Carnegie as a Metal Worker

"There is no doubt," said Mr. Carnegie, in reply to a question from me, "that it is becoming harder and harder, as business gravitates more and more to immense concerns, for a young man without capital to get a start for himself, and in the large cities it is especially so, where large capital is essential. Still it can be honestly said that there is no other country in the world, where able and energetic young men and women can so readily rise as in this.

"A president of a business college informed me, recently, that he has never been able to supply the demand for capable, first-class [Mark the adjective.] bookkeepers, and his college has over nine hundred students. In America, young men of ability rise with most astonishing rapidity."

"As quickly as when you were a boy?"

"Much more so. When I was a boy, there were but very few important positions that a boy could aspire to. Every position had to be made. Now a boy doesn't need to make the place—all he has to do is to fit himself to take it."

EARLY WORK AND WAGES

"Where did you begin life?"

"In Dunfermline, Scotland, during my earliest years. The service of my life has all been in this country."

"In Pittsburgh?"

"Largely so. My father settled in Allegheny City, when I was only ten years old, and I began to earn my way in Pittsburgh."

"Do you mind telling me what your first service was?"

"Not at all. I was a bobbin boy in a cotton factory, then an engineman or boy in the same place, and later still I was a messenger boy for a telegraph company."

"At small wages, I suppose?"

"One dollar and twenty cents a week was what I received as a bobbin boy, and I considered it pretty good, at that. When I was thirteen, I had learned to run a steam engine, and for that I received a dollar and eighty cents a week."

"You had no early schooling, then?"

"None except such as I gave myself."

COLONEL ANDERSON'S BOOKS

"There were no fine libraries then, but in Allegheny City, where I lived, there was a certain Colonel Anderson, who was well to do and of a philanthropic turn. He announced, about the time I first began to work, that he would be in his library at home, every Saturday, ready to lend books to working boys and men. He had only about four hundred volumes, but I doubt if ever so few books were put to better use. Only he who has longed, as I did for Saturday to come, that the spring of knowledge might be opened anew to him, can understand what Colonel Anderson did for me and others of the boys of Allegheny. Quite a number of them have risen to eminence, and I think their rise can be easily traced to this splendid opportunity."*

HIS FIRST GLIMPSE OF PARADISE

"How long did you remain an engine-boy?"

"Not very long," Mr. Carnegie replied; "perhaps a year."

"And then?"

"I entered a telegraph office as a messenger boy."

Although Mr. Carnegie did not dwell much on this period, he once described it at a dinner given in honor of the American Consul at Dunfermline, Scotland, when he said:

"I awake from a dream that has carried me away back to the days of my boyhood, the day when the little white-haired Scottish laddie, dressed in a blue jacket, walked with his father into the telegraph office in Pittsburgh to undergo examination as an applicant for a position as messenger boy.

"Well I remember when my uncle spoke to my parents about it, and my father objected, because I was then getting one dollar and eighty cents per week for running the small engine in a cellar in Allegheny City, but my uncle said a messenger's wages would be two dollars and fifty cents . . . If you want an idea as to heaven on earth, imagine what it is to be taken from a dark cellar, where I fired the boiler from morning until night, and dropped into an office, where light shone from all sides, with books, papers, and pencils in profusion around me, and oh, the tick of those mysterious brass instruments on the desk, annihilating space and conveying intelligence to the world. This was my first glimpse of paradise, and I walked on air."

"How did you manage to rise from this position?"

---

* It was Colonel Anderson's kindness that led Carnegie to bestow his wealth so generously for founding libraries, as he is now doing every year.

"I learned how to operate a telegraph instrument, and then waited an opportunity to show that I was fit to be an operator. Eventually my chance came."

The truth is that James D. Reid, the superintendent of the office, and himself a Scotchman, favored the ambitious lad. In his "History of the Telegraph," he says of him:

"I liked the boy's looks, and it was easy to see that, though he was little, he was full of spirit. He had not been with me a month when he asked me to teach him to telegraph. He spent all his spare time in practice, sending and receiving by sound and not by tape, as was the custom in those days. Pretty soon he could do as well as I could at the key."

INTRODUCED TO A BROOM

"As you look back upon it," I said to Mr. Carnegie, "do you consider that so lowly a beginning is better than one a little less trying?"

"For young men starting upon their life, work, it is much the best to begin as I did, at, the beginning, and occupy the most subordinate positions. Many of the present-day leading men of Pittsburgh had serious responsibility thrust upon them at the very threshold of their careers. They were introduced to the broom, and spent the first hours of their business life sweeping out the office. I notice we have janitors and janitresses now in offices, and our young men, unfortunately, miss that salutary branch of early education. It does not hurt the newest comer to sweep out the office."

"Did you?"

"Many's the time. And who do you suppose were my fellow sweepers? David McBargo, afterwards superintendent of the Allegheny Valley Railroad; Robert Pitcairn, afterwards superintendent of the Pennsylvania Railroad; and Mr. Mooreland, subsequently City Attorney of Pittsburgh. We all took turns, two each morning doing the sweeping; and now I remember Davie was so proud of his clean shirt bosom that he used to spread over it an old silk handkerchief which he kept for the purpose, and we other boys thought he was putting on airs. So he was. None of us had a silk handkerchief."

"After you had learned to telegraph, did you consider that you had reached high enough?"

"Just at that time my father died, and the burden of the support of the family fell upon me. I earned as an operator twenty-five dollars a month, and a little additional money by copying telegraphic messages for the newspapers, and managed to keep the family independent."

AN EXPERT TELEGRAPHER

More light on this period of Mr. Carnegie's career is given by the "Electric Age," which says: "As a telegraph operator he was abreast of older and experienced men; and, although receiving messages by sound was, at that time, forbidden by authority as being unsafe, young Carnegie quickly acquired the art, and he can still stand behind the ticker and understand its language. As an operator, he delighted in full employment and the prompt discharge of business, and a big day's work was his chief pleasure."

"How long did you remain with the telegraph company?"

"Until I was given a place by the Pennsylvania Railroad Company."

"As an operator?"

"At first—until I showed how the telegraph could minister to railroad safety and success; then I was made secretary to Thomas A. Scott, the superintendent; and not long afterwards, when Colonel Scott became vice-president, I was made superintendent of the western division."

Colonel Scott's attention was drawn to Carnegie by the operator's devising a plan for running trains by telegraph, so making the most of a single track. Up to this time no one had ever dreamed of running trains in opposite directions, towards each other, directing them by telegraph, one train being sidetracked while the other passed. The boy studied out a train-despatching system which was afterwards used on every single-track railroad in the country.

Nobody had ever thought of this before, and the officials were so pleased with the ingenious lad, that they placed him in charge of a division office, and before he was twenty made him superintendent of the western division of the road.

WHAT EMPLOYERS THINK OF YOUNG MEN

Concerning this period of his life, I asked Mr. Carnegie if his promotion was not a matter of chance, and whether he did not, at the time, feel it to be so. His answer was emphatic.

"Never. Young men give all kinds of reasons why, in their cases, failure is attributable to exceptional circumstances, which rendered success impossible. Some never had a chance, according to their own story. This is simply nonsense. No young man ever lived who had not a chance, and a splendid chance, too, if he was ever employed at all. He is assayed in the mind of his immediate superior, from the day he begins work, and, after a time, if he has merit, he is assayed in the council chambers of the firm. His ability, honesty, habits, associations, temper, disposition—all these are weighed and analyzed. The young man who never had a chance is the same young man who has been canvassed over and over again by his superiors, and found destitute of necessary qualifications, or is deemed unworthy of closer relations with the firm, owing to some objectionable act, habit or association, of which he thought his employers ignorant."

"It sounds true."

"It is."

THE RIGHT MEN IN DEMAND

"Another class of young men attributes failure to rise to employers having near relatives or favorites whom they advance unfairly. They also insist that their employers dislike brighter intelligences than their own and are disposed to discourage aspiring genius and delighted in keeping young men down There is nothing in this. On the contrary, there is no one suffering more for lack of the right man in the right place as the average employer, nor anyone more anxious to find him."

"Was this your theory on the subject when you began working for the railroad company?"

"I had no theory then, although I have formulated one since. It lies mainly in this: Instead of the question, 'What must I do for my employer?' substitute, 'What can I do?' Faithful and conscientious discharge of duties assigned you is all very well, but the verdict in such cases generally is that you perform your present duties so well, that you would better continue performing them. Now, this will not do. It will not do for the coming partners. There must be something beyond this. We make clerks, bookkeepers, treasurers, bank tellers of this class, and there they remain to the end of the chapter. *The rising man must do something exceptional, and beyond the range of his special department. He must attract attention.*"

HOW TO ATTRACT ATTENTION

"How can he do that?"

"Well, if he is a shipping clerk, he may do so by discovering in an invoice an error with which he has nothing to do and which has escaped the attention of the proper party. If a weighing clerk, he may save for the firm in questioning the adjustment of the scales, and having them corrected, even if this be the province of the master mechanic. If a messenger boy, he can lay the seed of promotion by going beyond the letter of his instructions in order to secure the desired reply. There is no service so low and simple, neither any so high, in which the young man of ability and willing disposition cannot readily and almost daily prove himself capable of greater trust and usefulness, and, what is equally important, show his invincible determination to rise."

"In what manner did you reach out to establish your present great fortune?" I asked.

"By saving my money. I put a little money aside, and it served me later as a matter of credit. Also, I invested in a sleeping-car industry, which paid me well."

SLEEPING-CAR INVENTION

Although I tried earnestly to get the great iron-king to talk of this, he said little, because the matter has been fully dealt with by him in his "Triumphant Democracy." From his own story there, it appears that one day at this time, when Mr. Carnegie still had his fortune to make, he was on a train examining the line from a rear window of a car, when a tall, spare man, accosted him and asked him to look at an invention he had made. He drew from a green bag a small model of a sleeping-berth for railway cars, and proceeded to point out its advantages. It was Mr. T. T. Woodruff, the inventor of the sleeping-car. As Mr. Carnegie tells the story:

"He had not spoken a moment before, like a flash, the whole range of the discovery burst upon me. 'Yes,' I said, 'that is something which this continent must have.'

"Upon my return, I laid it before Mr. Scott, declaring that it was one of the inventions of the age. He remarked: 'You are enthusiastic, young man, but you may ask the inventor to come and let me see it.' I did so, and arrangements were made to build two trial cars, and run them on the Pennsylvania Railroad. I was offered an interest in the venture, which I gladly accepted.

"The notice came that my share of the first payment was $217.50. How well I remember the exact sum. But two hundred and seventeen dollars and a half were as far beyond my means as if it had been millions. I was earning fifty dollars per month, however, and had prospects, or at least I always felt that I had. I decided to call on the local banker and boldly ask him to advance the sum upon my interest in the affair. He put his hand on my shoulder and said, 'Why, of course, Andie; you are all right. Go ahead. Here is the money.'

"It is a proud day for a man when he pays his last note but not to be named in comparison with the day in which he makes his first one and gets a banker to take it. I have tried both, and I know. The cars furnished the subsequent payments by their earnings. I paid my first note from my savings, so much per month, and thus I got my foot upon fortune's ladder. It was easy to climb after that."

THE MARK OF A MILLIONAIRE

"I would like some expression from you," I said to Mr. Carnegie, "in reference to the importance of laying aside money from one's earnings, as a young man."

"You can have it. There is one sure mark of the coming partner, the future millionaire; his revenues always exceed his expenditures. He begins to save early, almost as soon as he begins to earn. I should say to young men, no matter how little it may be possible to save, save that little. Invest it securely, not necessarily in bonds, but in anything which you have good reason to believe will be profitable. Some rare chance will soon present itself for investment. The little you have saved will prove the basis for an amount of credit utterly surprising to you. Capitalists trust the saving man. For every hundred dollars you can produce as the result of hard-won savings, Midas, in search of a partner, will lend or credit a thousand; for every thousand, fifty thousand. *It is not capital that your seniors require, it is the man who has proved that he has the business habits which create capital. So it is the first hundred dollars that tell.*"

AN OIL-FARM

"What," I asked Mr. Carnegie, "was the next enterprise with which you identified yourself?"

"In company with several others, I purchased the now famous Storey farm, on Oil Creek, Pennsylvania, where a well had been bored and natural oil struck the year before. This proved a very profitable investment."

In "Triumphant Democracy," Mr. Carnegie has expatiated most fully on this venture, which is so important. "When I first visited this famous well," he says, "the oil was running into the creek, where a few flat-bottomed scows lay filled with it, ready to be floated down the Allegheny River, on an agreed-upon day each week when the creek was flooded by means of a temporary dam. This was the beginning of the natural-oil business. We purchased the farm for $40,000, and so small was our faith in the ability of the earth to yield for any considerable time the hundred barrels per day, which the property was then producing, that we decided to make a pond capable of holding one hundred thousand barrels of oil which, we estimated, would be worth, when the supply ceased, $1,000,000.

"Unfortunately for us, the pond leaked fearfully; evaporation also caused much loss, but we continued to run oil in to make the losses good day after day, until several hundred thousand barrels had gone in this fashion. Our experience with the farm is worth reciting: its value rose to $5,000,000; that is—the shares of the company sold in the market upon this basis; and one year it paid cash dividends of $1,00,000—upon an investment off $40,000.

IRON BRIDGES

"Were you satisfied to rest with these enterprises in your hands?" I asked.

"No. Railway bridges were then built almost exclusively of wood, but the Pennsylvania Railroad had begun to experiment with cast-iron. It struck me that the bridge of the future must be of iron; and I organized, in Pittsburgh, a company for the construction of iron bridges. That was the Keystone Bridge Works. We built the first iron bridge across the Ohio."

His entrance of the realm of steel was much too long for Mr. Carnegie to discuss, although he was not unwilling to give information relating to the subject. It appears that he realized the immensity of the steel manufacturing business at once. The Union Iron Mills soon followed as one of the enterprises, and, later, the famous Edgar Thompson Steel Rail Mill. The last was the outcome of a visit to England, in 1868, when Carnegie noticed that English rail ways were discarding iron for steel rails. The Bessemer process had been then perfected, and was making its way in all the iron-producing countries. Carnegie, recognizing that it was destined to revolutionize the iron business, introduced it into his mills and made steel rails with which he was enabled to compete with English manufacturers.

HOMESTEAD STEEL WORKS

His next enterprise was the purchase of the Homestead Steel Works—his great rival in Pittsburgh. In 1888, he had built or acquired seven distinct iron and steel works, all of which are now included in the Carnegie Steel Company, Limited. All the plants of this great firm are within a radius of five miles of Pittsburgh. Probably in no other part of the world can be found such an aggregation of splendidly equipped steel works as those controlled by this association. It now comprises the Homestead Steel Works, the Edgar Thompson Steel Works and Furnaces, the Duquesne Steel Works and Furnaces, all within two miles of one another; the Lucy Furnaces, the Keystone Bridge Works, the Upper Union Rolling Mills, and the Lower Union Rolling Mills.

In all branches, including the great coke works, mines, etc., there are employed twenty-five thousand men. The monthly pay roll exceeds one million, one hundred and twenty-five thousand dollars, or nearly fifty thousand dollars for each working day. Including the Frick Coke Company, the united capital of the Carnegie Steel Company exceeds sixty million dollars.

A STRENGTHENING POLICY

"You believe in taking active measures," I said, "to make men successful."

"I believe in anything which will help men to help themselves. To induce them to save, every workman in our company is allowed to deposit part of his earnings, not exceeding two thousand dollars, with the firm, on which the high interest rate of six per cent is allowed. The firm also lends to any of its workmen to buy a lot, or to build a house, taking its pay by installments."

"Has this contributed to the success of your company?"

"I think so. The policy of giving a personal interest to the men who render exceptional service is strengthening. With us there are many such, and every year several more are added as partners. It is the policy of the concern to interest every superintendent in the works, every head of a department, every exceptional young man. Promotion follows exceptional service, and there is no favoritism."

PHILANTHROPY

"All you have said so far, merely gives the idea of getting money, without any suggestion as to the proper use of great wealth. Will you say something on that score?"

"My views are rather well known, I think. What a man owns is already subordinate, in America, to what he knows; but in the final aristocracy, the question will not be either of these, but what has he done for his fellows? Where has he shown generosity and self-abnegation?

"Where has he been a father to the fatherless? And the cause of the poor, where has he searched that out?"

That Mr. Carnegie has lived up in the past, and is still living up to this radical declaration of independence from the practice of men who have amassed fortunes around him, will be best shown by a brief enumeration of some of his almost unexampled philanthropies. His largest gift has been to the city of Pittsburgh, the scene of his early trials and later triumphs. There he has built, at a cost of more than a million dollars, a magnificent library, museum, concert hall and picture gallery, all under one roof, and endowed it with a fund of another million, the interest of which (fifty thousand dollars per annum) is being devoted to the purchase of the best works of American art. Other libraries, to be connected with this largest as a center, are now being constructed, which will make the city of Pittsburgh and its environs a beneficiary of his generosity to the extent of five million dollars.

While thus endowing the city where his fortune was made, he has not forgotten other places endeared to him by association or by interest. To the Allegheny Free Library he has given $375,000; to the Braddock Free Library, $250,000; to the Johnstown Free

Library, $50,000; and to the Fairfield (Iowa) Library, $40,000. To the Cooper Institute, New York, he has given $300,000.

To his native land he has been scarcely less generous. To the Edinburgh Free Library he has given $250,000, and to his native town of Dunfermline, $90,000. Other Scottish towns to the number of ten have received helpful donations of amounts not quite so large. He has given $50,000 to aid poor young men and women to gain a musical education at the Royal College of Music in London.

"THE MISFORTUNE OF BEING RICH MEN'S SONS"

"I should like to cause you to say some other important things for young men to learn and benefit by."

"Our young partners in the Carnegie company have all won their spurs by *showing that we did not know half as well what was wanted as they did*. Some of them have acted upon occasions with me as if they owned the firm and I was but some airy New Yorker, presuming to *advise upon what I knew very little about*. Well, they are not now interfered with. *They were the true bosses—the very men we were looking for.*"

"Is this all for the poor boy?"

"Every word. Those who have the misfortune to be rich men's sons are heavily weighted in the race. A basketful of bonds is the heaviest basket a young man ever had to carry. He generally gets to staggering under it. The vast majority of rich men's sons are unable to resist the temptations to which wealth subjects them, and they sink to unworthy lives; It is not from this class that the poor beginner has rivalry to fear. The partner's sons will never trouble you much, but look out that some boys poorer, much poorer, than yourselves, whose parents cannot afford to give them any schooling, do not challenge you at the post and pass you at the grand stand. Look out for the boy who has to plunge into work direct from the common school, and begins by sweeping out the office. He is the probable dark horse that will take all the money and win all the applause."*

---

* Mr. Carnegie's recent retirement from business, and the sale of his vast properties to the Morgan Syndicate, marks a new era in his remarkable career; and it gives him the more leisure to consider carefully every dollar he bestows in the series of magnificent charities that he has inaugurated.

CHAPTER XXVII

Herreshoff, The Yacht Builder

—ONE—
The Voyage of Life

Amid the ranks of the blind, we often find men and women of culture and general ability, but we do not look for world-renowned specialists. No one is surprised at a display of enterprise in a "booming" western town, where everybody is "hustling": but in a place which has once ranked as the third seaport in America, but has seen its maritime glory decline, a man who can establish a marine industry on a higher plane than was ever before known, and attract to his work such world-wide attention as to restore the vanished fame of his town, is no ordinary person.

Moreover, if such a man has laid his plans and done his work in the disheartening eclipse of total blindness, he must possess qualities of the highest order.

The office of the Herreshoff Manufacturing Company, at Bristol, Rhode Island, is in a building that formerly belonged to the Burnside Rifle Company. It is substantial, but unpretentious, and is entered by a short stairway on one side. The furniture throughout is also plain, but has been selected with excellent taste, and is suggestive of the most effective adaptation of means to ends in every detail. On the mantel and on the walls are numerous pictures, most of them of vessels, but very few relating directly to any of the great races for the "America's" cup. The first picture to arrest one's attention, indeed, is an excellent portrait of the late General Ambrose E. Burnside, who lived in Bristol, and was an intimate friend of John B. Herreshoff.

Previous inquiry had elicited the information that the members of the firm are very busy with various large orders, in addition to the rush of work on Cup Defenders; so it was a very agreeable surprise when I was invited into the tasteful private office, where the blind president sat, having just concluded a short conversation with an attorney.

"LET THE WORK SHOW"

"Well, sir," said he, rising and grasping my hand cordially, "what do you wish?"

"I realize how very busy you must be, Mr. Herreshoff," I replied, "and will try to be as brief as possible; but I venture to ask a few minutes of your time, to obtain suggestions and advice from you to young people."

"But why select me, in particular, as an adviser?"

This was "a poser," at first, especially when he added, noting my hesitation:

"We are frequently requested to give inter views in regard to our manufacturing business but, since as it is the settled policy of our house to do our work just as well as we possibly can and then leave it to speak for itself, we have felt obliged to decline all these requests. It would be repugnant to our sense of propriety to talk in public about our special industry. 'Let the work show!' seems to us a good motto."

THE VOYAGE OF LIFE

"True," said I. "But the readers of my books may not care to read of cutters or 'skimming dishes,' center-boards or fin keels, or copper coils *versus* steel tubes for boilers. They leave the choice in such matters s to you, realizing that you have always proved equal to the situation. What I want now is advice in regard to the race of life—the voyage in which each youth must be his own captain, but in which the words of others who have successfully sailed the sea before will help to avoid rocks and shoals, and to profit by favoring currents and trade winds. You have been handicapped in an unusual degree, sailing in total darkness, and beset by many other difficulties, but have, nevertheless, made a very prosperous voyage. In overcoming such serious obstacles, you must have learned much of the true philosophy of both success and failure, and I think you will be willing to help the young with suggestions drawn from your experience."

"I always want to help young people, or old people, either, for that matter, if anything I can say will do so. But what can I say?"

A MOTHER'S MIGHTY INFLUENCE

"What do you call the prime requisite of success?"

"I shall have to answer that by a somewhat humorous but very shrewd suggestion of another—select a good mother. Especially for boys, I consider an intelligent, affectionate but considerate mother an almost indispensable requisite to the highest success. If you would improve the rising generation to the utmost, appeal first to the mothers."

"In what way?"

"*Above all things else, show them that reasonable self-denial is a thousand-fold better for a boy than to have his every wish gratified. Teach them to encourage industry, economy, concentration of attention and purpose, and indomitable persistence.*"

"But most mothers try to do this, don't they?"

"Yes, in a measure; but many of them, perhaps most of them, do not emphasize the matter half enough. A mother may wish to teach all these lessons to her son, but she thinks too much of him, or believes she does, to have him suffer any deprivation, and so indulges him in things which are luxuries for him, under the circumstances, rather than necessaries. Many a boy, born with ordinary intellect, would follow the example of an industrious father, were it not that his mother wishes him to appear as well as any boy in the neighborhood. So, without exactly meaning it, she gets to making a show of her boy, and brings him up with a habit of idling away valuable time, to keep up appearances. The prudent mother, however, sees the folly of this course, and teaches her son to excel in study and work, rather than in vain display. The difference in mothers makes all the difference in the world to children, who like brooks, can be turned very easily in their course of life."

SELF HELP

"What ranks next in importance?"

"Boys and girls themselves, especially as they grow older, and have a chance to understand what life means, should not only help their parents as a matter of duty, but should learn to help themselves, for their own good. I would not have them forego recreation, a reasonable amount every day, but let them learn the reality and earnestness of existence, and resolve to do the whole work and the very best work of thorough, reliable young men and women."

WHAT CAREER

"What would you advise as to choosing a career?"

"In that I should be governed largely by the bent of each youth. What he likes to do best of all, that he should do; and he should try to do it better than anyone else. That is legitimate emulation. Let him devote his full energy to his work; with the provision, however, that he needs change or recreation more in proportion as he uses his brain more. The more muscular the work, if not too heavy, the more hours, is a good rule: the more brain work, the fewer hours. Children at school should not be expected to work so long or so hard as if engaged in manual labor. Temperament, too, should be considered. A highly organized, nervous person, like a racehorse, may display intense activity for a short time, but it should be followed by a long period of rest; while the phlegmatic person, like the ox or the draft horse, can go all day without injury."

EDUCATION

"I believe in education most thoroughly, and think no one can have too much knowledge, if properly digested. But in many of our colleges, I have often thought, not more than one in five is radically improved by the course. Most collegiates waste too much time in frivolity, and somehow there seems to be little restraining power in the college to prevent this. I agree that students should have self-restraint and application themselves, but, in the absence of these, the college should supply more compulsion than is now the rule."

APPRENTICES

"Do you favor reviving the old apprentice system for would-be mechanics?"

"Only in rare cases. As a rule, we have special machines now that do as perfect work as the market requires; some of them, indeed, better work than can be done by hand. A boy or man can soon learn to tend one of these, when he becomes, for ordinary purposes, a specialist. Very few shops now have apprentices. No rule, however, will apply to all, and it may still be best for one to serve an apprenticeship in a trade in which he wishes to advance beyond any predecessor or competitor."

PREPARE TO THE UTMOST: THEN DO YOUR BEST

"Is success dependent more upon ability or opportunity?"

"Of course, opportunity is necessary. You couldn't run a mammoth department store on the desert of Sahara. But, given the possibility, the right man can make his opportunity, and should do so, if it is not at hand, or does not come, after reasonable waiting. Even Napoleon had to wait for his. On the other hand, if there is no ability, none can display itself, and the best opportunity must pass by unimproved. The true way is to first develop your ability to the last ounce, and then you will be ready for your opportunity, when it comes, or to make one, if none offers."

PRESENT OPPORTUNITIES

"Is the chance for a youth as good as it was twenty-five or fifty years ago?"

"Yes, and no. In any country, as it becomes more thickly populated, the chance for purely individual enterprises is almost sure to diminish. One notices this more as he travels through other and older countries, where, far more than with us, boys follow in the footsteps of their fathers, generation after generation. But for those who are willing to adapt themselves to circumstances, the chance, today, at least from a pecuniary standpoint, is better than ever before, for those starting in life. There was doubtless more chance for the individual boat-builder, in the days of King Philip, when each Indian made his own canoe; but there is certainly more profit now for an employee of our firm of boat-builders."

NATURAL EXECUTIVE ABILITY

"Granted, however, that he can find employment, how do his chances of rising compare with those of your youth?"

"They still depend largely upon the individual. *Some seem to have natural executive ability, and others develop it, while most men never possess it. Those who lack it cannot hope to rise far, and never could.* Jefferson's idea that all men are created equal is true enough, perhaps, so far as their political rights are concerned, but from the point of view of efficiency in business, it is ridiculous. In any shop of one hundred men, you will find one who is acknowledged, at least tacitly, as the leader, and he sooner or later becomes so in fact. A rich boy may get and hold a place in an office, on account of his wealth or influence; but in the works, merit alone will enable a man to hold a place long."

THE DEVELOPMENT OF POWER

"But what is his chance of becoming a proprietor?"

"That is smaller, of course, as establishments grow larger and more valuable. It is all bosh for every man to expect to become a Vanderbilt or a Rockefeller, or to be President. But, in the long run, a man will still rise and prosper in almost exact proportion to his real value to the business world. He will rise or fall according to his ability."

"Can he develop ability?"

"Yes, to a certain extent. As I have said, we are not all alike, and no amount of cultivation will make some minds equal to those of others who have had but little training. But, whether great or small, everyone has some weak point; let him first study to overcome that."

"How can he do it?"

"The only way I know of is to—do it. But this brings me back to what I told you at first. A good mother will show one how to guard against his weak points. She should study each child and develop his individual character, for character is the true foundation, after all. She should check extravagance and encourage industry and self-respect. My mother is one of the best, and I feel I owe her a debt I can never repay."

"MY MOTHER"

"Your mother? Why, I thought you had been a boat builder for half a century! How old is she?"

"She is eighty-eight, and still enjoys good health. If I have one thing more than another to be thankful for, it is her care in childhood and her advice and sympathy through life. How often have I thought of her wisdom when I have seen mothers from Europe (where they were satisfied to be peasants), seek to outshine all their neighbors after they have been in America a few years, and so bring financial ruin to their husbands or even goad them into crime, and curse their children with contempt for honest labor in positions for which they are fitted, and a foolish desire to keep up appearances, even by living beyond their means and by seeking positions they cannot fill properly."

A BOAT BUILDER IN YOUTH

"You must have been quite young, when you began to build boats?"

"About thirteen or fourteen years old. You see, my father was an amateur boat-builder, in a small way, and did very good work, but usually not for sale. But I began the work as a business thirty-six years ago, when I was about twenty-two."

HE WOULD NOT BE DISCOURAGED

"You must have been terribly handicapped by your blindness."

"It was an obstacle, but I simply would not allow it to discourage me, and did my best, just the same as if I could see. My mother had taught me to think, and so I made thought and memory take the place of eyes. I acquired a kind of habit of mental projection which has enabled me to see models in my mind, as it were, and to consider their good and bad points intelligently. Besides, I cultivated my powers of observation to the utmost, in other respects. Even now, I take an occasional trip of observation, for I like to see what others are doing, and so keep abreast of the progress of the age. But I must stop or I shall get to 'talking shop,' the thing I declined to do at first.

THE SUM OF IT ALL

"The main thing for a boy is to have a good mother, to heed her advice, to do his best, and not get a 'swelled head' as he rises—in other words, not to expect to put a gallon into a pint cup, or a bushel into a peck measure. Concentration, decision, industry and economy should be his watchwords, and invincible determination and persistence his rule of action."

With another cordial handshake, he bade me good-by.

—TWO—
What the Herreshoff Brothers Have Been Doing

Their recent Cup Defenders have made their names familiar to all, but shipping circles have long known them. The business of the firm was long confined almost wholly to the creation of boats with single masts, each craft from twenty to thirty-six feet long. In their first ten years of associated work, they built nearly two thousand of these. But they were wonderful little boats, and of unrivaled swiftness. Then they made as wonderful a success in building steam fishing yachts. Then came torpedo boats.

And in 1881 their proposal to the British government to build two vedette boats was accepted on condition they should outmatch the work of White, the naval launch builder at Cowes. No firm had ever been able to compete with White. But in the following July the two Herreshoff boats were in the Portsmouth dockyard, England, ready for trial. They were each forty-eight feet long, nine feet in beam, and five feet deep, exactly the same size as White's. They made fifteen and one half knots an hour, while White's only recorded twelve and two-fifths knots. "With all their machinery coal and water in place the Herreshoff boats were filled with water, and then twenty men were put aboard each, that human load being just so much in excess the admiralty test, and even then each had a floating capacity of three tons. The examiners pronounced enthusiastically in favor of the Herreshoff safety coil boilers as unexplodable, less liable to injury from shock, capable of raising steam more quickly, far lighter, and in all respects superior to those that had been formerly used for the purpose." The boats were accepted, and orders given at once for two pinnaces, each thirty-three feet long. Again John Samuel White competed, but his new boats could only make seven and one-eighth knots, while the Herreshoff's easily scored nine and one-quarter.

RACING JAY GOULD

In July, 1883, Jay Gould was highly elated over the speed of his beautiful steam yacht *Atalanta*, which had several times met and distanced Edward S. Jaffray's wonderful *Stranger*; but, on the twentieth

PART III: LIFE STORIES OF SUCCESSFUL MEN AND WOMEN... 319

of that month, his happiness, as the story is told, was very suddenly dashed.

After a hard day's work, the jaded Jay boarded the *Atalanta* and began to shake out his pin-feathers a little, figuratively speaking. But before his boat had gone far on her run to Irvington, the bold manipulator of Wall Street made out a craft on his weather-quarter that seemed to be gliding after the *Atalanta* with intent to overhaul her. He had a good start, however, and sang out to the captain to keep a sharp eye on the persistent little stranger, so unlike the *Stranger* he had vanquished.

"I wonder what it is!" he exclaimed to a friend beside him.

The friend looked long and carefully at the oncoming boat, then turned a quizzical eye on Jay, remarking:

"In a little while we can tell."

"Will she get that close?"

"I think she will."

It was not long before the strange boat was abreast of the *Atalanta*, and Jay was then able to make out the mystical number "100" on her. He rubbed his eyes. Those were the very figures he had long hoped to see on the stock ticker, after the words "Western Union," but that day they had lost their charm. Before long he was not only able to see the broadside of the *100*, but also had a good view of the stern of the vessel, whereon the same figures soon appeared and nearly as soon disappeared, as the *100* bade good-by to the *Atalanta*, which was burning every pound of coal that could possibly be carried without putting Mr. Gould or some efficient substitute on the safety valve.

"He seems to be out of humor tonight," said his coachman, after leaving his employer at the door of his Irvington mansion.

The mystic *100* which, by the way, was just one hundred feet over all, was merely the hundredth steamer built by the Herreshoffs, but on her first trip up the Hudson she attracted as much attention as the *Half Moon* of Henry Hudson or the *Clermont* of Robert Fulton. She was the fastest yacht in the world, and was beaten on the river by only one vessel, the *Mary Powell*—four and one-half minutes in twenty miles.

Although Mr. Gould was considerably irritated at his defeat, he knew a good thing when he saw it, and the next year he ordered a small steam launch of the Herreshoffs.

The *100* made a great stir in Boston Harbor. Later on she steamed through the Erie canal and the Great Lakes, and made her home with the millionaire Mark Hopkins.

THE *STILETTO*

The versatility of the Herreshoffs has appeared in their famous boiler improvement, and in the great variety of vessels they have built. The *Stiletto* only ninety-four feet long, over all, astonished the yachting world in 1885. On June 10, she beat the *Mary Powell* two miles in a race of twenty-eight miles on the Hudson. At one time, the *Stiletto* circled completely around the big steamer and then moved rapidly away from her.

Secretary Whitney bought the *Stiletto* for the United States navy, in which she has done valuable service. She was followed, in 1890, by the still faster *Cushing*, whose record in the recent Spanish-American war is so well known.

Admiral Porter wrote to Secretary of the Navy Chandler, that the little Herreshoff steam launches were faster than any other owned by the government, their great superiority showing especially against a strong head wind and sea when they would remain dry while their rivals required constant bailing. They were better trimmed, lighter, more buoyant, and in every way superior in nautical qualities, and twice as fast as others in a gale.

Nineteen vessels have been built by this firm for the United States government. "There is a certain speed that attaches to every vessel, which may be called its natural rate," says Lewis Herreshoff. "It is mainly governed by its length and the length of the carrier wave which always accompanies a vessel parallel to her line of motion. When she reaches a speed great enough to form a wave of the same length as the moving body, then that vessel has reached her natural rate of speed, and all that can be obtained above that is done by sheer brute force. The natural limit of speed of a boat forty feet long is about ten miles an hour; of a vessel sixty feet in length, twelve and one-quarter miles; of one a hundred feet long, fifteen and three-fourths miles; of one two hundred feet long, twenty-two miles."

As the speed is increased, this double or carrier wave, one-half on either side of the yacht, lengthens in such a way that the vessel seems to settle more the faster she goes, and so has to climb the very wave she makes. Hence the motive power must be increased much faster than the speed increases. Further, in order to avoid this settling and consequent climbing as much as possible, lightness of construction, next to correct proportions, is made the great desideratum in the Herreshoffs' ideal boat. They use wood wherever possible, as it is not only lighter than metal, but is reasonably strong and generally much more durable. Wherever heavy strains come, a bracing form of construction is adopted, and metal is used also.

The engine of the *Stiletto* weighs ten pounds for each indicated horse-power; that of the *Cushing*, fifteen. The entire motive plant of the *Cushing* weighs sixty-five pounds for each horse-power; that of the *City of Paris*, two hundred. Comparing displacement, the former has eight times the power of the latter.

For four years our government kept a staff of officers stationed at the Herreshoff works to experiment with high-speed machinery, in which the firm then led the country. One of their steamers, ascending the St. Lawrence River to the Thousand Islands, ran up all the rapids except the Lachine, where a detour by canal was made. The Canadians were deeply impressed by this triumph.

THE BLIND BROTHERS

One of the Herreshoff sisters is blind and a remarkable musician; and one brother blind who studied music in Berlin, and who conducts a school of music in Providence. Lewis Herreshoff, one of the boat-builders, is also blind. He, too, is a fine musician and an excellent bass singer, having received careful vocal training in Europe. He has fine literary taste, a very clear style, and writes for magazines, especially on boat-building and engineering. He has a large foreign correspondence, all of which he answers personally on the typewriter. It would be difficult to find a greater favorite with young people, to whom he devotes much of his time, teaching them games or lessons, also how to sail or row a boat, how to swim or float, and how to save each other from drowning. When walking along the street with a group of chatting children, he will ask, "What time is it by the clock on St. Michael's Church?" pointing right at the steeple. He will wind a clock and set it exactly, and regulate it, if it does not go right.

THE PERSONALITY OF JOHN B. HERRESHOFF

From his boyhood, John B. Herreshoff evinced a great fondness for boats and machinery, finding most pleasure, in his leisure hours, when boys of his age usually think only of play, in haunting boat-builders' yards and machine shops, studying how and why things were done, and reading what had been clone elsewhere in those branches of industry, beyond his field of observation.

At the age of eleven, he was studying the best lines for vessels' hulls and making models and three years later he began building boats.

His terrible affliction has never seemed to weaken his self-reliance or turn him aside from following the chosen pursuit of his life, but has rather strengthened his devotion to it and his capacity for it by concentrating all his faculties upon it.

His many years of blindness have given him not only the serious, patient, introspective look common to those who suffer like him, and their gentle, clearly modulated voice, but have also developed all his other faculties to such an extent as to largely replace the missing sense.

He can tell as much about an ordinary-sized steam launch, her lines, methods of construction, etc., by feeling, as others can by seeing, and he goes on inventing and building just as if his eyes were not closed forever. He is a tall, big-brained man, who couldn't help inventing and working if he tried. Such a man would have to suffer the loss of more than one of his senses before his mental efficiency would be impaired. When he wanted to build some steam launches for the government, he went to the navy yard at Washington and felt of the government launches, to discover their shape and how they were made. Then he went to Bristol and made better launches suitable for the government's use.

HAS HE A SIXTH SENSE?

He reads and understands the most delicate intonations and modulations of voices addressing him, as others read and understand facial expression. His sensitive fingers detect differences in metals, and follow, as if with a gift of perception, the lines, of models submitted to him, and his mind sees even more clearly than by mere physical sight the intricacies of the most complicated machinery intelligently described to him, or over which his fingers are allowed to move. "That is a good stick," he will say, examining a pile of lumber with his fingers. "Here's a shaky piece, throw it out; it won't do for this work," may come next, or, "Saw off this end; it's poor stock. The rest is all right." On hearing him criticize, direct, and explain things within his province, a stranger finds it hard to believe he cannot see at least a little—out of one eye.

SEEING WITH THE FINGERS

By the constant practice, he has, as he expresses it, learned to see with his hands, not quite so quickly, but he believes as perfectly, as he could with his eyes, and this means more than it does in the case of an ordinary blind man; for, by a touch, he can tell whether the graceful double curves of a boat's bottom are in correct proportion, one with another, and then, by a few rapid sweeps of his hands, over all, he can instantly judge of the symmetry and perfection of the whole. Even more than this, he will give minute directions to the carpenters and mechanics, running his hand along the piece of work one had produced, will immediately detect the slightest deviation from the instruction he has given. If at all impatient, he will seize the plane or other tool, and do the work himself. And yet the world calls this man "blind!"

While skill plays a material part, one of John B. Herreshoff's boats is a product of the mind, in a very great degree. Psychologists tell us that we do not see with our eyes, but with the brain proper. This blind man sees, and constructs, not that which is objective and real to others, but that which is evolved from a transcendental intelligence applied to the most practical purposes.

BROTHER NAT

One of the brothers, who has good eyes, is a prominent chemist in New York; and one who can see is Nat the designer for the boat building.

Nathaniel G., the great yacht designer, was born in 1848. When he was not more than two years old, he was often found asleep on the sand along shore, with the rising tide washing his bare feet. Whenever he was missing, he was sought for first on the shore, where he would generally be found watching the ships or playing with toy boats.

At nine years of age, he was an excellent helmsman, and at twelve he sailed the *Sprite* to her first victory and won a prize. When older grown, he was known as a vigilant watcher of every chance as well as a skillful sailor. Once, when steering the *Ianthe* in a failing wind, he veered widely from a crowd of contestants, so as to run into a good breeze he noted far to starboard, and won the race.

He took a four years' course at the Massachusetts Institute of Technology, and then served an apprenticeship with the famous Corliss Engine Company. He worked on the great engine at the Centennial Exposition, and took a course of engineering abroad, visiting many noted shipyards. He first joined the firm in 1877, fourteen years after the works were opened.

Nathaniel Greene Herreshoff, named for General Greene of Revolutionary fame, is seven years younger, and only less famous than his blind brother as a boat-builder—only second to John B. in about the same way that Greene was second to Washington. "General Greene is second to no one," said Washington. John B. would have done splendid work without Nat as he did for years before the latter joined the firm, but it would have been in a smaller way.

For years John B., his father, and his brothers, James B. or Lewis, and Nathaniel G., were accustomed to get together frequently in the dining-room of the old homestead, and talk and plan together in regard to boat-building. Nat would usually make the first model on lines previously agreed upon, and then John B. would feel it over and suggest changes, which would he made, and the consultation continued until all was satisfactory.

Nathaniel is described as "a tall, thin man, with a full beard and a stoop," the latter said to have been acquired in "watching his rivals in his races, craning his head in order to see them from under the boom."

"We have been always together from boyhood," said John B., speaking of "Nat."

"We have had the same pleasures, the same purposes, the same aspirations; in fact, we have almost been one, and we have achieved nothing for which a full share of credit is not his just due. Nothing has ever been done by one without the other. Whenever one found an obstacle or difficulty, the other helped him to remove it; and he, being without the disadvantage I have, never makes a mistake."

CHAPTER XXVIII

A Successful Novelist: Fame After Fifty*

PRACTICAL HINTS TO YOUNG AUTHORS

By Mrs. Amelia E. Barr

To be successful! That is the legitimate ideal every true worker seeks to realize. But success is not the open secret which it appears to be; its elements are often uncomprehended; and its roots generally go deep down, into the very beginnings of life. I can compel my soul to look back into that twilight which shrouds my earliest years, and perceive, even in them, monitions and tendencies working for that future, which in my destiny was fashioned and shaped when as yet there was neither hint nor dream of it. Fortunately, I had parents who understood the

VALUE OF BIBLICAL AND IMAGINATIVE LITERATURE

in the formation of the intellect. The men and women whom I knew first and best were those of the Hebrew world. Sitting before the nursery fire, while the snow fell softly and ceaselessly, and all the

---

* This is a most remarkable story, communicated to me by Mrs. Barr, and related for the first time in this article. The distinguished novelist, being a perfect housekeeper and the mother of a large family, yet earns $20,0000 a year by her books, which have been translated into the language of almost every civilized country. O. S. M

mountains round were white, and the streets of the little English town choked with drifts, I could see the camels and the caravans of the Ishmaelitish merchants, passing through the hot, sandy desert. I could see Hagar weeping under the palm, and the waters of the Red Sea standing up like a wall. Miriam clashing the timbrels, and Deborah singing under the oak, and Ruth gleaning in the wheat-fields of Bethlehem, were as real to me as were the women of my own home. Before I was six years old, I had been with Christian to the Celestial City, and had watched, with Crusoe, the mysterious footprint on the sand, and the advent of the savages. Then came the wonders of afrites and genii, and all the marvels and miracles of the Arabian tales.

These were the mind-builders, and though schools and teachers and text-hooks did much afterwards, I can never nor will forget the glorious company of men and women from the sacred world, and that marvelous company of caliphs and kings and princesses from Wonder Land and Fairy Land, that expanded my whole nature, and fitted me for the future miracles of Nature and Science, and all the marvelous people of the Poet's realm.

For eighteen years I was amassing facts and fancies, developing a crude intelligence, waiting for the vitalization of the heart. Then Love, the Supreme Teacher, came; and his first lesson was,

RENUNCIATION.

I was to give up father, and mother, home and kindred, friends and country, and follow where he would lead me, into a land strange and far off. Child-bearing and child-losing; the limitations and delights of frontier life; the intimate society of such great and individual men as Sam Houston, and the men who fought with him; the intense feelings induced by war, its uncertainties and possibilities, and the awful abiding in the Valley of the Shadow of Death, with the pestilence that walked in darkness and the sickness that destroyed at noonday—all these events with their inevitable "asides" were instrumental in the education and preparation of the seventeen years of my married life.

The calamitous lesson of widowhood, under peculiarly tragic circumstances, was the last initiation of a heart already broken and humbled before Him who doeth all things well, no matter how hard the stroke may be. I thought all was over then; yet all was just beginning. It was the open door to a new life—a life full of comforts, and serene, still,

DELIGHTFUL STUDIES.

Though I had written stories to please my children, and many things to please myself, it had never occurred to me that money could be made by writing. The late William Libbey, a man of singular wisdom and kindness, first made me understand that my brain and my ten fingers were security for a good living. From my first effort I began to gather in the harvest of all my years of study and reading and private writing. For there is this peculiarity about writing—that if in any direction it has merit, it will certainly find a market. For fifteen years I wrote short stories, poems, editorials, and articles on every conceivable subject, from Herbert Spencer's theories, to gentlemen's walking sticks; but bringing to every piece of work, if it was only ten lines, the best of my knowledge and ability; and so earning, with a great deal of pleasure, a very good living.

During the earlier years of this time I worked and read on an average

FIFTEEN HOURS A DAY;

for I knew that, to make good work, I must have constant fresh material; must keep up to date in style and method; and must therefore read far more than I wrote. But I have been an omnivorous reader all my life long, and no changes, no cares of home and children, have ever interfered with this mental necessity. In the most unlikely places and circumstances, I looked for books, and found them. These fifteen years on the weekly and monthly periodicals gave me the widest opportunities for information. I had an alcove in the Astor Library, and I practically lived in it. I slept and ate at home, but I lived in that City of Books. I was in the prime of life, but neither society, amusements, nor pleasures of any kind, could draw me away from the source of all my happiness and profit.

Suddenly, after this long novition, I received the "call" for a different work. I had AN ACCIDENT which confined me to my room, and which, I knew, would keep me from active work for some months. I fretted for my work, as dry wood frets an inch from the flame, and said, "I shall lose all I have gained; I shall fall behind in the race; all these things are against me." They were all for me. A little story of what seemed exceptional merit, had been laid away, in the hope that I might some day find time to extend it into a novel. A prisoner in my chair, I finished the book in six weeks, and sent it to Dodd, Mead & Co. On Thanksgiving morning, a letter came, accepting the book, and any of my readers can imagine what a happy Thanksgiving Day that was! This book was *Jan Vedder's Wife*, and its great and immediate success indicated to me the work I was at length ready for. I was then in my fifty-second year, and every year had been a preparation for the work I have since pursued. I went out from that sick room sure of my

VOCATION;

and, with a confidence founded on the certainty of my equipment, and a determination to trust humanity, and take my readers only into green pastures and ways of purity and heroism, I ventured on my new path as a novelist.

I cannot close this paper without a few words to those who wish to profit by it. I want them to be sure of a few points which, in my narrative, I may not have emphasized sufficiently.

WORDS OF COUNSEL

Men and women succeed *because they take pains to succeed*. Industry and patience are almost genius; and successful people are often more distinguished for resolution and perseverance than for unusual gifts. They make determination and unity of purpose supply the place of ability.

Success is the reward of those who "spurn delights and live laborious days." We learn to do things by *doing them. One of the great secrets of success is "pegging away."* No disappointment must discourage, and a run back must often be allowed, in order to take a longer leap forward.

No opposition must be taken to heart. Our enemies often help us more than our friends. Besides, a head-wind is better than no wind. Who ever got anywhere in a dead calm?

A fatal mistake is to imagine that success is some stroke of luck. This world is run with far too tight a rein for luck to interfere. Fortune sells her wares; she never gives them. In some form or other, we pay for her favors; or we go empty away.

We have been told, for centuries, to watch for opportunities, and to strike while the iron is hot. Very good; but I think better of Oliver Cromwell's amendment—*"make the iron hot by striking it."*

Everything good needs time. Don't do work in a hurry. Go into details; it pays in every way. *Time means power for your work.* Mediocrity is always in a rush; but whatever is worth doing at all is worth doing with consideration. For genius is nothing more nor less than doing well what anyone can do badly.

Be orderly. Slatternly work is never good work. It is either affectation, or there is some radical defect in the intellect. I would distrust even the spiritual life of one whose methods and work were dirty, untidy, and without clearness and order.

Never be above your profession. I have had many letters from people who wanted all the emoluments and honors of literature, and who yet said, "Literature is the accident of my life; I am a lawyer, or a doctor, or a lady, or a gentleman." *Literature is no accident. She is a mistress who demands the whole heart, the whole intellect, and the whole time of a devotee.*

Don't fail through defects of temper and over-sensitiveness at moments of trial. *One of the great helps to success is to be cheerful*; to go to work with a full sense of life; to be determined to put hindrances out of the way; to prevail over them and to get the mastery. *Above all things else, be cheerful*; there is no beatitude for the despairing.

Apparent success may be reached by sheer impudence, in defiance of offensive demerit. But men who get what they are manifestly unfit for, are made to feel what people think of them. Charlatanry may flourish; but when its bay tree is greenest, it is held far lower than genuine effort. The world is just; it may, it does, patronize quacks; but *it never puts them on a level with true men.*

It is better to have the opportunity of victory, than to be spared the struggle; for success comes but as the result of arduous experience. The foundations of my success were laid before I can well remember; *it was after at least forty-five years of conscious labor that I reached the object of my hope.* Many a time my head failed me, my hands failed me, my feet failed me, but, thank God, my *heart* never failed me. Because *I knew that no extremity would find God's arm shortened.*

CHAPTER XXIX
John Burroughs at Home: The Hut on the Hill Top

When I visited the hill-top retreat of John Burroughs, the distinguished writer upon nature, at West Park, New York, it was with the feeling that all success is not material; that mere dollars are nothing, and that the influential man is the successful man, whether he be rich or poor. John Burroughs is unquestionably both influential and poor. Relatively poor: being an owner of some real estate, and having a modest income from copyrights. He is content: knowing when he has enough. On the wooden porch of his little bark-covered cabin I waited, one June afternoon, until he should come back from the woods and fields, where he had gone for a ramble. It was so still that the sound of my rocker moving to and fro on the rough boards of the little porch seemed to shock the perfect quiet. From afar off came the plaintive cry of a wood dove, and then all was still again. Presently the interpreter of out-door life appeared in the distance, and, seeing a stranger at his door, hurried homeward. He was without coat or vest and looked cool in his white outing shirt and large straw hat. After some formalities of introduction we reached the subject which I had called to discuss, and he said:

"It is not customary to interview men of my vocation concerning success."

"Any one who has made a lasting impression on the minds of his contemporaries," I began, "and influenced men and women."

"Do you refer to me?" he interrupted, naively.

I nodded and he laughed. "I have not endowed a university nor made a fortune, nor conquered an enemy in battle," he said.

"And those who have done such things have not written *Locusts and Wild Honey* and *Wake Robin*."

"I recognize," he said quietly, "that success is not always where people think it is. There are many ways of being successful; and I do not approve of the mistake which causes many to consider that a great fortune acquired means a great success achieved. On the contrary, our greatest men need very little money to accomplish the greatest work."

"I thought that anyone leading a life so wholly at variance with the ordinary ideas and customs would see success in life from a different point of view," I observed. "Money is really no object with you?"

"The subject of wealth never disturbs me."

"You lead a very simple life here."

"Such as you see."

The sight would impress anyone. So far is this disciple of nature away from the ordinary mode of the world, that his little cabin, set in the cup-shaped top of a hill, is practically bare of luxuries and the so called comforts of life. His surroundings are of the rudest, the very rocks and bushes encroaching upon his back door. All about, the crest of the hill encircles him, and shuts out the world. Only the birds of the air venture to invade his retreat from the various sides of the mountain; and there is only one approach by a straggling, narrow path. In his house are no decorations but such as can be hung upon the exposed wood. The fireplace is of brick, and quite wide; the floor, rough boards scrubbed white; the ceiling, a rough array of exposed rafters; and his bed rudely constructed. Very few and very simple chairs, a plain table and some shelves for books make the wealth of the retreat and serve for his ordinary use.*

"Many people," I said, "think that your method of living is an ideal example of the way people ought to live."

"There is nothing remarkable in that. A great many people are very weary of the way they think themselves compelled to live. They are mistaken in believing that the disagreeable things they find themselves doing, are the things they ought to do. A great many take their ideas of a proper aim in life from what other people say and do. Consequently, they are unhappy, and an independent existence such as mine strikes them as ideal. As a matter of fact, it is very natural."

"Would you say that to work so as to be able to live like this should be the aim of a young man?"

"By no means. On the contrary, his aim should be to live in such a way as will give his mind the greatest freedom and peace. This can be very often obtained by wanting less of material things and more of intellectual ones. A man who achieved such an aim would be as well off as the most distinguished man in any field. Money-getting is half a mania, and some other 'getting' propensities are manias also. The man who gets content comes nearest to being reasonable."

"I should, like," I said, "to illustrate your point of view from the details of your own life."

"Students of nature do not, as a rule, have eventful lives. I was born at Roxbury, New York, in 1837. That was a time when condi-

---

* This hut on the hill-top is situated in an old lake bed, some three hundred yards wide, half filled with peat and decomposed matter, swampy and overgrown. This area was devoted by Mr. Burroughs to the raising of celery for the market, when he set out to earn a living upon the land.

tions were rather primitive. My father was a farmer, and I was raised among the woods and fields. I came from an uncultivated, unreading class of society, and grew up among surroundings the least calculated to awaken the literary faculty. I have no doubt that daily contact with the woods and fields awakened my interest in the wonders of nature, and gave me a bent toward investigation in that direction."*

"Did you begin early to make notes and write upon nature?" I questioned.

"Not before I was sixteen or seventeen. Earlier than that, the art of composition had anything but charms for me. I remember that while at school, at the age of fourteen, I was required, like other students, to write 'compositions' at stated times, but I usually evaded the duty one way or another. On one occasion, I copied something from a comic almanac, and unblushingly handed it in as my own. But the teacher detected the fraud, and ordered me to produce a twelve-line composition before I left school. I remember I racked my brain in vain, and the short winter clay was almost closing when Jay Gould, who sat in the seat behind me, wrote twelve lines of doggerel on his slate and passed it slyly over to me. I had so little taste for writing that I coolly copied that, and handed it in as my own."

"You were friendly with Gould then?"

"Oh, yes. 'Chummy,' they call it now. His father's farm was only a little way from ours, and we were fast friends, going home together every night."

---

* "Blessed is he whose youth was passed upon a farm," writes Mr. Burroughs; "and if it was a dairy farm his memories will be all the more fragrant. The driving of the cows to and from the pasture every day and every season for years, how much of summer and of nature he got into him on these journeys! What rambles and excursions did this errand furnish the excuse for! The birds and birds' nests, the berries, the squirrels, the woodchucks, the beech woods into which the cows loved so to wander and browse, the fragrant wintergreens and a hundred nameless adventures, all strung upon that brief journey of half a mile to and from the remote pasture."

"His view of life must have been considerably different from yours."

"It was. I always looked upon success as being a matter of mind, not money; but Jay wanted the material appearances. I remember that once we had a wrestling match, and as we were about even in strength, we agreed to abide by certain rules—taking what we called 'holts' in the beginning and not breaking them until one or the other was thrown. I kept to this in the struggle, but when Jay realized that he was in danger of losing the contest, he broke the 'holt' and threw me. When I remarked that he had broken his agreement, he only laughed and said, 'I threw you, didn't I?' And to every objection I made, he made the same answer. The fact of having won was pleasing to him. It satisfied him, although it wouldn't have contented me."

"Did you ever talk over success in life with him?"

"Yes, quite often. He was bent on making money, and did considerable trading among us schoolboys—sold me some of his books. I felt then that my view of life was more satisfactory to me than his would have been. I wanted to obtain a competence, and then devote myself to high thinking instead of to moneymaking."*

"How did you plan to attain this end?"

"By study. I began in my sixteenth or seventeenth year to try to express myself on paper, and when, after I had left the country school, I attended the seminary at Ashland and at Cooperstown, I often received the highest marks in composition, though only standing about the average in general scholarship. My taste ran to essays, and I picked up the great works in that field at a bookstore, from time

---

* An old schoolmate in the little red schoolhouse has said, that "John and Jay were not like the other boys. They learned their lessons easier; and at recess they looked on the games, but did not join in them. John always knew where to find the largest trout; he could show you birds' nests, and name all the flowers. He was fond of reading, and would walk five miles to borrow a book. Roxbury is proud of John Burroughs. We celebrated 'Burroughs Day' instead of Arbor Day here last spring, in the high school, in honor of him."

to time, and filled my mind with the essay idea. I bought the whole of Dr. Johnson's works at a second-hand bookstore in New York, because, on looking into them I found his essays appeared to be solid literature, which I thought was just the thing. Almost my first literary attempts were moral reflections, somewhat in the Johnsonian style."

"You were supporting yourself during these years?"

"I taught six months and 'boarded round' before I went to the seminary. That put fifty dollars into my pocket, and the fifty paid my way at the seminary.* Working on the farm, studying and teaching filled up the years until 1863, when I went to Washington and found employment in the Treasury Department."

"You were connected with the Treasury then?"**

"Oh, yes; for nearly nine years. I left the department in 1872, to become receiver of a bank, and subsequently for several years I performed the work of a bank examiner. I considered it only as an opportunity to earn and save up a little money on which I could retire. I managed to do that, and came back to this region, where I bought a fruit farm. I worked that into paying condition, and then gave all my time to the pursuit of the studies I like."

---

* It was when he was attending the academy, that young Burroughs first saw that wonderful being—a living author: "I distinctly remember with what emotion I gazed upon him," he said, "and followed him about in the twilight, keeping on the other side of the street. He was of little account, a man who had failed as a lawyer, and then had written a history of Poland, which I have never heard of since that time; but to me he was the embodiment of the august spirit of authorship, and I looked upon him with tore reverence and enthusiasm than I had ever before looked upon any man with. I cannot divine why I should have stood in such worshipful fear and awe of this obscure individual, but I suppose it was the instinctive tribute of a timid and imaginative youth to a power he was just beginning to see—or to feel—the power of letters."

** "My first book, *Wake-Robin*, was written while I was a government clerk in Washington," says Mr. Burroughs. "It enabled me to live over again the days I had passed with the birds, and in the scenes of my youth. I wrote the book while sitting at a desk in front of an iron wall. I was the keeper of a vault in which many million of bank-notes were stored. During my long periods of leisure, I took refuge in my pen. How my mind reacted from the iron wall in front of me, and sought solace in memories of the birds and of summer fields and woods."

"Had you abandoned your interest in nature during your Washington life?"

"No. I gave as much time to the study of nature and literature as I had to spare. When I was twenty-three I wrote an essay on 'Expression,' and sent it to the *Atlantic*. It was so Emersonian in style, owing to my enthusiasm for Emerson at that time, that the editor thought some one was trying to palm off on him an early essay of Emerson's which he had not seen. He found that Emerson had not published any such paper, however, and printed it, though it had not much merit. I wrote off and on for the magazines."

The editor in question was James Russell Lowell, who, instead of considering it without merit, often expressed afterwards the delight with which he read this contribution from an unknown hand, and the swift impression of the author's future distinction which came to him with that reading.

"Your successful work, then, has been in what direction?" I said.

"In studying nature. It has all come by living close to the plants and animals of the woods and fields, and coming to understand them. There I have been successful. Men who, like myself, are deficient in self-assertion, or whose personalities are flexible and yielding, make a poor show in business, but in certain other fields these defects become advantages. Certainly it is so in my case. I can succeed with bird or beast, for I have cultivated my ability in that direction. I can look in the eye of an ugly dog or cow and win, but with an ugly man I have less success. I consider the desire which most individuals have for the luxuries which money can buy, an error of mind" he added. "Those things do not mean anything except a lack of higher tastes.

"Such wants are not necessary wants, nor honorable wants. If you cannot get wealth with a noble purpose, it is better to abandon it and get something else. Peace of mind is one of the best things to seek, and finer tastes and feelings. The man who gets these, and maintains himself comfortably, is much more admirable and successful than the man who gets money and neglects these. The realm of power has no fascination for me. I would rather have my seclusion and peace of mind. This log hut, with its bare floors, is sufficient. I am set down among the beauties of nature and in no danger of losing the riches that are scattered all about. No one will take my walks or my brook away from me. The flowers, birds and animals are plentifully provided. I have enough to eat and wear, and time to see how beautiful the world is, and to enjoy it. The entire world is after your money, or the things you have bought with your money. It is trying to keep them that makes them seem so precious. I live to broaden and enjoy my own life, believing that in so doing I do what is best for everyone. If I ran after birds only to write about them, I should never have written anything that anyone else would have cared to read. I must write from sympathy and love—that is, from enjoyment—or not at all. I come gradually to have a feeling that I want to write upon a given theme. Whenever the subject recurs to me, it awakens a warm, personal response. My confidence that I ought to write comes from the feeling or attraction which some subjects exercise over me. The work is pleasure, and the result gives pleasure."

"And your work as a naturalist is what?"

"Climbing trees to study birds, lying by the waterside to watch the fishes, sitting still in the grass for hours to study the insects, and tramping here and there, always to observe and study whatever is common to the woods and fields."

"Men think you have done a great work," I said.

"I have done a pleasant work," he said, modestly.

"And the achievements of your schoolmate Gould do not appeal to you as having anything in them worth aiming for?" I questioned.

"Not for me. I think my life is better for having escaped such vast and difficult interests."

The gentle, light-hearted naturalist and recluse came down the long hillside with me, "to put me right" on the main road. I watched him as he retraced his steps up the steep, dark path, lantern in hand. His sixty years sat lightly upon him, and as he ascended I heard him singing.

Long after the light melody had died away, I saw the serene little light bobbing up and down in his hand, disappearing and reappearing, as the lone philosopher repaired to his but and his couch of content.

CHAPTER XXX

How James Whitcomb Riley Came to be Master of the Hoosier Dialect

It is doubtful if there is in the literary world, today, a personage whose boyhood and young manhood can approach in romance and unusual circumstances that of the author of "The Old Swimmin' Hole."

All tradition was against his accomplishing anything in the world. How, indeed, said the good folks of the little town of Greenfield, Indiana, could anything be expected of a boy who cared nothing for school, and deserted it at the first opportunity, to take up a wandering life.

THROWN ON HIS OWN RESOURCES

The boy's father wanted the boy to follow in his footsteps, in the legal profession, and he held out alluring hopes of the possibility of scaling even greater heights than any to which he had yet attained. Better still—from the standpoint of the restless James—he took the youngster with him as he made his circuit from court to court.

These excursions, for they were indeed such to the boy, sowed deep in his heart the seed of a determination to become a nomad;

and it was not long until he started out as a strolling sign-painter, determined upon the realization of his ideals.

Oftentimes business was worse than dull, and, on one occasion, hunger drove him for recourse to his wits, and lo, he blossomed forth as a "blind sign-painter," led from place to place by a little boy, and showered with sympathy and trade in such abundance that he could hardly bear the thought of the relinquishment of a pretense so ingenious and successful, entered on at first as a joke.

Then came another epoch. The young man fell in with a patent-medicine man, with whom he joined fortunes, and here the young Indianian, who had been scribbling more or less poetry, found a new use for his talent; for his duties in the partnership were to beguile the people with joke and song, while his co-worker plied the sales of his cure-all. There were many times when, but for his fancy, the young poet might have seen his audience dwindle rapidly away. It was while thus engaged, that he had the opportunities which enabled him to master thoroughly the Hoosier dialect.

When the glamor of the patent-medicine career had faded somewhat, the nomadic Riley joined a band of strolling Thespians, and, in this brief portion of his life, after the wont of players of his class, played many parts.

At length, he began to give a little more attention to his literary work; and, later, obtained a place on an Indianapolis paper, where he published his first poems, and they won their author almost instant success.

WHY HE LONGED TO BE A BARER

When I drew Mr. Riley out to talk still further of those interesting days, and the strange experiences which came to him therein, the conversation finally turned on the subject of his youthful ambition.

"I think my earliest remembered one," he said, "was an insatiate longing to become a baker. I don't know what prompted it, unless it were the visions of the mountains of alluring 'goodies,' which, as they are ranged in the windows of the pastry shops, appear doubly tempting to the youth whose mother not only counsels moderation, but enforces it.

"Next, I imagined that I would like to become a showman of some sort.

"Then, my shifting fancy conjured up visions of how grand it would be to work as a painter, and decorate houses and fences in glowing colors.

"Finally, as I grew a little older, there returned my old longing to become an actor. When, however, my dreams were realized, and I became a member of a traveling theatrical company, I found that the life was full of hardships, with very little chance of rising in the world.

"I never had any literary ambition whatever, so far as I can remember. I wrote, primarily, simply because I desired to have something to read, and could not find selections that exactly suited me. Gradually I found a demand for my little efforts springing up; and so my brother—who could write legibly transcribed them."

PERSISTENCE

At this point I asked Mr. Riley his idea of the prime requisites for success in the field of letters.

"The most essential factor," he replied "is persistence—the determination never to allow your energy or enthusiasm to be dampened by the discouragement that must inevitably come. I believe that he is richer for the battle with the world, in any vocation, who has great determination and little talent, rather than his seemingly more fortunate brother with great talent, perhaps, but little determination. As for the field of literature, I cannot but express my conviction that

PART III: LIFE STORIES OF SUCCESSFUL MEN AND WOMEN... 345

meteoric flights, such as have been taken, of recent years, by some young writers with whose names almost everybody is familiar, cannot fail to be detrimental, unless the man to whom success comes thus early and suddenly is an exceptionally evenly-balanced and sensible person.

"Many persons have spoken to me about Kipling's work, and remarked how wonderful a thing is the fact that such achievements could have been possible for a man comparatively so young. I say, not at all. What do we find when we investigate? Simply that Kipling began working on a newspaper when he was only thirteen years of age, and he has been toiling ever since. So you see, even that case confirms my theory that every man must be 'tried in the fire,' as it were.

"He may begin early or late-and in some cases the fight is longer than in others—but of one thing I feel sure, that there is no short-cut to permanent, self-satisfying success in literature, or anything else."

TWENTY YEARS OF REJECTED MANUSCRIPTS

"Mr. Riley," I asked, "would you mind saying something about the obstacles over which you climbed to success?"

"I am afraid it would not be a very pleasant story," he replied. "A friend came to me once, completely heartbroken, saying that his manuscripts were constantly returned, and that he was the most miserable wretch alive. I asked him how long he had been trying? 'Three years,' he said. 'My dear man,' I answered, laughing, 'go on, keep on trying till you have spent as many years at it as I did.' 'As many as you did!' he exclaimed. 'Yes, as long as I did.' 'What, you struggled for years!' 'Yes, sir; through years, through sleepless nights, through almost hopeless days. For twenty years I tried to get into one magazine; back came my manuscripts eternally. I kept on. In the twentieth year, that magazine accepted one of my articles.'

"I was not a believer in the theory that one man does a thing much easier than any other man. Continuous, unflagging effort, persistence and determination will win. Let not the man be discouraged who has these."

"What would you advise one to do with his constantly rejected manuscript?" I asked.

"Put it away awhile; then remodel it. Young writers make the mistake I made."

"What mistake?" I asked.

"Hurrying a manuscript off before it was dry from my pen, as if the world were just waiting for that article and must have it. Now it can hardly be drawn from me with a pair of tweezers. Yes, lay it aside awhile. Reread. There is a rotten spot somewhere. Perhaps it is full of hackneyed phrases, or lacks in sparkle and originality. Search, examine, rewrite, simplify. Make it lucid. *I am glad, now, that my manuscripts did come back.* Presently I would discover this defect, then that. Perhaps three or four sleepless nights would show my failure to be in an unsymmetrical arrangement of the verses.

"See these books?" he said, rapping upon the book case with the back of his hand. "Classics! But of what do they tell? Of the things of their own day. Let us write the things of our day. Literary fields exhausted! Nonsense. If we write well enough, ours will be the classics of tomorrow. Our young Americans have, right at hand, the richest material any country ever offered. Let them be brave and work in earnest."

A COLLEGE EDUCATION

Answering other questions, the poet said, "A college education for the aspirant for literary success is, of course, an advantage, provided he does not let education foster a false culture that will lead him away from the ideals he ought to cling to.

"There is another thing that the young man in any artistic pursuit must have a care for; and that is, to be practical. This is a practical world, and it is always ready to take advantage of this sort of people: so that one must try to cultivate a practical business sense as well as an artistic sense. We have only a few men like Rudyard Kipling and F. Hopkinson Smith, who seem to combine these diverse elements of character in just the right proportions; but I believe that it is unfortunate for the happiness and peace of mind of our authors, and artists, and musicians, that we have not more of them."

RILEY'S POPULARITY

Riley's poetry is popular because it goes right to the feelings of the people. He could not have written as he does, but for the schooling of that wandering life, which gave him an insight into the struggle for existence among the great unnumbered multitude of his fellow men. He learned in his travels and journeys, in his hard experience as a strolling sign-painter and patent-medicine peddler the freemasonry of poverty. His poems are natural; they are those of a man who feels as he writes. As Thoreau painted nature in the woods, and streams, and lakes, so Riley depicts the incidents of everyday life, and brightens each familiar lineament with that touch that makes all the world akin.

SELF-ASSESSMENT

The following is not meant to be a professional, diagnostic tool. For that reason, the questions are not numbered—there is no "proper" sequence in which to consider them, and nor is there a "score." These questions are meant simply to stimulate your thinking regarding the sorts of things that fulfill you . . . the nature and surroundings of the sort of activity that would most be an expression of self-expression for you. You'll notice that these questions are not about aptitudes but about interests—in a word, personality. There's a reason for this: As in love, so too in work—personality characteristics have more to do with compatibility than external characteristics or specific aptitudes/skills.

For example, you'll see several questions that ask you to think about the things you like to talk about. Customarily, we don't consciously think about this when thinking about a job we'd like. But in fact, it plays an important role. If the people in a particular workplace have a certain vocabulary, a certain jargon, a certain outlook on things that you feel no comfort with—say it's a grocery store and the employees spend a considerable time talking about the correct way to stock the shelves for customer appeal, or talk about attitudes of certain annoying customers, and are indifferent to the food that's disposed of daily because of its expiration date, and you find these subjects boring or disturbing—you will not feel content in that job setting, even if the pay is good and you have the skills to do the work. You will also see items in this list that ask you to look at certain assumptions you may have about success, or making money, or work—assumptions that could affect the ways and opportunities you have for career fulfillment. The intent is not for you to denigrate yourself or brow-beat yourself, but just to know yourself. What you do with that knowledge you gain is an individual matter.

- What hobbies, interests, activities did you most enjoy as a child? Which ones gave you the greatest feeling of self-esteem? of joy?
- If we could look into your life as a child, what would we see you doing that you were completely absorbed in, oblivious of time, your surroundings, etc.?
- Imagine a room filled with the type of people you would most enjoy spending an evening with—having a dialogue with about your beliefs, interests, philosophy of life, most heart-felt concerns, etc. What type of people would be in this room? What sort of jobs would they have? What work would they be doing in this world?
- Who, among the living or those deceased are your heroes? Who are the people you admire? Why do you admire them? What is it they said, did, believed that you admire them for?
- If money and time and family obligations were no object—if, in other words, you did not feel that you had limitations, restrictions—what would you do right now with your life?
- If you knew you were only going to life for the next 4–6 months, what sort of people would you want to spend your time with? Doing what?

- What are the dreams you've put aside because you were led to believe they were "too idealistic"? told that you'd never be able to succeed "at that"?
- If you and another person were trapped in an elevator for 12 hours, what would you want to be that other person's favorite things to talk about?
- Do you prefer having others set up the tasks that you then successfully complete? Or do you prefer setting up your own tasks and assignments?
- Do you prefer working by yourself or in a group (team)? If a group/team, a small one or a mid-sized one, or a large one?
- If you had the education, training, etc., required, what work would you most love doing?
- What sorts of books do you find interesting? (Novels? Is there a particular genre? Nonfiction? Is there a particular subject?)
- What part of the newspaper do you turn to first? Why?
- If you were in a library, or a waiting room, and the day's newspaper was there and you opened it and found a section of it was missing, what section would it be that would most disappoint you if it weren't there?
- What attitudes about work did you learn from your parents? From the way one or both spoke about work? About money? From the way they came home from work (on week nights? on weekends?) and returned to work (on week days? after a weekend? after a vacation?)?
- If you have a job now, what do you like about it? Why? What do you not like about it? Why?
- What things, if they occurred, could you not walk away from but would have to fight for? (Keep the list short: 5–10 items)
- If you were told that you were going to die tomorrow, what would you say you most regretted not having accomplished? What would you say was your greatest accomplishment?

- True or False: I believe that to rich/successful you must be ruthless, egotistical, etc.
- True or False: I believe that as people become more successful, their behaviors, actions, morals, values, etc., become more corrupted.
- True or False: I believe that in order to be successful, you must sacrifice time from your family and loved ones.
- True or False: It is more important for me to have the time to do things I enjoy than to strive to get ahead in a career.
- True or False: I believe that the pursuit of achievement and "being a success" are over-rated and over-emphasized . . . there are other, more important pursuits.
- True or False: I believe that the older you get, the less opportunities there are to change . . . to achieve success if you haven't already.
- If I had the ideal job, it would consist of . . . being outdoors/indoors? being self-employed/working for someone else? working day shifts/night shifts? working in a group/by myself? working with the public/working away from the public? working with people/things/ideas/machines? selling a product/service? Etc.

Continue this list, thinking of all the things your ideal job would consist of. Be playful, here. Don't worry about whether there is or isn't such a job. Now, you're just trying to know yourself. Later, you can look at what is "realistic" and what isn't, what is available and what isn't, what can be and what cannot be. Later, you can look at whether there is such a job waiting in the world, or whether you will create one for yourself.